ANGLO-SAXON AGE

THE
ANGLO-SAXON AGE

THE BIRTH OF ENGLAND

MARTIN WALL

AMBERLEY

First published 2015
This edition published 2016

Amberley Publishing
The Hill, Stroud
Gloucestershire, GL5 4EP

www.amberley-books.com

ISBN 978 1 4456 6034 9 (paperback)
ISBN 978 1 4456 4773 9 (ebook)

British Library Cataloguing in Publication Data.
A catalogue record for this book is available
from the British Library.

Typesetting and Origination by Amberley
Publishing
Printed in the UK.

CONTENTS

ACKNOWLEDGEMENTS

I wish to thank all the kind people who have assisted me in the production of this book, without whose help it would have been difficult or impossible to complete, particularly Justin Clarke, Alastair Perkins, Simon Rathbone, Jim Walker and Kurt Fretchson. Thanks too to John Gibbons for his encouragement and help as the project developed over time.

The author and publisher would like to thank the following people/organisations for permission to use copyright material in this book. Individual photographers are credited alongside the captions. Every attempt has been made to seek permission for copyright material used in this book. However, if we have inadvertently used copyright material without permission/acknowledgement we apologise and we will make the necessary correction at the first opportunity.

Please note that throughout the book, the *Anglo-Saxon Chronicle* is referred to as the *Chronicle*.

INTRODUCTION

This book came about in an odd way. In July 2009 when the Staffordshire Hoard was unearthed I was about to enter upon a period of personal darkness. The details of my personal tribulations need not trouble the reader here, but suffice to say they were life-changing. I was then living with my parents in South Staffordshire, just over twenty miles from Hammerwich, near Lichfield, where the treasures came to light thanks to the endeavours of Terry Herbert, a metal detector enthusiast. Due to the need for absolute secrecy about the find to prevent interference at the site, it was some months before the discovery was announced on *Midlands Today*, our local TV news programme. I was sitting in the living room of our cottage with my father, whose lifelong interest in local ancient history I have inherited. There were few things that could arouse his interest in those ominous times, or to distract us both from anticipation of forthcoming troubles, but when the news-reader gave sketchy details of the mystery of this extraordinary seventh-century Anglo-Saxon find, we immediately looked at each other, and he exclaimed, 'Penda's treasure!' For the next five years the painstaking process of conservation was undertaken, but as the questions multiplied, answers were few and far between as to the context of the find, arguably the most important hoard ever discovered in Britain. For the first time in my life I had both the time and the resources to devote to researching the mystery, and in 2014 I gave a lecture to a local historical society giving a conjectural and radical context for it, based on a theory that ancient Welsh poetry records a battle with English forces at Caer Luitcoit, modern-day Wall-by-Lichfield, at exactly the time when we think the hoard was deposited, less than two miles from where it was found. It is one among many theories, of course, and subsequently I have examined many other credible scenarios, all of them just as valid as my own. The lecture was politely received but left me with an impression that the history of this period is somehow culturally alien to us, perhaps even dangerous for us to contemplate. Yet, for me and my father before me, it constituted *the* most formative period in the story of this island, and it seemed that the ignorance and mystification about it amounted to a form of cultural impoverishment. Exasperated to some extent by this, I finally approached the City of Birmingham Museum and Art Gallery with an idea of volunteering to interpret the finds for visitors to the Birmingham section of the Staffordshire Hoard exhibition. By incredible serendipity and immense good fortune, I was selected to be among the first volunteer gallery interpreters for the exhibition when it first went on permanent display in October 2014. I count it a singular honour to act in this role, to explain what we know about the hoard, to admit what we don't know (yet) and to listen to the ideas and theories visitors bring with them. I would not be human if I did not put forward my own ideas, and the great glory of the discovery is that everyone is free to make of it what they will. Some things we do know, however. Mercia was real; it did exist. It was not some fictional territory like those in J. R. R Tolkien's stories. The Staffordshire Hoard has shifted the centre of gravity for our understanding of the formation of England and has placed a new emphasis on Mercia's part in that process. The people who lived in it were real too, and when we see the exquisite art the Anglo-Saxons made in their crude workshops with their primitive tools, we must surely wonder, what manner of people were these folk? What kind of world was it that they lived in? Why have they been so overlooked by the culture that owes nearly all it is to the foundations they laid almost 1,400 years ago? I hope to answer these questions and show that the mysterious 'Dark Ages' are a canard, a redundant term, obscuring much that may yet illuminate our own benighted times.

Martin Wall

I

INTO THE MISTS OF OBLIVION

For the first four centuries of the Christian era, Britain, excluding the most remote and wild upland areas, formed four provinces of the mighty Roman Empire. Collectively they were called Britannia. In the third century BC, a traveller named Pytheas made his way from the Greek port now called Marseilles in France to the Bay of Biscay, where he took ship on a mission to explore the British Isles. After a few days, he sighted Ierne (Ireland) before coming to Albionon (Great Britain). The natives of both islands wore painted designs on their skin, so he called them Pretanike or people of the designs or patterns. Over time Pretani, the Greek word for the island, became Latinised as Britannia. Both the Romans and the Greeks were fascinated by these mysterious, and in their eyes savage, people, splendidly isolated across the stormy seas. To glorify himself, Julius Caesar attempted a desultory invasion and then a punitive military expedition, but nearly a century was to pass before the Emperor Claudius sent Aulus Plautius, his best general, with 40,000 soldiers in 800 ships to finally bring Britain under Roman rule. Resistance was savage, desperate but ultimately futile. It is worth mentioning, however, that sporadic resistance went on for a long time, even in what is now England and Wales. Caledonia, or Scotland, and large parts of what we now call Wales, were so barren and of such little agricultural value (and the former so troublesome) that the Romans were content to leave them be. Ireland, although it had trading contacts with Britain and Europe, was even less attractive for them and escaped Roman occupation altogether. So, for 400 years, Britain became an integral part of the larger Roman scheme, with all the benefits that entailed: a level of civilisation so sophisticated, in fact, that only in the last 200 years – some would say less – have we attained anything to equal it.

This wealthy, powerful system was doomed. Its dissolution has been well documented elsewhere and was gradual. Britain was especially vulnerable as the Roman power waned. As rival contenders for the imperial title warred against each other, an admiral named Carausius declared himself independent emperor of Britain. The Emperor Constantius recaptured Britannia, and his son, Constantine, was proclaimed emperor at York in 306 AD. It was he who made Christianity into the state religion, and Britain was Christian, at least in theory, by the time of the Roman collapse, with its own churches and bishops. There had always been political and economic upheavals to contend with all through the Roman occupation, but perhaps precisely because it was so insular Britain could scarcely imagine the catastrophe that was about to befall it. In 367 AD, the Picts, a coalition of tribes from the desolate north, which lay outside Roman authority, broke through Hadrian's Wall. They advanced deep into the Roman provinces, sacking and burning and slaughtering as they came. News of this mayhem travelled fast and far. The Scotti, notorious slave raiders from Ireland, now raided along the western coasts in their *currachs*, flimsy but surprisingly sea-worthy boats. Informants among the Laeti, or barbarian soldiers in Roman service, may have also sent word to their cousins in their continental homelands of the chaos in Britain. Frisian traders would certainly have been aware of the crisis. Soon, these coastal raiders arrived too, to add to the miseries of the British. Ammianus, a contemporary

Roman historian, thought that the three barbarian peoples had acted in concert, what he called a *conspiratio barbarum*, a grand alliance, to destroy Britain. This concatenation of disasters so damaged Britannia that it never truly recovered, and in the year 410 AD, Rome finally abandoned its responsibility to defend Britain, advising that it should look to its own defence. There was little else it could do. In that very year, Alaric, the King of the Visigoths, sacked the Eternal City itself. Now, Britannia was on its own against the most fearsome enemies that could possibly be imagined, for unlike the Vandals, Alans, Burgundians and Suevi, or the Franks and Goths who had overwhelmed Western Europe, the Angles, Saxons and Jutes who descended upon the stricken island were not even heretical Christians. These latter three tribes (and there were certainly others too) had never come under Roman influence and so were heathens, whose entire lifestyle was geared to war. To them, as Brian Bates notes in his *The Real Middle Earth*, Rome was a cursed culture, effete and decadent, out of harmony with nature. Its religion was a thing above all to be despised, along with its philosophy of peace and love, justice and order. Its cities, prostituted to commerce, profit and luxurious living, predicated on slavery, seemed like an effrontery to all they held sacred. Nothing Rome had stood for was of value to them, and since Britain was now undefended, they began a process of gradual settlement of the island. The people we call Anglo-Saxons had arrived, but who were they?

Bede, the so-called father of English history, says that they were from three of the most eminent and powerful of the German tribes, the Angles, Saxons and Jutes. There is no reason to doubt that he was correct, for his was a considerable intellect and he would have possessed all relevant information, including orally transmitted lists of English royal lineages. The Saxons, a very fearsome tribe, named for their national weapon, a short-bladed, single-edged dagger, or Seax, came from the north German coast between the rivers Elbe and Weser. The Angles came from Angeln, modern-day Schleswig-Holstein, and the Jutes from Jutland and into modern

Denmark. Although all three were Germanic or Teutonic and spoke very similar languages, we should not allow this to conceal their own perceived differences to one another. They were proud, independent peoples with strong kin-bonds and tribal chiefs whom they believed to be descended from Nordic deities such as Woden, which meant that they were as likely to war against each other as to act in concert. The sudden breakdown of Roman authority in Britain began to focus all their minds westwards. These were not the only Germanic peoples associated with Britain. Procopius of Caesarea, a Byzantine historian writing in the early sixth century, tells us that 'three populous nations inhabit the island of Britain, each of them ruled by a king. These nations are named the Angliloi, the Frissones, and the Brittones, from whom the island is named'. The people he calls Frissones (Frisians) were almost certainly the Jutes. However, none of these were the first Germans to come to Britain. The emergency between 367 and 369 AD may have been resolved in large part by the arrival of German auxiliary troops. The Alemanni a very troublesome and large tribe, had been moved to Britain en masse in 372 AD under their king, Fraomar. He was given the rank of tribune with full authority to restore order and repel interlopers from the sea. So, later, when we come to the story of Vortigern, the British tyrant whose treachery led to the legendary settlement myth, it is worth remembering that for many generations there had been thousands of *foederati*, *laeti* or *numeri* German soldiers in the Roman army, settled in Britain, many of whom had British wives and children of mixed heritage. Ultimately they were here to defend Britain and had a stake in it. The British were no more shocked to see Germans around than any other of the troops and traders who were settled in Britain from all over the Roman Empire.

Apart from opportunities in Britain and beyond, there were other pressing reasons which impelled these Germanic folk to emigration. Climate change and coastal inundation, combined with over-population, forced them in upon each other, so to speak. For the first 300 years of the Roman occupation, Britain and northern Europe had been warm and temperate, but as if to announce forthcoming hardships, this now began to change. The climate became colder and wetter, and peat deposits (according to Brian Fagan, an archaeologist specialising in the impact of climate change) began to accumulate along the low-lying coastal regions of the Anglo-Saxon homelands. Perhaps it was this same climate change which had forced the nomadic tribes of central Asia, called Huns or Avars, to move westward with their flocks in search of fresh pastures. They drove before them those other tribes, such as the Goths, who were to overwhelm the Western Roman Empire, and the pressure exerted by these numerous and warlike tribes began to be felt by the Angles, Saxons and Jutes. Rather than dissipate their forces in inter-tribal wars they focussed their energies outwards, to the rich cleared lands just a few days sailing away. Compressed in villages built on raised mounds above the marshes, their lives must have been constrained and austere, but we should not draw analogies with modern economic migrants. The reaction of these tribes to these problems was a cult of militaristic piracy. At first they came in just this way, as simple raiders, but as time went on they began to see the potential for mass settlement. All that was needed was some sort of incident that would tip the balance in favour of permanent settlement, and we have powerful stories which have come down to us about how this happened. A sixth-century British historian named Gildas set down a fairly contemporary account of the process by which Britain had been overwhelmed. Although he is looking at things from a British Christian perspective, he is our best witness, and his main work, *De Excidio et conquestu Britanniae*, gives a bitter account of the decline of Britain, which he attributes to the apostasy and sin of its people and their petty warrior kings, and it is one of these post-Roman rulers who he tells us was above all responsible for the great catastrophe that had ruined Britain.

It is important to stress that with the Roman withdrawal we are entering upon a period where conventional history begins to fail us. Much of what we think we know about the fifth century in Britain is based on legends and folk-myths transmitted orally by means of bardic storytelling and poetry. This is why, for all his shortcomings and omissions, Gildas is so vitally important, because he was an educated man with strong opinions writing about the cultural and political transition which concerns us. However, and as I hope to show in a later chapter, we should not look down our noses at the folk traditions which culminated in the Arthurian myth cycle, for instance. It is very hard for us to appreciate the completeness of the disaster which engulfed the British in the wake of the English settlement, and I am not among those who conceive of it as a gradual, mainly non-violent experiment in multiculturalism, with the two peoples blending harmoniously together. Gildas, who was almost contemporary with the events, tells us the reality, and grim reading it makes. What he says is that a person he calls a *superbus tyrannus*, who had been selected to exercise complete authority, chose to invite Saxon war-bands into Britain to defend against the marauding Picts. As we have already seen, this was a long-established practice, and in the absence of a professional army his options were limited. The half-trained and poorly equipped militias he could put in the field would have been completely inadequate even for a partial defence of lowland Britain, but the real deficiency was the lack of an effective fleet or coastal fortifications which could alert him to major incursions. Carausius, the usurper emperor, had strengthened a system of Saxon Shore fortifications, under a commander called Comes Litoris Saxonici, ostensibly to defend against Saxon raids but with the added bonus that they defended his autonomous empire in Britain against a re-assertion of Roman power. In recent years, some experts have claimed that the Saxon Shore was so named because it had a history of Saxon occupation and was named after people already in situ before 410 who manned the defences. However, the defences called the Gothic Bank on the Danube were so called because they formed a defence *against* the Goths, and much evidence suggests that the Saxon Shore forts existed to counter the threat of Saxon piracy and intrusions. Economic and military collapse rendered these mighty strongholds useless for their original purpose. The solution, to hire mercenary Saxon warriors with a legendary facility for seamanship, would perhaps have been seen by us as a perfectly practical one if it had not gone so terribly wrong. Vortigern is almost certainly not a personal name but a title held by this *superbus tyrannus*. Welsh texts call him a *guletic* or chief. Vor means great and tigern means clan-chief, so this was his role, the great leader or father, the kind of petty dictator to which people resort in desperate times. It has been asserted that his power base may have been in the former territory of the province called Britannia Prima, perhaps in Powys and the Severn Valley, or even deeper into wild Wales. He was confronted not only by external enemies but also by a religious controversy that was dividing the British – the Pelagian heresy which originated in the island. Although Roman military power was by now redundant, the Roman Church was still operating and was determined to eliminate schism and heretical beliefs. In essence, the Pelagian doctrines amounted to a denial of original sin, combined with a social egalitarianism which especially appealed to the freed slaves and the urban poor, such elements as have been known to initiate insurrections throughout history. It is not difficult to see why the Catholic Church was determined to eradicate it, and we have good reasons to think that Vortigern was in fact a Pelagian sympathiser. So the scene was set for the total disintegration of what remained of Romano-British culture.

In setting down his thoughts in writing, Gildas has an entirely different agenda to that of a conventional historian. His book is an invective against the corrupt and over-mighty rulers of the patchwork of Celtic state-lets who have neglected their moral and religious duties. What he is trying to emphasise is that Britain is analogous to the Israel of the Old Testament. So, just as Daniel and Jeremiah had denounced the feckless rulers of Israel and uttered dire prophesies of doom in the face of their irresponsible attitudes to holy writ, Gildas is taking this prophetic task upon himself. Unless the British repent, he is saying, then the heathen English plague will bring them low, as due punishment from God. Rather than simply recording historical facts, he is concerned to inculcate a stern adherence to the moral adjuncts in the scriptures, which he sees as the only hope of saving his country. His stern critique and apocalyptic warnings proved remarkably prescient. The Saxon advent (he claims) came in the form of three keels of warriors, a mere handful, but they were the thin end of an exceptionally large wedge. Gildas pulls no punches and says that the ferocious Saxons were let in by the tyrant-like 'wolves', set to guard the sheepfold. It is not specified where these Saxons were billeted, but traditionally it was in Kent, though this hardly seems an appropriate base from which to counter Pictish raids. The possible solution to this anomaly is that Vortigern now had a powerful rival in Britain itself, Ambrosius Aurelianus, whose power base was, we think, in what is now Wiltshire. His august name implies that he was from the cream of the Romano-British aristocracy, and there is a tradition that his ancestors had worn the purple. The historian J. N. L Myers, in his *The English Settlements*, points out that the father of the Bishop of Milan, Saint Ambrose, whose cult was very influential at this time, was called Aurelius Ambrosius. We can infer from this that Ambrosius was a Catholic, wealthy and strongly imbued with traditional Roman values; he was the sort of high-ranking and influential figure who would have despised the heretical and double-dealing great leader Vortigern. If Ambrosius was engaged in correspondence with like-minded people of his class in Gaul, which is highly likely, then Vortigern's strategy becomes clearer. Under the pretext of introducing *foederati* to defend against the Picts, Vortigern had called in hard men who could guard against Romano-Gaulish, Catholic support for his rival, Ambrosius. As has so often proven the case, he had under-estimated how dangerous these henchmen were, with disastrous consequences.

The alleged leader of the Saxon pioneers was Hengist, an exiled Jutish adventurer very much in the mould of the legendary Beowulf. We know from the Roman historian Tacitus that the history of the

German tribes amounted to ancient songs about gods and heroes from whose descendants they chose their kings. The dragon-slayer Beowulf exemplifies this heroic culture, in which enterprising warriors hired themselves out to perform heroic deeds in exchange for tributes of treasure. Indeed, if the saga about Beowulf was based on an actual person from Sweden or thereabouts, then he was probably a near contemporary of Hengist. One of the main lessons we can take from the Staffordshire Hoard is that these sagas, long held to be outlandish exaggerations for poetic effect, actually record a cultural reality. Scholars are coming to the view that this culture of heroic itinerancy may have its roots in a folk movement of the Angles and Jutes into Frisia. Frisia had long-standing contacts with Roman Britain and these continued even after the departure of the Roman military and bureaucracy. The *Anglo-Saxon Chronicle* mentions an appeal made by the Britons (meaning the British governing authorities) to Anglian chieftains in the 440s. What this implies is that Vortigern had a policy of recruiting these restless peoples so as to use their military muscle to shore up his disintegrating state.

A clue to the chaos that was happening in Britain is that Saint Germanus of Auxerre, a former soldier turned churchman, made two trips to Britain at just this time. Ostensibly his purpose was to purge the country of the Pelagian heresy, but if, as some accounts suggest, his visits coincided with Vortigern's rule, there may have been a political subtext. Certainly the old soldier was not averse to using his military skills, for we are told he led the people out against a barbarian incursion in a well-organised ambush which ended in a bloodless victory. He made a visit to the shrine of St Alban at Verulamium, where he met civic and Church dignitaries who were richly attired and still capable of a show of pomp and display. For some people at least, life in Britain was still good. Unfortunately these powerful magnates were very reluctant to finance such small matters as a means of national defence. Traditionally, this had been the responsibility of the imperial authorities. Perhaps Germanus, by leading them in this expedition against a barbarian raid, was trying to suggest that in these desperate times they would have to accept more responsibility for themselves. Was one of those he led into battle Ambrosius? Where was Vortigern? Although we can't answer these questions for sure, these visits have every appearance of some sort of response to a national crisis in Britain which demanded outside assistance. It was probably this political emergency which formed the backdrop to the incident which Hengist exploited to his advantage. If Vortigern had fallen out of political favour, or if a revolt against his rule had taken place, he would have retired to his stronghold of Castell Gwerthryniawn in his own lands. The desperate appeals to Anglian chiefs may well have been issued by him. There is a tradition that he married Hengist's daughter to ingratiate himself. This would have seemed a disgraceful act to his compatriots. Moreover, Ambrosius, his rival, had now emerged as a national resistance leader, whose policy was to crush heresy and end appeasement of the barbarians. If, as Bede thought, Anglo-Saxon immigration had become a flood, sufficient to empty Angeln of its entire population, then there must have come a point at which the supplies and tributes Vortigern had agreed to provide to them simply stopped arriving or were no longer sufficient to feed a growing population. Gildas says that the Saxons complained when their monthly tribute was withheld, and that in response they threatened to plunder and burn the entire island. If all this sounds like the dramatic spin of one in the grip of a fanatical hatred of a national enemy (and there is some truth in this), perhaps we should recall the events which followed the coming of the Great Army of the Vikings 400 years later. This is a matter of historical record, involving peoples from a very similar racial and cultural background. In fact, for all intents and purposes they were almost identical to their Anglo-Saxon predecessors. In the space of a few short years this marauding army destroyed three long established English kingdoms, and it was only by a miracle that the last, Wessex, survived, and then only thanks to the efforts of our greatest national hero, Alfred the Great. Before we dismiss Gildas and his tales of devastation, pillage and national disintegration as propaganda, we need to think long and hard. As Martin Welch in his *Anglo-Saxon England* (for English Heritage) puts it,

> In recent years (some archaeologists) seem determined to believe, that very few immigrants from northern Germany and southern Scandinavia were involved in the creation of Anglo-Saxon England from post-Roman Britain ... there are real problems in accepting such a viewpoint. Firstly it argues that we know much better than contemporary and slightly later commentators who wrote about the events in Britain ... Bede felt secure in the belief that he was not of British descent and that his people, the Northumbrians, were Angles.

However, some modern scholars have tended to disagree. As Timothy Venning states in his *The Anglo-Saxon Kings*, DNA evidence does not tally with a mass extermination of the British population. At least on the maternal line many British folk have a lineage to the indigenous population. But this is to conflate the later mass settlements with the earlier Anglo-Saxon ingress which Gildas wrote about. The two were actually completely separate events. The fact that women were taken as sex-slaves and their menfolk slain in the eastern parts of Britain does not imply that the newcomers were introducing a culture of community welfare. The Anglo-Saxons did not come as charitable organisations. Even the *Anglo-Saxon Chronicle* admits as much. In AD 473 'Hengist and Aesc took immense booty and the Welsh fled from the English like fire'. In 477 'Aelle came to Britain ... there they slew many of the Welsh; and some in flight they drove into the wood called Andred'. In AD 490 'Aelle and Cissa besieged the city of Andred. They slew all that were therein; nor was there even one Briton left alive there'. By withholding the agreed tribute Vortigern had violated the code of honour that underpinned Germanic tribal societies inviting vengeance and retribution and this was enacted with ruthless celerity. The fact that British DNA survives in the lowlands does not exonerate the Anglo-Saxons of genocide, rather it may speak of an aristocracy as cruel as the later Norman Conquest, exerting a rule over a people entirely cowed. New research by the University of Oxford suggests that the main determinant of regional DNA profiles is specifically linked to the patchwork of small kingdoms which preceded the formation of larger states, and this will be a particular theme of this book.

Gildas says that the Saxons 'burnt and devastated all the neighbouring cities and lands, until the entire island, even unto the western Ocean felt it's red and savage tongue'. The British, like so many other refugees in living memory, fled overseas mostly to Armorica, the part of France still called Brittany. Presumably these were of the wealthiest class with some of their retainers. The poorer sort were enslaved or slain, and those more enterprising found refuge in the extensive forests of the west, but more often they sought refuge in the 'high hills, steep and fortified', by which is meant the re-fortified Iron Age hill-forts such as Cadbury Castle. These we must presume, were more like refugee reception centres than bastions against the 'wolf-like villains'. Those who protected them, regional Celtic warlords, were probably only slightly less unscrupulous than the foreign interlopers from which they were fleeing. But a new paradigm was emerging. The south-east was coming under the sway of the invaders, but the north and west were, as yet, beyond their reach.

However, although the absence of Anglo-Saxon infiltration and penetration of the British-held areas meant that the warlords there could maintain a shaky independence of sorts, there was no escape from the impact of wider changes which erased the 400 years of Roman hegemony. The collapse of a money economy and the virtual eclipse of external, and to some extent internal, trade, meant that the major cities, as well as the villa economy which had brought prosperity to its zenith in the fourth and early fifth centuries, were virtually obliterated. Roman coins ceased to be issued and wheel-thrown pottery formerly produced by kilns licensed by the legions was no longer produced. Now that the skilled Roman masons had departed, people were no longer able to build sophisticated structures in stone. The Roman system had been based on urban centres and the Christian churches and diocesan centres located in the cities. In the countryside people remained pagan, from the Latin *pagani* meaning rustic, and in these remote areas, where people spoke in Celtic dialects which were the ancestors of modern Welsh, Cornish and Breton, local deities were still worshipped. Christianity was either remote or only present in a hybrid form. This is why we still refer to non-Christians as pagans. The original name of the British kingdom of Powys seems to derive from the Latin Pagenses, or country districts, and Salopium the Latin for Shropshire means something like the bush or the outback. It was in these places where Roman manners were most easily abandoned and swiftly replaced by a Celtic cultural revival which had little time for the sophistry of Catholic theology. This was the background of Vortigern the *superbus tyrannus*. His name appears in the genealogies of Powys, and the historian Michael Wood postulates that it was he who ordered the refurbishment of Wroxeter, the former Roman Viriconium, albeit in timber and within a reduced circuit of walls in the late fifth century. As Caer Guricon it continued to function as a major urban centre long after such towns had been abandoned in the south and east. As the British population drifted west, they encountered this neo-Celtic revival in the form of myths, legends, *genii loci* or local guardian spirits, which merged with half-remembered Christian doctrines to become the template for the strange cult of King Arthur. Such myths are more emotionally and psychologically potent than mere history, and this accounts for their enduring appeal. In a time when physical resistance had ceased to be a realistic option, the British resorted to magic, but in fact the time that was bought in order that these traditions and folk-myths might coalesce was provided by a very real military victory over the Anglo-Saxons which gave the natives a respite for fifty, perhaps more, years. This was the Battle of Mons Badonicus and thanks to Gildas we know something at least about it. Had it not been for this crucial victory there may well have been no indigenous contribution to our modern culture whatsoever.

Because the Arthurian legends have obscured our conventional historical understanding of this crucial period, it is often not understood that this 'last great victory of the fatherland' as Gildas called it, actually happened. By a supreme national effort Ambrosius Aurelianus, or another unnamed leader, managed to rally his countrymen and prevent the Anglo-Saxons establishing hegemony over the entire island. It is unfortunate, to say the least, that Gildas does not name this British leader or the Anglo-Saxon kings who were his adversaries. Neither does he give a precise date for the 'siege' of Badon Hill. The village of Amesbury in Wiltshire was known in a ninth-century charter as Ambresbyrig and I concur with the opinion of J. N. L Myers that this must have been derived from a place name meaning 'the stronghold of Ambrosius'. If a coalition of Anglo-Saxons, led by King Aelle of Sussex, and including Cerdic, the leader of the West Saxons, intended to strike a knock-out blow to Ambrosius or perhaps tantalisingly, Arthur, or both, then they must have advanced into modern Wiltshire using the ancient Ridgeway or Ermine Street. The historian John Morris in his *The Age of Arthur* presented a convincing scenario for such a campaign. There are many contenders for Mount Badon, almost all re-occupied hill forts such as Barbury Castle, Liddington Castle near Badbury, Solsbury Hill near Batheaston, Great Bedwyn or Dyrham Camp in Gloucestershire. We will never know for certain, and the interest in attributing certainty has come about through a desire to vindicate a passage in a ninth-century text by a Welsh scribe called Nennius where he claims Badon as the last and greatest of King Arthur's twelve battles: 'The twelfth battle was on Badon Hill where 960 men were killed at Arthur's onset; none slew them but he alone, and in all the battles he was the victor ...'. Whether or not a historical Arthur existed is a subject beyond the remit of this book, and there are many theories about this. What is pertinent and relevant to this introductory preamble is that the Anglo-Saxon advance was stopped in its tracks, and indeed reversed for a while. Sir Frank Merry Stenton in his classic *Anglo-Saxon England* adduces evidence that some English settlers decided to try their luck on the Continent rather than remain in a country where dangerous foes, perhaps utilising cavalry, might attack them at any time. John Morris, whose extensive research into this period should perhaps be more generously recognised, thought that in essence the British effort could not be extended into more vigorous offensive operations and that some kind of territorial partition must have been agreed. Unfortunately this entire period is so ill attested that we must content ourselves with a broad outline of probable events.

The armistice between the two peoples may well have consolidated the Celtic myth of an Arthurian golden age, but it was not to last. Britain, already beset by every conceivable misfortune was at last undone by one final cataclysm. In faraway Indonesia, in the 530s, a volcano, probably Krakatoa, erupted. It spewed so much debris into the atmosphere that climatic extremes followed for twenty years, as is evidenced by tree ring growth, or rather the absence of it. Then a voracious epidemic, the Yellow Plague, spread from Africa, entering the British and Irish ports. The Celtic countries still traded with the Eastern Roman Empire, whereas the Anglo-Saxons had no such contacts and remained immune. Up to 60 per cent of the British population perished. Those who argue for a peaceful admixture of British and Anglo-Saxon cultures cannot explain how it was that the former did not infect the incomers. The answer is simple. So terrorised and psychically violated did the British feel by their Anglo-Saxon neighbours that they would not mix with them on any account, even refusing to eat from the same plates they had used and shunning inns where they had stayed when on pilgrimage abroad. They steadfastly refused to proselytise to them about the Christian faith, for which they were admonished by St Augustine. The famous story about the Celtic holy man Beuno is a case in point. He was said to have been walking along the west bank of the River Severn (or Hafren) one day when he heard a man on the east bank calling to his hounds in a language he did not understand. Immediately he realised that the heathen foreigners had penetrated into the Cymric lands of the west. So appalled was he at this prospect that he fled to the Lleyn Peninsula, as far into Wales as it was possible to go. This speaks of an intense bitterness and hatred for the 'wolfish villains', as Gildas called them, which was a corollary of the savage events which were a consequence of the Anglo-Saxon influx, but there was no doubt which of the two peoples would eventually prevail in the country we now call England. Once the temporary peace was over, the Anglo-Saxon folk consolidated and extended their territories and founded strong new kingdoms which would endure for many centuries. In the next chapter we will look at this heptarchy, as it is called, and at one kingdom which was for a time to become the mightiest of them all: Mercia.

2

THE ANGLO-SAXON
HEPTARCHY

In the aftermath of the initial Anglo-Saxon settlements, seven major proto-English kingdoms emerged. These were Kent, Wessex, East Anglia, Sussex, Essex, Northumbria and Mercia. However, the process of state formation was by no means a simple one and did not take place at a uniform chronological rate. In the case of Northumbria, two smaller kingdoms, Deira and Bernicia, eventually merged, and it incorporated parts of former Celtic kingdoms such as Elmet and Rheged. Lindsey, the part of the country comprising much of modern Lincolnshire, was for a long time the second most populous part of England, and control of it fluctuated between Northumbria and Mercia according to the fortunes of war. Originally, and as I will later explain in more detail, Mercia did not have a defined political existence. Rather, it was an outgrowth of an earlier kingdom of Middle-Anglia. In the area of modern Gloucestershire and Worcestershire a tribe of somewhat mixed Germanic folk had established a kingdom of their own, the kingdom of the Hwicce. It would be some time before they acknowledged Mercian overlordship. The bedrock of these emerging states were the smaller areas of local settlement, effectively clan cantons like the

Wilsaetan in Wiltshire, the Magonsaetan in Herefordshire and South Shropshire, the Wreocensaetan around the Wrekin in Shropshire, or the Tomsaetan, around the headwaters of the Tame near Tamworth. *Saetan* means literally settlement place. The Anglo-Saxons were used to a system of autonomy based upon kinship bonds and homage to dynastic rulers claiming descent from gods, as we have seen. It was only when the struggle against the indigenous British was finally over (and this took much longer time than is commonly understood) that these smaller state-lets coalesced into the larger heptarchic realms. Particularly in the north and west, there were still Celtic kingdoms surviving within modern England well into the seventh century. Powys, or at least its sister principalities of Pengwern and Luitcoit, still maintained a precarious existence until the mid-seventh century. Dumnonia, (Devon and Cornwall) was still unconquered as were parts of Somerset. Only in AD 577 following the Battle of Deorham or Dyrham north of Bath were the British expelled from the old villa heartlands around the Cotswolds. In the north, the British kingdom of Rheged was only destroyed after an epic war against two famous Celtic princes, Urien and Owain.

The pressure that forged these loosely organised local cantons into powerful English kingdoms was war. As the different Anglo-Saxon groupings consolidated, they immediately commenced armed conflict with each other and this went on for many generations on a more or less continual basis. If we are to understand the context of the Staffordshire Hoard it is absolutely crucial for us to bear this in mind. To these Teutonic peoples, war was a test of the potency of the tribe, personified by their kings and attested by their capacity to accumulate plunder *especially* treasures of gold and other precious metals and finely wrought jewellery incorporating precious stones. The essence of the cult of Woden was similar in many ways to the belief system of the Samurai warriors of medieval Japan. All men ultimately die, but by acquitting themselves heroically in battle, preferably by dying in the service of their lord, they could gain everlasting fame by their deeds which would be recounted in the mead halls to encourage the next generation of potential heroes.

The ultimate status symbol of these kings and their noble retinues was the sword, which was not, as we may imagine from modern cinematic depictions, the everyday weapon of the common soldier. Swords were extremely rare and valuable, requiring delicate and painstaking work to produce by skilled smiths. They were like helmets: the preserve of elite warriors. Therefore, to mark them out as the possessions of royal or noble exemplars, they were further embellished and decorated utilising exquisite craftsmanship, using the most lavish materials available. Such trappings transcended the constraints of mere life and death, and warriors of elite rank or kings took their weapons and other treasures with them into the otherworld. Consider this description of a burial from *Beowulf*: 'within the barrow they placed collars, brooches and all the trappings which they had plundered from the treasure hoard. They buried the gold and left that princely treasure to the keeping of the earth, where it yet remains.' This ostentatious display of wealth and power was designed not only to overawe the enemies of the Anglo-Saxon kings, but to impress upon their own tribes and allied folk that they were to be considered literally divine, invulnerable beings. Unlike the preceding Romans, they did not as yet mint coins and when old Roman coinage was used this was usually for display, suspended on necklaces and the like. When they were occasionally unearthed by the plough, they were thought to be 'fairy money' deposited by elves or similar supernatural entities. We may feel ourselves a little superior to this barbarism, but are our psychical impulses really so different, when we queue to see the Crown Jewels in the Tower of London? Indeed, we are not yet free of the mystique of the Anglo-Saxon dynastic legacy, for our reigning monarch is, through the marriage of Henry I to a descendant of the royal House of Wessex, a descendant of Woden. It has become fashionable among modern historians to mock these legendary pretensions, but before we disrespect the most elemental beliefs of our forebears, perhaps we should take pause. Such stories as the glorious reign of King Arthur we dismiss as compensation fantasies of a defeated people, but the ancestors of the English kings were themselves semi-legendary figures, whose sagas were declaimed by storytellers in the smoky mead halls. We must remember also, that the Anglo-Saxons had left all they knew of their ancient past behind them in the tribal homelands across the seas. This profound psychological break caused them to venerate the dimly remembered god-kings, men such as Offa of Angeln, or his (possible) great-grandson, Icel, who was the first Anglian ruler in Britain, all the more. If Sir Frank Stenton was correct in thinking that the Mercian kings were pre-eminent in some way among the other English kings, this may well have been due to their having preserved a more credible link to the overseas ancestors by asserting their connection to rulers whose deeds were objectively recalled by other German tribes, rather than quasi-mythical figures like Hengist or Cerdic. The *Anglo-Saxon Chronicle* itself must have originally been compiled as a means of preserving sacred genealogies, victories won by powerful warrior kings, their campaigns and conquests, initially against the Welsh, later against their English rivals. So, in fact, the establishment of the English kingdoms has as little hard evidence to commend it from a historical point of view as the Celtic myths and legends. Once again, we must content ourselves with a broad outline of probable events. A useful place to pick up our story is the end of the armistice following the battle at Mount Badon in the mid-sixth century, for it was in this area where hostilities were renewed, by the West Saxons under a ruler called Cynric.

Cynric is not an Anglo-Saxon name, but an Irish or British one. This may seem puzzling, especially in view of the marked hostility between the two peoples which I have posited. In fact, there is something a little odd about the origins of the West Saxon royalty. Its alleged founder, Cerdic, also has a British name. It has been conjectured that some British chieftain of that name may have taken control of the former tribal heartland of the Belgae folk around the Solent in the aftermath of the Roman withdrawal and that he supplemented Laeti foreign troops in his service by hiring Saxon mercenaries, or permitting limited settlement, much in the manner of Vortigern. If like Vortigern he then inter-married with a Saxon princess this may explain the apparent anomaly. Such a leader may well have recruited Irish pirates into his service too. However, there is a growing consensus that there is something not quite right about the story of Cerdic. The area which he is supposed to have ruled is almost devoid of Saxon archaeology, but there is evidence of Jutish settlement. Perhaps he was actually a king of the Gewissae of the Thames Valley. A British name would not be unknown among these people, who may have comprised Germanic Laeti already long settled among the British before the Saxon advent. British folk were seemingly living unmolested in what is now Hampshire just at the time when the *Chronicle* says Cerdic reigned. The attitude of the West Saxons to the conquered Welsh was somewhat more liberal than we would expect from an aggressive leader of Saxon war bands, and they survived in Wessex right into the reign of King Athelstan. It was felt necessary to make provision for them in West Saxon law codes (though they were almost invariably *theows* or bond-slaves). At least in the West Saxon context the English word *walh* meaning foreigner or stranger came to mean slave. Thus Wales means 'the land of the foreigners'. There was something deep in the Germanic race-consciousness about the term. Caesar tells us that the first Celtic tribe which the Germans encountered on the continent were the Volcae. They were incapable of differentiating between the separate Celtic peoples and so the term came to apply to any who they subsequently encountered, especially if they offered resistance to their expansionism. As one who bears a personal surname derived from the word, I have always been struck by the irony that these Germanic immigrants regarded those folk who had resided here for well over a thousand years as foreigners. I make this point because it will later become crucial to my argument, for the term did not just apply to people, but to the places where they lived, places such as Walton, Walcot, Walsall or Wall-by-Lichfield in Staffordshire. At any rate, Cerdic, if he existed, is a mysterious figure, whose existence we must take on trust. The *Anglo-Saxon Chronicle* was, of course, far from incredulous. This is the entry for the year 495 AD:

This year came two leaders into Britain, Cerdic and his son Cynric, with five ships... and they fought with the Welsh the same day. Then he died, and his son Cynric succeeded, and reigned six and twenty winters. Then he died; and Ceawlin, his son, succeeded, who reigned seventeen years. Then he died; and Ceol succeeded to the government, and reigned five years. When he died, Ceolwulf, his brother succeeded, and reigned seventeen years. Their kin goeth to Cerdic ...

So, clearly, the *Chronicle* is attempting to establish unbroken proof of dynastic succession. It should not be treated as unimpeachable historical fact any more than the wearisome lists of begats in the Old Testament, but on the other hand it is not to be considered worthless, because it must have been constructed from some distant folk memories of early rulers and their doings. Like Cerdic, Cynric is a shadowy figure, he is said to have fought a battle at Old Sarum in Wiltshire in AD 552 and four years later at Beranbyrg together with his son, Ceawlin. All we can really conclude from this is that the West Saxons were in arms against the British. With Ceawlin we are at last on surer ground historically speaking because his reign was the subject of a detailed saga recounting the progress of his wars. This implies that the centre of his operations had shifted north, into the Thames Valley area, into the Cotswolds and also east across to Kent. It is clear that he was attempting not only to eject the British from their last strongholds on his borders, but also to intimidate his Anglo-Saxon neighbours. Bede calls him a Bretwalda a term meaning 'wide-ruler', which meant he could compel other rulers to supply levies for his armies. One of the most important of these neighbouring tribes were the Gewissae who seem to have been established at an early date in the Thames Valley area, possibly as Laeti to protect the Romano-British population. These folk seem to have been partially subsumed by Ceawlin, or otherwise displaced into the southern Midlands as a result of his campaigns. They may well have morphed into the Hwicce who assumed control of the former lands of the British Dobunni tribe. J. N. L Myers proposed that the assertion in the *Chronicle* that Ceawlin was Cynric's son was an invention, and that he was in fact more likely to have been a ruler of the Gewissae, a tribe with a long-established military pedigree. Such an interpolation was designed to establish him as a descendant of Cerdic, for purely political purposes. Upon his succession in AD 560 he determined to eliminate the king of Kent, and their two armies met at Wibbandun, possibly Wimbledon, in 568. Ceawlin was the victor and was soon in a position to attempt a campaign against the remaining British in the Cotswolds area. At Dyrham, in 577, three British kings were slain by Ceawlin and his ally Cuthwine. This effectively drove a wedge between the British of Wales and the West Midlands, and Dumnonia, Devon and Cornwall, and this indicates that Ceawlin was much more than a barbarian warlord. His was a grand strategy, designed to end the Anglo-British wars once and for all. But in 584 he overreached himself, and at the Battle of Fethanleag outside Stoke Lyne in Oxfordshire, his ally Cuthwine (or Cutha) was killed, and he suffered a humiliating reverse. This was the turning point in the renewed war, for at a place called Wodnesbeorh in north Wiltshire, he was confronted by a nephew, Ceol, who had rebelled against him. The aging Bretwalda was heavily defeated, and the following year he was hunted down with his surviving retainers and killed. The surviving British must have breathed a huge sigh of relief.

In the aftermath of the great Yellow Plague, the British position must have been truly wretched, and it is extraordinary that they maintained a courageous resistance for as long as they did. It may have been this perceived vulnerability which had stimulated the West Saxon campaigns, and in northern Britain it was the same story. According to Bede, who must have had access to all the relevant information, the first Bernician king, Ida, landed on the Northumbrian coast in AD 547 just as the plague was at its most intense (according to Irish annals). The *Chronicle* concurs, and true to form gives an exhaustive list of his illustrious ancestors:

Ida was the son of Eoppa, Eoppa of Esa, Esa of Ingwy, Ingwy of Angenwit, Angenwit of Alloc, Alloc of Bennoc, Bennoc of Brand,

Brand of Balday, Balday of Woden... Ida reigned twelve years. He built the fortress of Bamburgh, which was surrounded with a hedge, and afterwards with a wall.

He was not the only Anglian invader in the north country. Aelle, a king of Deira, a region comprising much of the coast nearby the mouth of the Humber, had established himself during the 560s and subdued the independent British kingdom of York within twenty years. In the vicinity of modern Lincolnshire another Anglian kingdom, Lindsey, was consolidated at about the same time under a king called Critta or Creoda, possibly a kinsman of Icel. Once again it was the exigencies of war which brought about a merger of these different (though related) peoples into a more powerful state, Northumbria. Just before the turn of the seventh century a ruthless military leader, Aethelric, son of Ida, was busily consolidating this new state, and like Ceawlin of Wessex, he aspired to nothing less than total victory over the remaining Britons. By the time of his accession the British were recovering from the ravages of the plague and were becoming a real threat to the northern Anglian settlements. This threat came from Urien, king of Rheged, a Celtic nation extending from Galloway in modern Scotland as far south as Rochdale near Manchester (originally Recedham). The centre of Urien's power lay near Carlisle, and although Arthur and his gallantry may be fictitious or at least exaggerated, Urien was a real leader straight out of Celtic legend. His son, Owain, was no less gallant, so much so that he passed into Celtic folklore as a companion of King Arthur in the guise of Sir Yvain of the Round Table. But he too was quite real, a rival whose existence was a very dangerous reality for Northumbria. The Roman province of Britannia Inferior had always been heavily militarised, mainly due to the immense garrison (30,000 men) required to man Hadrian's Wall. This debatable land bred tough men, with a tradition of serving under (sometimes foreign) chieftains who had been sponsored by Rome to keep the peace – men with Roman names which may originally have been military titles, such as Paternus of the Red Cloak indicating the scarlet military cloak worn by Roman soldiers. To dislodge these hardy folk was no easy prospect.

Aethelric had already attempted to destroy Rheged by striking over the Pennines into Argoed Llwyfein probably the Forest of Leven in Cumbria. There, on a bleak Saturday morning, he met with a severe defeat at the hands of Urien and the Gwr y Gogledd, the men of the north as these north-country Celts were known. Urien promptly gathered a coalition consisting of war bands from all the northern Celtic realms, and struck back, forcing the Northumbrians onto the island of Metcawt, now called Lindisfarne, in 590. But in one of those odd twists of fate so characteristic of the Celts, one of Urien's allies, Morcant, became so insanely jealous of Urien's growing fame that he hired a traitor, Llovan Llawdivro – meaning landless, which perhaps explains his motive – to assassinate Urien. The hope of Britain lay dead and the bards lamented his passing in these haunting lines;

> I bear within my cloak the head of Urien most generous of princes
> On his white breast a raven feeds, great were his deeds
> And far from the fame of Urien from Rhiw I have borne a head
> Whose lips are red with blood ... woe to Rheged this day
> His slender white body will be buried this day
> Beneath earth and blue stones, sorrow to me and sad disgrace ...

Owain was determined to avenge his murdered father. He slew Aethelric in battle in 593 but Aethelfrith, Aethelric's son, avenged him in his turn. In one last attempt to repulse the Northumbrians, Owain made an alliance with Mynydog, king of Din Eidyn (around modern Edinburgh). A British cavalry force attempted to storm Catraeth, most likely modern Catterick in Yorkshire, but Aethelfrith lay in wait for them behind prepared defences. This swan-song of the men of the north was a suicide mission, leaving only a handful of survivors to tell the tale, among them fortunately, the bard Aneirin:

> Men went to Catraeth, shouting for battle
> A squadron of horse,
> Blue their armour, lances poised and sharp
> Mail and sword glinting
> Though they were slain they slew,
> None to his homeland returned
> Short their lives, long the grief of their kinfolk
> Seven times their number the English they slew,
> Many the widows they made, many the mothers who wept
> After the wine and the mead they left us armoured in mail,
> I know the sorrow of their death
> They were slain and never grew grey,
> From the army of Myndog, grief unbounded,
> Of three hundred, but one returned.

This heavy British defeat left Aethelfrith in a commanding position, and at a place called Degsastan a combination of forces from Rheged and Dal Riada (modern Argyll) were beaten in similar fashion. Now the tables had been turned, for Northumbrian power had become an Anglo-Saxon steamroller, threatening to overwhelm all Britain. It was at around this time, at the commencement of the seventh century, that a crucial development occurred which was to have profound consequences for all the peoples of the island, and which I believe may well provide crucial clues as to the context for the Staffordshire Hoard.

In the process of annexing Deira, Aethelfrith had driven King Aethelric's brother, Edwin, into exile. According to a tradition recorded by Geoffrey of Monmouth, his protectors were Cadfan ap Iago of Gwynedd and Selyf ap Cynan of Powys, which was then a mighty kingdom with strong ties to Ireland. The kings of Gwynedd had traditionally regarded themselves as High Kings of Britain for reasons which I will outline in a following chapter. According to the *Chronicle* in AD 607, but probably some years later, Aethelfrith attacked Selyf and killed him at the Battle of Chester. In blind fury, Aethelfrith also slew many hundreds of unarmed British monks, who had gone to pray for a British victory. This was said to have fulfilled a prophesy made by Saint Augustine that the Welsh, because of their failure to evangelise the English, should suffer death at their hands. So, this was a triple blow. The British had lost their high king, been entirely cut off from the men of the north and now suffered a callous insult from Roman Catholic propagandists siding with their, until very recently, heathen enemies. This incident had dramatic consequences which were to play out in the coming years. Edwin was next forced to flee to the Mercian court of King Ceorl, but fearing to risk war with the mighty Aethelfrith, Ceorl forced him to flee for refuge yet again, to the court of King Raedwald of East Anglia (he did, however, marry off his daughter to Edwin first). This gave Aethelfrith a *casus belli* against Raedwald, but East Anglia was a strong military power in its own right. Raedwald took the initiative and marched on Northumbria, where in Lindsey and Deira he was greeted as a liberator from Aethelfrith's tyranny. At a battle on the River Idle, Raedwald (probably the king whose ship burial was excavated at Sutton Hoo in 1939) had the victory, and Aethelfrith was killed. Raedwald effectively installed Edwin as the new king of Northumbria, and the scene was set for the drama which then unfolded, and which I believe must surely form the backdrop for the Staffordshire Hoard's deposition. But, for the time being, we must turn from these momentous events to consider another emergent kingdom: Mercia.

The origins of the Mercians are unfortunately extremely obscure. We have virtually no written evidence to act as a guide because their late conversion to Christianity (in the 650s) meant that they had no tradition of literacy. There are, it is true, genealogies of its rulers, and a most important later document, the *Tribal Hideage*, which describes the different constituent territories of the region in terms of how many hides of land they consisted of. Since one hide was thought a sufficient amount of land to support an extended family group, we can make guesstimates as to population. There is another reason why they have been consistently overlooked and underestimated in English historical terms. The father of English history as we have seen before was the Venerable Bede. He was a polymath, a genius of his time, a giant intellect, but he was also human. His kingdom, Northumbria, had been invaded by the Mercians and their British allies in the 630s and so brutally devastated that as a patriot it was almost his duty to despise them. To add to this, Mercia was also a heathen country at that time and so to Bede Mercians had been enemies of God, almost devils incarnate. He especially demonised Penda the last pagan king of Mercia who will play such a large part in this story. It is true that he ransacked monasteries and left Northumbria a wasteland and that he committed the cardinal sin of allying himself to the British against another Anglo-Saxon kingdom. But there is surely more to Penda than this depiction of a one-dimensional villain, as I hope to show. Bede hardly ever ventured more than a few miles from his monastery at Jarrow and the compilation of his *Historia Ecclesiastica* was largely facilitated by correspondence with other eminent monks and churchmen in other Anglo-Saxon nations who supplied him with the information he needed. Mercia, of course, had little to contribute to this intellectual enterprise and the information he received about it was second hand from informants who had their own prejudices. When he compiled a list of the kings who had ruled supreme in England, Bede ended his list with Oswy, his own countryman, and entirely ignored the Mercian kings. The *Anglo-Saxon Chronicle* falsified history in this way also, stressing the supremacy of the West Saxons. I do not think it unfair to say that the barely concealed cultural contempt towards the region, which has endured up until our own times, has its origins in this exclusion of Mercia from the foundations of England's national story, Bede's *Historia* and to a lesser extent the *Chronicle*. I am aware that this may seem a contentious statement, and the debate about it lies more in the field of cultural studies than history, but I ask the reader to merely note that Mercia was no ordinary Anglo-Saxon kingdom. Its history has been obfuscated, overlooked, misrepresented and subjected to mystification for so long that it had almost vanished from public perception even in what was Mercia itself, but the discovery in a farmer's field in Staffordshire in July 2009 may as well have been a detonation of unexploded subsoil ordnance. The Staffordshire Hoard cannot be ignored. It forces us to take Mercia seriously. The acquisition of the finds by Birmingham City Council and Stoke on Trent City Council, made possible by unprecedented public generosity, seemed almost the expression of a sublimated 'national' will to preserve the heritage of a country which ceased to exist in AD 918.

The most famous of the Mercian rulers, and the one whose name is synonymous with the extraordinary monument he ordered to be built, was Offa who came to the throne in AD 757. He treated as an equal the mighty Charlemagne and ruled over most of southern England as well as Mercia, when Mercian supremacy was at its zenith. Such a man certainly desired that he should have a noble pedigree, and the construction of Offa's Dyke was very possibly an attempt to emulate a king of the same name, Offa of Angeln, in the ancestral homelands. This other Offa had achieved fame in a very similar way, for according to an ancient saga, 'When he was but a youth he gained the greatest of kingdoms, none of his age achieved greater deeds of valour in battle; by the power of his sword he fixed the boundary against the Myrgings of Fifledor.' Offa of Mercia had more than just an egotistical motive in trying to emulate Offa of Angeln and his achievement of fixing the boundary. He had come to power as a result of a civil war, by force of arms, and desperately needed to establish legitimacy. He was descended from Penda's brother, Eowa, and was a cousin of the murdered King Aethelbald, but his right to the succession was by no means clear. Aethelbald had been the mightiest king in southern England, as he himself states in the Ismere Diploma a charter of AD 736 now in the British Library. But any dispute over Offa's ancestry brought into question to what extent other conquered English kingdoms owed him tribute. Almost certainly, Offa's claim to be descended from the mighty Offa of Angeln was fabricated to address this ticklish problem. But it tells us something very important. There must have been a preceding tradition of Mercian kings being descended from Offa of Angeln, through his great-grandson, Icel. The coalition of Mercian tribes were so disparate and, indeed, inter-bred with other peoples, including the native British, and their early history so obscure (for the reasons discussed above), that virtually the only proof of their right to rule were ancient traditions from sagas. That they settled on Offa and his heirs does at least tell us that they were Angles, with an original territory in East Anglia and around the Wash.

No one really knows why these Angles decided to push west. Overpopulation, inter-dynastic conflict and sheer opportunism all seem likely. An East Anglian chronicle states that around the year AD 527 there was a fresh influx of immigrants from northern Germany who 'invaded Mercia and fought many battles against the British. But they were not yet organised under a single king. Many leaders occupied these regions by force, and fought many wars from there. But since their leaders were many, they have no name of their own'. These bands of intrepid settlers were clearly adventurers, no longer content to live the settled comfortable life of the East Anglian folks. We may perhaps compare them to 'the American settlers moving west, and we can imagine these wandering groups of invaders following either a primitive track or a small brook to a place where good drainage and clear springs gave them hope of a settled life. Here they staked out a claim as a family or group, chopped down trees and built their elementary stockade to keep out the rest of the world …' (Edward Chitham, The Black Country). Their mindset was one of risk-taking and enterprise, and what they sought above all, as the above passage eloquently demonstrates, was a place of their own where they could be independent, farm and rear livestock and keep out the rest of the world. Just like the American pioneers, they were in hostile country where the natives might become truculent, even deadly. Their attitude to the Celts was just the same as that of the American settlers to the Native Americans. They gave them a name, the 'Welsh' which implied a lower social status and which had nothing to do with the cultural reality of the hostiles. In fairness, the opposite case was true. To the British, all Germanic folk were Saxons, as J. N. L Myers observed:

Thus the Celtic peoples, following in this respect the usage of their Latin-speaking ancestors, continued for centuries to label all Germanic inhabitants of Britain as Saxons. Even Penda of Mercia, sprung apparently from the purest Angle stock in England, the old royal family of Angeln itself, appears in the Welsh annals as 'Panta the Saxon' ... however inconvenient this may be for modern scholarship, it was quite natural that a single name should be given to the whole group of north German peoples whose homes lay along the coastline beyond the Franks, and whose behaviour was associated in the popular mind with desperate valour and barbarity, and their appearance with a trail of burning farmsteads, wrecked villages and a panic-stricken countryside. To the frightened provincial the precise ethnology of those who looted his villa was a matter of indifference: Angles and Jutes, they were all Saxons to him.

The Mercians avoided the British if possible, but when they encountered them they were treated as potentially dangerous. Just as in the Wild West, there were some brave men who had contact with them for trade and suchlike, and bilingual interpreters known as *walhstods* became valuable intermediaries. Some small groups may have been tolerated within areas where the British were still in the majority, possibly as protection against other hostile British tribes. The British were notorious for their internecine warfare and in Worcestershire there is the intriguing place name of Pensax, 'the Hill of the Saxons'. Professor Patrick Sims-Williams thinks that this may have constituted a boundary between the two peoples, but others have taken it to be a small Anglo-Saxon enclave surrounded by Britons. It was also a practice to corral local Welsh folk in reservations where they could get on with their lives separately, a kind of apartheid. These places sometimes bear the indigenous name of the folk who dwelt there, such as Comberton, but more often bear the English word for them, such as Walcot or Walton etc., as we have seen. But as they moved further and further west, they came to frontiers, usually demarcated by forests and marshes, beyond which lay lands where the natives were in the majority and were more than capable of attacking them with overwhelming force. There was only one counter to this threat: they had to rely on some force which would either support them in time to save them, or avenge them with brutal violence if they were killed. This was why the Mercians eventually formed a confederation for mutual protection, as we will see in due course.

The means of ingress into the Midlands were the rivers. The founder of the City of Nottingham on the Trent was a leader called Snot or Snota, and early Anglo-Saxon influence was probably confined to the East Midlands. A king claiming descent from Icel, and by extension Offa of Angeln, seems to have differentiated himself from the Middle-Angles about the turn of the seventh century. His name is extremely interesting: Ceorl. This name means *churl*, which was the lowest class of free men in the Anglo-Saxon hierarchy. It has been postulated that the Mercians had been in a kind of cultural rebellion against the notion of autocratic monarchy, represented by such men as Offa and Icel, and that this may have led to their expulsion from East Anglia. It seems natural that folk of a lower social class, whose kinfolk had risked everything to make a new life in a new land, should not wish to endure the old-fashioned social arrangements of their ancestors but strike out on their own. Perhaps the requirements of military service or taxation seemed to them out of date in the new world. Perhaps Ceorl was making a political statement of some sort, that among the Mierce, the 'border folk', the old class distinctions no longer applied. Certainly their later success and supremacy was due in large part to the fact that they accepted the concept of diversity within an organic whole, what the European Union now calls subsidiarity. It has also been postulated that Icel may have taken his name from the original Iceni tribe of East Anglia, and that the proto-Mercian population were already a folk of mixed-race. This would perhaps explain their more tolerant attitude to the British natives.

However, much of the above is speculation. The bare facts are these: small groups of settlers originating to the east had pushed into central Britain in the late sixth century, consisting of about thirty different tribes, the Noxgaga, Hendrica, Unecungga and many others. Their numbers were not great and they remained at first relatively isolated from one another. They had perforce the need of rapid military assistance from some strong central base, and had recognised kings, such as Creoda, Pybba, or Ceorl, whose authority was predicated upon their capacity to respond. By the turn of the seventh century they had overwhelmed the old Celtic kingdom of Cynwidion or Calchwynedd in Northamptonshire, and a royal centre had been established at Tamworth in Staffordshire from which offensive operations could be conducted as proved necessary. They were in contact with powerful and warlike British kingdoms and stood in constant danger of raiding from them. It was in this context that they took a new name for themselves, 'the border people' and this border was located in the West Midlands, as Sir Frank Stenton pointed out in his *Anglo-Saxon England*:

It is clear that the people as a whole had come to adopt a name which originally described the portion of the race in contact with its British enemies. Already in the heathen age, the Angles of the northern midlands, following the course of the Trent, had reached the water-parting between the Trent and the Severn. The names Wednesbury and Wednesfield ... 'Woden's fortress' and 'Woden's plain'... prove that the country above the head-waters of the Tame had been sacred ground in the heathen time. The boundary from which the Mercians took their name may well have been the belt of high land connecting the hills of Cannock Chase with the Forest of Arden. To the west of this belt, there stretched forests which bore British names, such as Morfe and Kinver, and which even in the eighth century had not yet been divided out among English settlers. Immediately to the east lay the country which formed the centre of the historic Mercian kingdom, and contained Lichfield, the seat of its bishopric, and Tamworth, the chief residence of its kings.

So Staffordshire was the lynch-pin of the Mercian realm in every respect, but in the early seventh century it did not yet contain

Lichfield because the diocese was not established until AD 669. As well as this, the Celtic frontier was not marked out merely by forests and marshes such as Kinver and Morfe but by a militant Celtic nation, the kingdom of Pengwern. It is a little-known fact that in the 650s, the time when it is most likely the Staffordshire Hoard was buried, the place where it was deposited may not actually have been part of Mercia at all. John Morris in his *The Age of Arthur* was explicit when he said, 'pagan Saxon (*sic*) burials, that last into the early seventh century, stop short at Tamworth, the future Mercian capital, seven miles east of Lichfield, and also at Yoxall and Wichnor, the same distance to the north, where the Trent formed the frontier.' There was a reason for this abrupt halt to Mercian influence. A British state-let, Caer Luitcoit, called by the Mercians Wall because of its British inhabitants, had developed from an old Roman town called Letocetum. It stood directly on the Roman road known as Watling Street (more prosaically the A5). The Celts possibly devised a system of elastic defence utilising former Roman posting stations situated on major routes enabling reinforcement by mounted troops. Caer Luitcoit would have been a place of vital strategic importance. As well as this, it was the centre of an ancient British shrine, a holy place, venerated long before the Romans came to Britain. So here was a place where the friction between the two peoples was building just at the time when the hoard was probably buried at a place called Hammerwich, less than two miles from Wall-by-Lichfield, Caer Luitcoit. Was there some connection, an event almost forgotten by history, which linked the hoard to something important that happened there? I believe there was, and in a forthcoming chapter I will expand on this. Meanwhile, there had been a major cultural change in the Anglo-Saxon countries in the shape of a resurgent Christianity which changed the entire spiritual and political landscape of the times. In the next chapter, I propose to look at this new religious influence, focussing especially on how it affected the obdurately pagan Mercians.

3

THE ANGLO-SAXON CONVERSION

Many of us will recall the famous story from our schooldays. The year was AD 597, the place Thanet in Kent. A party of monks had been permitted to land there by King Aethelbert of Kent. Solemnly and with great trepidation, they processed inland singing the litany, following a silver cross and an image of Christ painted on a board. The king was awaiting them, not at his royal hall, but out of doors seated beneath an oak tree surrounded by bodyguards. He feared the potential for magical spells these strangers might cast. Eventually, the fierce pagan king was persuaded to allow the holy men to preach and win converts among his people and granted them land around the ruined old Roman church of St Martin in Canterbury which they were allowed to restore. A handful of intrepid monks led by Augustine had dared the dangerous sea crossing, risking their lives in a barbarian realm to spread the light of Christ to an uncivilised pagan island. It is a charming vignette but it is not quite as simple as it may seem.

Firstly, there had already been a Roman Catholic presence in Kent for some time. Aethelbert was married to a Catholic Frankish princess, Bertha, who brought with her Bishop Liudhard, her personal chaplain. His influence was not just confined to the spiritual guidance and comfort of his royal charge and it seems he may have been allowed to refurbish St Martin's at Canterbury, before Augustine's mission had even set foot in Kent, and from this base he had been allowed to proselytise in a limited way with the tacit support of the king. This toleration must have been a signal to Pope Gregory the Great that here was a king ready to do business. Gregory had taken an interest in the affairs of the English for a long time. As a young man he had seen blonde-haired, blue-eyed children for sale in the slave market at Rome, and, enquiring as to their origins, had been told that they were Angles from Deira, one of the territories of Northumbria. He is said to have replied that they looked more like angels from God. Aethelbert had his eye on developing wider trade with the Franks and imitating their law codes, their coinage and their planned towns. All these innovations were predicated on the unifying role of Roman Catholic religion, and there must have been many among the pagan priesthood and the warrior nobility who drew the line at abandoning the ways of their forefathers. But in 601 Aethelbert was finally baptised, and where a king went, his subjects were bound to follow. Gregory had not realised how much change had taken place in Britain and still thought there were grand cities there as in Gaul, in which new sees could be implanted. In fact, as we have seen, urban life had all but collapsed and the London he imagined as the centre for an archbishopric was a collection of half-timbered settlements located outside the Roman ruins. Soon, Canterbury and Rochester were diocesan centres and London followed, but it was not directly under Aethelbert's control. Instead, Canterbury, Augustine's first see, became the seat of the archbishop.

Secondly, there were of course Christians among the British in the far-off western lands. Columba, the Irishman whose distinctive Celtic Christianity was one day to spread the faith to the people of the north, had died in the same year that Augustine's mission had arrived. It was a signal of which way the winds of faith were blowing. Augustine presumed that the British Church would immediately bow to his authority and expected their cooperation in his project, but like Gregory, whose view of the English was based on the charms of pretty, wide-eyed children and maps of Roman provinces with grand cities which no longer existed, Augustine simply failed to understand the political realities of the island he had come to evangelise. In his mind, the relations between Britons and Anglo-Saxons did not seem so very different to those of the Gauls to the Franks, but the enmity between the two peoples was so toxic that it threatened to undermine even Christian unity. However, seven British bishops, when they received a summons to meet with Augustine at a place on the borders between the English and the Cymric lands, agreed to meet with him to discuss terms. Where the meeting took place is unclear. Aust in Gloucestershire may be a contraction of Augustine, but there is a tradition that it could have been near Great Witley in the Abberley Hills of Worcestershire. Before going out to meet Augustine, the British bishops had visited a holy man, a hermit visionary, to take advice from him about how they should approach negotiations. The hermit's wise policy was to test the Catholic archbishop. If, when they arrived to meet him, he rose from the episcopal seat to greet them courteously then he was a man to be trusted, and to whom they should offer obedience, but if he remained seated then he was a proud haughty man whose arrogance precluded further discussions. Augustine, of course, remained in his chair, and the chance for Christian unity had been lost. Augustine was not happy to be rebuffed in this way and is said to have prophesied that the British would 'suffer the vengeance of death' at English hands. The independent-minded British and Irish Christians of the west who had guarded the light of Christianity against every peril and fierce pagan foes for so long alone were not about to conform with Augustine's plan unless they received due respect from him. His mission had been a beginning, that was all, and for all they knew Kent could just as swiftly become apostate. So, the conversion was not going to be easy, and as the seventh century commenced there were three religious influences at work in the island. In the south-east, Augustine's mission; in the far north and the west, British and Irish Celtic Christianity; and in the vast majority of the English speaking areas, Germanic paganism. Two kingdoms were to prove particularly resistant to Christianity: Sussex and Mercia.

In the context of the unceasing warfare between the Anglo-Saxon kingdoms, there was another reason for conversion to Christianity. It promised the faithful victory in battle. In fact, Christianity had become the state religion as a direct result of a vision the Emperor Constantine had experienced at the Battle of the Milvian Bridge in AD 312 where he had attributed his subsequent victory to divine aid from the Christian God. But victory did not always follow with conversion, and as a practical people the Anglo-Saxons soon fell away from the faith when the lord of hosts proved ineffectual. As soon as Aethelbert died (about 616), Kent threw off the new faith. The bishops of London and Rochester fled England but the new Archbishop of Canterbury, Laurentius, was preparing to abandon his see when he had a vision of St Peter which troubled his conscience. He bravely stuck his ground, and the precarious Catholic foothold was maintained. However, Augustine's early gains were almost set at naught. The new impetus in English Christianity came from the north. As in Kent, Northumbria had a Christian queen (from Kent) and through her bishop, Paulinus of York, was eventually able to convert the most powerful of the English kingdoms (at that time) to Christianity. This was an especially valuable coup for Rome. King Edwin of Northumbria, after many adventures, as we have already seen, had inherited the powerful military machine which was the Northumbrian army and had conferred upon him the title Bretwalda or wide ruler. Now this old English distinction was given another, perhaps more prestigious meaning: 'Britain ruler'. Edwin, possibly encouraged by Roman Catholic clergymen, took himself to be the inheritor of the ancient Roman imperial tradition. It is not difficult to see how this might have come about. York had been one of the largest military bases in the entire Roman Empire and large edifices such as the Roman walls and the Principia or barracks of the resident Roman legion were still standing even into Viking times. Hadrian's Wall was, of course, a constant reminder of Roman might, and all these monuments formed stone-quarries to build the earliest Northumbrian churches and monasteries. Edwin took to processing through the streets with a *tufa*, or Roman-style symbol of authority, borne before him, implying that he was the heir to the Dux Britanniarum, the old Roman military governor of the north country. His conversion during Easter 627 (he had prevaricated for some time) caused him to consider himself to be not only militarily invincible, but also to be performing a sacred destiny of uniting all Britain (not just the English) under an *imperium* sanctioned by God. Edwin's decision to accept baptism was encouraged even by the pagan high-priest Coifi and his chief men in council. Bishop Paulinus baptised thousands of the king's chief men and retainers in the River Glen beside Yeavering, one of the most impressive royal residences. Just as in Kent, these conversions were half-hearted and were entirely contingent on the good fortunes of the king. As soon as Edwin died, Paulinus fled for his life, though his faithful deacon, James, remained even during the horrors of invasion by the Mercian/ British alliance. Edwin's pretensions to hegemony threatened all the other free peoples of the island, whether English or British. His intention to install Paulinus as Archbishop of York was a threat to the authority of the Archbishop of Canterbury. The Church was deeply involved in intrigues against King Cwichelm of Wessex, and Edwin's promise to convert was conditional on prayers for victory being said when he sent his army on a punitive raid against them in reprisal for the attempt on his life instigated by Cwichelm in 626. His fleet attacked the Isle of Man and Anglesey and must have intimidated even the Irish kings. Before very long it became clear that those who stood in his way alone would be crushed beneath the Northumbrian juggernaut. Small wonder then that the weaker realms soon began to look to building alliances against him, and there was one king in particular who was determined to destroy Edwin: Cadwallon ap Cadfan of Gwynedd.

It may well be asked why Gwynedd, a remote mountainous region comprising much of Snowdonia, and the island of Anglesey, sparsely inhabited by people scratching a living from the poor soil, should figure so largely in the story which will now unfold. The background is extremely complex and contested, but in simple terms, the answer may be as follows. While the south and east of Britain were being colonised by the Anglo-Saxons, the western seaboard, particularly what is now Wales, had been under constant attack from the Irish. There is some reason to think that initially the Irish threat was a more serious problem for the post-Roman authorities. If we accept that Vortigern existed and that he had sufficient influence to entice Saxon mercenaries to settle in Britain as a defence against the Picts, then it seems reasonable to assume that some similar policy was followed in respect of the western seaboard against the Irish. Moreover, Vortigern had large issues at stake in this part of the world, which tradition states was his personal power base. Where could he turn to find war bands who could operate in this role? In Welsh tradition the answer was the Votadini, a tribe from modern Clackmannanshire on the Scottish borders. The Romans had struggled to maintain control in that area for many generations. Hadrian's Wall, formidable though it was, had had its garrison depleted and whittled down, and many of the garrison troops were auxiliaries from all over the empire for whom the strict regulations against marrying and raising a family which applied to the legionaries were not enforced. As a result they had gone native to some extent and their cohorts were often raised from their own male children within the forts. Economic pressures probably led to chronic underinvestment in the infrastructure of the fortifications too. Archaeological research seems to confirm that one solution to the problem of maintaining order on the frontier had been to pay off the tribes immediately north of Hadrian's Wall, dignifying their chieftains with Roman military titles such as 'Paternus of the Red Cloak'. It was probably a descendant of this man, Cunedda, to whom Vortigern turned when he was looking for a strong-arm against the Irish. According to Nennius, a Welsh scribe of the ninth century, Cunedda and his people were settled in Ynys Mon, or Anglesey, and Snowdonia and the North Wales coastal area, where he founded a dynasty of kings. He was said to have married the daughter of a British war leader in northern Britain, Coel Hen Guotepauc, or Old Coel the Splendid, the original 'Old King Cole' of nursery rhyme fame.

If all this sounds more the stuff of legend than of history, that is because it is. It forms part of no ordinary legend but the sacred lore known as the 'matter of Britain', the pseudo-historical magical underpinning of the British people. Venedotia, or Gwynedd, had always been the holiest, most sacred, most magical of all the kingdoms of Britain, and Ynys Mon had been the ancient centre of the Druidic priesthood. There was a reason why Anglesey had been such a dominant religious centre. It was accessible by sea from all the Celtic realms, Alba or Scotland, Ireland, Cornwall and also Gaul. Now, because of the mass-British emigration, there was a kingdom of the British in Armorica, or Brittany, which was also connected by sea. The Celtic power was therefore inextricably linked to the sea, and so Gwynedd's importance was as a nexus of international Celtic culture, trade and diplomacy. The kings of Gwynedd made much of their connections to the former Roman Empire and they did not see themselves as petty sectional rulers, but as high kings of Britain. Their close relationships with Ireland caused them to emulate many ancient Irish customs, especially the notion of a high king. Urien of Rheged had been 'a whelp of Coel's breed' and so the kings of Gwynedd, under the influence of inspired bards, aspired to rule these territories, which they felt belonged to them by right. These bardic prophesies and visions promised that the lost lands of Lloegr, or England, would one day be restored by God to their rightful owners. The power of this ancient legendary lore should not be underestimated. It was as potent as Zionism or National Socialism in its way, and a failure to appreciate this has resulted in great misunderstanding by Anglo-centric historians who simply dismiss all this as myth. To Cadwallon ap Cadfan it was much more than that, and as he grew up, tutored by eloquent and highly educated bards, he would have been inculcated with these traditions to the point of saturation. As far as he was concerned, his destiny was to be the high king of Britain, but from a young age it became clear he had a rival: Edwin, exiled prince of Deira. Geoffrey of Monmouth's story that Edwin sought sanctuary with the king of Gwynedd at Aberffraw, the royal court, has been dismissed as an interpolation invented to add extra dramatic tension to bardic tales about the subsequent war between Cadwallon and Edwin. The fact that such a tale was invented speaks of a deep-seated enmity. The battle between these two men was to become one of the most dramatic struggles in all British history.

However, the out-workings of this personal duel lay in the future. Meanwhile, what was happening in central England, particularly Mercia? It should be understood that the Mercia which existed at the turn of the seventh century was by no means as extensive as the later kingdom of Aethelbald or Offa. Its extent was limited to the west by British/Welsh kingdoms, on the south by the kingdom of the West Saxons, in the east by East Anglia and in the north by the British kingdom of Elmet and Anglian Northumbria. The Mercians continued in their folk-religion, Germanic paganism, and since the British do not appear to have made any attempt to evangelise them they had as yet hardly any contact with the Christian faith. All this was about to change. Yet there was one area where there may have been significant interaction between Christians and Anglo-Saxons. This was the kingdom of the Hwicce tribe of modern day Gloucestershire and Worcestershire. During the Roman occupation, this had been an area of considerable wealth and influence, with large and successful towns such as Glevum (Gloucester), Vertis (Worcester) and Salinis (Droitwich). These and other towns formed nodal points on the Roman system of roads, and an even more ancient and well-used system of salt ways radiated from Droitwich to carry precious salt to communities who relied upon its preservative powers. Moreover, this region seems to have been partitioned between Germanic and British tribes on an east–west basis. Patrick Sims-Williams, a scholar who has conducted a special study of the area at this time, noted that 'No sixth-century Anglo-Saxon graves have been recognised in the Severn valley and beyond, in the southern Cotswolds and Vale of Gloucester and in the valley of the (Bristol) Avon'. Among his many other complaints of his times, Gildas especially regretted that the partition had made it impossible for British pilgrims to visit *martyria*, local shrines to the many 'saints' the British venerated. As a rule, these were located in rural areas, and British churches, called *egles* from the Latin *ecclesia*, must have existed in areas in which they still formed the majority, giving rise to modern place names such as Eccles, Eccleshall, Eccleswall etc. Also, in Gloucestershire especially, large Roman villas, which were in effect palaces requiring large numbers of slaves, would have had their own church within the villa complex so the network of British places of Christian worship was probably very extensive. As well as the native British Church, this region had also been penetrated by Irish monks at an early stage, and so the silence of Bede regarding a survival of Christianity can only have come about through ignorance or because it did not fit in with his own grand narrative. Sims-Williams postulated that as the Hwicce and Magonsaetan moved further west, into Herefordshire and Shropshire, they may have been converted to Christianity by the native British.

Now, these possibilities are interesting, because the man who was to bring Mercia out of obscurity and lay the foundations of its future greatness, Penda, is thought to have been a native of the Cotswolds. The place name Pinvin, near Pershore in Worcestershire, may mean 'Penda's Fen'. Yet he was clearly completely uninfluenced by the Christian faith, remaining staunchly pagan till he died. A fascinating theory has been put forward by Stephen J. Yeates which may illuminate this problem. While his theory is conjectural, it is ingenious. In his *The Tribe of Witches*, and subsequent studies, Yeates asserts that the Dobunni, a British tribe which had been settled in the area for many centuries, perhaps millennia, had venerated a local deity called Cuda, perhaps related to Godda. This cult, he believes, survived right through the Roman occupation, and gave its name to the Cotswolds. When the Hwicce tribe invaded, or were displaced into the area, emerging from the forest which still bears their name, Wychwood, their aristocracy were absorbed into these ancient folk practices which they then continued into the early medieval period. Principally, the cult venerated rivers, forests and Nemetons, or hill-top groves; they were what we might call a nature religion. This scholarly work raises as many questions as it answers, but offers a distinct possibility that while some Anglo-Saxon folk were converting to Christianity in the area, others may have encountered an elemental form of paganism, incorporating magical rituals which would have been anathema to Christians. To Germanic pagans, however, they would have come quite naturally. Did Penda partake in these recondite ceremonies, and was his stubborn rejection of Christianity predicated on devotion to this older, elemental faith? At any rate, the mysterious kingdom of the Hwicce is intriguing, because its incorporation by Mercia was almost certainly brought about by Penda, whose doings will shortly assume very great importance in this story.

From the obscure, long-forgotten kingdom of the Hwicce, we must now turn to events on Mercia's northern frontiers, which were to have profound political consequences. As soon as Edwin had been installed as king of Northumbria in AD 616, he immediately began a campaign of aggressive expansionism. The first victim, and relatively easy meat, was the small British kingdom of Elmet. Its name seems to mean 'Elm Forest' and it extended from Olicana (Ilkley) in the north to Danum (Doncaster) in the south, on high ground of the southern Pennines, interspersed with wooded valleys around the Rivers Don and Calder. Its royal centre may well have been in or near Loidis, modern Leeds. Its ruler, Ceretic, was extremely exposed to the aggressive potential of both the Northumbrian Angles and the Mercian Angles. Edwin moved first, using as his pretext the alleged poisoning of Hereric, father of St Hilda, by agents of Ceretic. His situation was hopeless, and eventually he made a final stand on the River Idle near Bawtry, where the hugely outnumbered British warriors were swept aside by overwhelmingly superior forces. Ceretic escaped, but died in exile in 619. This may have been a mere footnote in history had it not been for the effect it had further south.

Mercia had overlordship of a remote highland folk calling themselves the Peak People in the Peak District of North Staffordshire and Derbyshire. The complex system of mutual defence which underpinned Mercian independence was immediately put in jeopardy by this Northumbrian take-over. However, for the time being, Mercia was in no position to challenge Edwin, but the political situation set in train covert negotiations which would in normal times have been unthinkable. Mercia now began to actively consider alliances with the British state-lets which were its traditional enemies – Pengwern, Luitcoit, Powys and, most importantly, Gwynedd. The kings of Gwynedd, through their shared bloodline with Urien of Rheged and their claims to high kingship of Britain, had claims on Elmet of their own, and now the bardic lore which prophesied a coming liberation of the lost lands, particularly a poem attributed to Myrddyn, or Merlin, called 'Cyfoesi Myrddyn a Gwynddydd ei chwaer' ('A conversation between Merlin and his sister Gwynddydd'), took on a bellicose British nationalistic fervour. Edwin's next move was by sea. As we have seen, Gwynedd, and to some extent all the British kingdoms, were held together by a common culture which absolutely depended upon mastery of the sea-ways and maritime trade routes, and Edwin's construction of a large fleet threatened their very existence. This fleet invaded and captured the Mevanian Islands, the Isle of Man and Anglesey, and menaced Irish traders. In 629 Cadwallon was taken by surprise at Penmon on Anglesey and forced to seek refuge on the tiny island of Glannauc, now called Priestholm, from Edwin's invading forces. The time for political manoeuvring was over, and open war had commenced. Miraculously (according to the 'Moliant Cadwallon', a Welsh poem) Cadwallon was spirited away and conveyed to Ireland, where he pondered his next moves. The Northumbrian blitzkrieg seemed unstoppable, and Edwin seemed poised to establish himself as Bretwalda, a new Emperor of Britain, while the high king licked his wounds in exile. But into this complex interplay of forces a new player was introduced: a relatively obscure warrior chief called Penda.

He was the grandson of the founder of the Mercian dynasty, Creoda, and therefore could trace his ancestors to Icel, Offa of Angeln and, ultimately, to Woden. The lineage was important, because Wodenism was a religion of heroic warrior dynasts, and such a pedigree was especially important for a people in constant strife against powerful enemies surrounding them on all sides. The Mercian royal family was a relatively recent development, and, unlike the centralised authoritarian and Christian kingdoms of Northumbria and Gwynedd, it was a confederation of many disparate peoples under their own regional leaders. The core of Mercian influence lay around the valley of the Trent, and this formed an internal boundary between the northern and southern Mercians. In the *Historia Brittonum*, which was compiled in Wales sometime in the ninth century, it is stated that Penda 'was the first to separate the Mercians from the Regnum Nordurum'. We must presume that by this it is meant that a state of dependency or tribute or tacit overlordship had up to Penda's time existed, whereby the Mercians recognised the Northumbrians as being the supreme Anglian folk in Britain. Their heartland was Leicestershire, Nottinghamshire, Northamptonshire and parts of Warwickshire, Staffordshire, the Peak District of Derbyshire, Hertfordshire, parts of Oxfordshire and, significantly, on the extreme western boundary with the Hwicce and Magonsaetan, a group calling themselves the Westerne, in east Worcestershire. There must have been some pressure on the Hwicce to join the Mercian confederation at this time, and it seems that Penda, as a prince from an august line of kings, was chosen to rule over this crucial area as a sub-king of the Mercians. We have no clue as to when he came to power, but Bede gives us some information at least: 'Cadwallon was aided by

Penda, a very able fighting man of the royal stock of the Mercians, who ruled the people of that region through various fortunes for twenty-two years from that time'. But before 633, and possibly after it, Mercia was ruled jointly by Penda in the south and Eowa, his brother, in the north. Certainly, the next time he appears in the historical record, in the *Chronicle*, the theme of a warlike fighting man is continued: 'In this year Cynegils and Chwichelm fought against Penda at Cirencester, and afterwards came to terms'. This entry for 628 looks as if the West Saxons had been worsted by Penda, which says much about the vitality and charisma of this obscure sub-king who had now overcome the mighty kingdom of Wessex. The momentum to join Mercia must have now become irresistible to the kingdoms of the Hwicce and the Magonsaetan. It was probably around this time that they became incorporated into the Mercian sphere of influence, if not full members, subordinating their rulers to Penda. His royal estates may have been located near Pebworth on the River Avon, and clearly his initial hostilities were directed against the West Saxons. The kings of Wessex had clearly underestimated the Mercians, because their strategy was predicated upon a campaign to eliminate Edwin of Northumbria, who, in the grand scheme of things, was the principal obstacle to their ambitions. King Cwichelm had sponsored an assassination attempt on Edwin in 626 which left him incapacitated, and so it would have been with Edwin's tacit approval that Penda had marched on Wessex. Northumbria may have sent troops, for there is a tradition that Penda settled an exiled Northumbrian war band in Worcestershire which had continuing influence on the royal family of the Hwicce and which appears to have kept up their Christian devotions. Edwin's reprisal campaign against Wessex had severely weakened it in any case. Edwin had promised that if he had victory against the West Saxons, he would convert to the Christian faith. His powerful army had marched on Wessex through Mercia, and at this stage Penda and Eowa were in no position to dissent. In Penda's later campaign, his ravaging extended as far south-west as Exeter, which he was said to have been besieging when Cadwallon, possibly in response to appeals from the men of Dumnonia (Devon) for aid, landed with an army of Breton and Irish mercenaries. Dumnonia and Brittany were close kinsmen, and in the vacuum left by the collapse of West Saxon power, Cadwallon saw his chance to reclaim his great inheritance.

This left Penda, the Panta ap Pyd, or 'Son of Danger', as the British called him, in an exposed position. The details are obscure and half-legendary but they seem to add up to this: warfare in these times was very different from the total wars of our own times. Military expeditions were not on a Napoleonic scale but consisted of small armies led by warrior elites. A war band may have comprised between 300 and 700 men, and a large army, utilising men called from toil in the fields for temporary military service who supplemented the hard core of noble warriors, may not have exceeded 5,000 men or so. The imperative to get back to the agricultural duties on which their communities depended entirely for survival meant that the rank and file, poor men with a basic spear, a shield, perhaps a dagger or club, had to return after a few months service at the most. Campaigns were seasonal, in the late spring and early summer, usually concluded quickly in savage, bloody contests where victory was usually decisive. Penda had calculated that he could deliver such a knock-out blow to the West Saxons, but the sudden arrival of Cadwallon was an event for which he had no contingency plan. He was now faced with a choice: he could withdraw and lose face, which would have thrown away all that he had gained in the preceding years, or he could remain and fight it out with Cadwallon, but he was in a hostile country, evidently low on supplies, faced by potential mutiny if he attempted to extend the traditional period of service of his levies. There was, however, a third choice. Cadwallon must have sent emissaries to Penda offering a mutual alliance. If he would switch his allegiance to him, assisting him in his war of revenge on Edwin, together they could invade and destroy Northumbria. Cadwallon's hatred was personal and political and his only objective was to kill Edwin, eliminate the Northumbrian state and succeed where Urien had failed, by driving the Northumbrians into the sea, 'exterminating the whole English race within the boundaries of Britain'. For Penda there was the chance of further glories and booty beyond his wildest dreams. His pagan marauders would be unleashed on the Northumbrian churches and monasteries, which had a subsidiary function as the equivalent of modern banks. All this Cadwallon would have offered to Penda if he would unite with him. Penda must have calculated that a showdown between Mercia and Northumbria was anyway inevitable, and so he acceded. The high king of Britain had returned and now had for his right-hand man the most feared warrior in all Britain. There now commenced a war on an epic scale, ferocious in its intensity and unprecedented in its duration; there could only be one victor, and to him would go the spoils of war, treasures to dazzle the imagination.

4

THE WAR OF THE HIGH KINGS

Cadwallon's approach to Penda came about for a very important reason. This was the fact that his homeland of Gwynedd was still under occupation by Northumbrian forces. The only practical way to expel them was by means of a direct assault on North Wales from Mercian territory. A Welsh tradition claims that Cadwallon fought Penda and that the battle took place at a very interesting location, Onnenau Meigion, now called Six Ashes on the border between Staffordshire and Shropshire, on the high road between Bridgnorth and Kinver. What I believe is that there never was any such battle, but something else that happened there which may offer some insight into the nature of Cadwallon's campaign and his war aims.

Onnenau Meigion was a sanctified grove within the Forest of Morfe, beside the River Severn. The Romans had constructed a bridge in the neighbourhood of Bridgnorth which was probably still serviceable. However, there was another reason why Cadwallon would have especially revered the place. The power of inspired prophesy in Celtic culture has been discussed previously. There were two visionary poets whose prophetic powers were particularly revered: Taliesin and Myrddyn (now known as Merlin). Merlin is an invented character from medieval romances, based on Myrddyn, but the latter did really exist. He was the chief court bard of Gwenddoleu ap Ceidio and in the Battle of Arfderydd (sometimes called Arthuret) in Cumbria, his master and patron had been slain. Therefore, Myrddyn had wandered insane in the Forest of Celidon on the Scottish borders, literally a wild man of the woods. Poetic and visionary inspiration was thought to be conferred upon those who isolated themselves amid the arboreal wilderness, and Myrddyn transformed into Llallogan, or Lailoken, meaning 'song master', implying that his utterances conveyed magical power and the ability to divine future events or indeed command their occurrence. An account of the process of enchantment using ritual song can be found in an old Welsh document known as *The Triads of Britain*. One of the prophesies is contained in a poem called 'Cyfoesi Myrddyn a Gwynddydd ei chwaer' which translates as 'A conversation between Myrddyn and his sister Gwynddydd' in *The Red Book of Hergest*, now kept in trust by the Bodleian Library for Jesus College Oxford. The manuscript is from the fourteenth century but is a compilation drawn from much older texts. In Celtic culture, twins (as they were) were especially sacred, particularly if they consisted of a boy and girl. Gwynddydd questions Myrddyn about future kings of Britain and the national destiny, and he replies that 'there will be resurgence', before listing the rulers to come. In the poem Myrddyn prophesies that the lost lands of England, or Lloegr, would one day be recovered and that a Celtic army would be summoned by a 'great eagle' to host at Onnenau Meigion, or 'the ash trees of Meigion'. They would then recapture the sources of the Trent and Mersey and a new frontier would be drawn up which would follow the course of the Severn to its mouth. Eagles symbolised exemplary rulers in Celtic mythology and so Cadwallon presented himself as the one who would fulfil the prophesy by gathering his host at the appointed place: the 'great eagle'. If all this seems fanciful to us, consider this: on 28 February 1405, the Welsh insurgent Owain Glyndwr

attested the famous document known as the Tri-Partite Indenture
by the terms of which he would have become the ruler of an
enlarged Welsh state extending far into western England. Glyndwr
had been subjected to exactly the same bardic propaganda by his
bard, Iolo Goch, and almost 800 years after the events I describe,
he demanded explicitly that the frontier should be drawn at
Onnenau Meigion. These were sacred ideas of the Celtic people
which they confidently expected would come to pass, not mere
dreams or fancies. It also tells us something important about the
territorial configuration that existed in the region at this time.
Cadwallon's claims would have left areas of Mercian settlement
virtually intact, and from this we must infer that this did not yet
extend westwards beyond the Severn to any great extent, with
the exception of the Magonsaetan of Herefordshire. Cadwallon's
'war of extermination against the whole English race within the
boundaries of Britain' did not apply to Mercia; indeed, it could not,
for without Penda's aid Cadwallon had little prospect of success.
The important thing about the prophesy was its references to the
sources of rivers. Watersheds and springs were in ancient times the
most important consideration in the creation of tribal boundaries.
Peoples were defined by reference to which river they lived beside,
and who controlled its flow. The bards, who were inheritors of
the ancient druids, expounded a mystical doctrine too complex to
explicate here, but in essence they saw that rivers formed arteries
into the flesh of the nation. The Trent flows into the Humber
and the North Sea, and the Mersey into the Irish Sea, while the
Severn flows into the Mor Hafren in Welsh, translating as the
Severn Sea. The number three was absolutely sacred to the Celts.
The story of Sabrina the princess reputed to have been sacrificed
in the Severn in Celtic myth is a complicated legend explaining
the entire foundation of the matter of Britain. By controlling the
sources of the great rivers, it was felt that the fate of Britain as an
independent nation would be secured. Cadwallon's ambitions were
influenced by this strange magical lore which informed his strategy
right from the start.

If I am correct, then the allied British and Mercian forces would have commenced the campaign to liberate Gwynedd from Onnenau Meigion. For the British it was a place of powerful omen, but practically it lay on an ancient route into mid-Wales, the Hen Fford, which ran through territory friendly to Cadwallon, namely Pengwern, a sub-kingdom of Powys. Gathering levies along the way, Cadwallon and Penda finally confronted the Northumbrian occupying forces at Cefn Digoll, Long Mountain near Welshpool. It is possible that Edwin was present in person to lead his army. The alliance triumphed and the Northumbrians were driven from North Wales. Now that their union had been sealed in blood, it was time to destroy Northumbria, and at the head of a vast army the two leaders rode out to invade their mutual enemy. The campaign was launched not in spring, the traditional season for martial ventures, but around the autumnal equinox for maximum surprise. On 12 October 633, Edwin confronted the allies at a place Bede called Haethfelth, or Heathfield. It was William Camden 900 years later who claimed that the battlefield could be identified as Hatfield Chase near Doncaster. A barrow called Sley-Burr Hill was said to contain the remains of the fallen warriors from the battle. But Haethfelth was actually a large region, not a particular place. In 1951 excavations by the National Coal Board revealed over 200 male skeletons adjacent to St Mary's church at Cuckney near Warsop, not far from the village bearing Edwin's name, Edwinstowe. A local historian, Stanley Revill, thought these remains, combined with suitable approaches to the place on old Roman roads, suggest that Cuckney was the field of slaughter. Certainly it is en route to Lindsey, the territory most likely to defect to Mercia, or at least to offer least resistance to Penda and Cadwallon. In any event, Edwin suffered a catastrophic defeat and was killed in the battle alongside his son Osfrith. His demise came only a few miles from the River Idle, where Raedwald had defeated Aethelfrith in AD 616 to install Edwin as king of Northumbria. Edwin's other son, Eadfrith, survived but was ruthlessly pursued by Penda into the far north. A huge ransom was offered to Penda at a place called Atbret Iudeu, probably Stirling in modern Scotland. This says something about Penda's reach, and also, perhaps, about his motives. He knew that Eadfrith would attempt to buy his life with treasure. In other histories the incident at Atbret Iudeu involves the later Northumbrian king Oswy. Nennius, tells us that Oswy 'reduced to the last extremity, tried to buy peace from Penda with a great treasure, which was refused'. Bede has it differently: 'Oswy, who was besieged in a fortress called Iudeu, surrendered all the treasures in that place to Penda, who then distributed them among his British allies'. As Sir Frank Stenton commented, 'These statements cannot be reconciled.' On the whole, Bede's account seems the most suspect of the two. As the junior partner in the alliance, it would have been strange if Penda were to have distributed treasures to the British in the original campaign of 632/633. We know that in a later campaign Penda besieged Oswy at Bamburgh, so it looks as if Bede, writing some years later, has confused the two expeditions. What does ring true is the desperation of the Northumbrians, whether Eadfrith or Oswy, in the face of this ravaging pagan leader and his army. Every scrap of gold, every jewel, even the holiest relics, had to be sacrificed to raise the necessary tribute. In the end none of this was sufficient to save Eadfrith. As a grandson of the Mercian King Ceorl he posed a threat to Penda and his heirs by way of lineage, and later, when King Oswald of Northumbria also desired his elimination, his fate was sealed and he was ruthlessly killed.

These accounts, garbled and irreconcilable as they are, paint a vivid picture of the power of tributes of great treasure. We are nowadays so used to seeing the economy in terms of trade, that we forget that in these times it was a peripheral activity compared to tributes and ransoms payable to kings. These kings were not misers hoarding their gold, and the immense booty they gained was distributed among their most faithful nobles, allies and those who had made a name for themselves by deeds of valour on the battlefield. It spoke well of a Celtic king if he was called by his warriors Hael, which meant generous, and this quality was especially praised by the bards. At this time, the Mercians did not mint coins of their own, and looted war booty and ransomed gold and silver served as a rough and ready currency. Even trade of luxury goods was done on a basis of barter. The alert reader will already have seen the point of all this. Northumbria was the richest, best-organised country in all of Britain. As well as royal tributes and ransoms, the plundering of the royal treasury (which may well have accompanied the royal personage onto the battlefields) and the churches and monasteries must have amounted to vast quantities of precious loot. Then there were the grim opportunities which came from the stripping of deceased enemies after the battle: swords, helmets, adorned horse-tack, shield fittings, hilts and pommels of swords and daggers etc. Just the kind of objects, in fact, which make up the Staffordshire Hoard.

Was there some other reason why the Mercians turned to plundering their neighbours at this time, besides the political manoeuvring of more powerful and sophisticated states? Just possibly there was. Gold was mainly derived from melting down coins, either old Roman ones or, more commonly, from coins imported from the Eastern Roman Empire. Traders knew the English tastes well and trading routes existed from the Adriatic Sea, utilising the Alpine passes and the River Rhine, which eventually ended in Kent. Garnets, the precious stones most favoured by the English for decoration of weapons and personal adornment, also had to travel far: some came from Bohemia, but others from India and Ceylon. Bright red garnets, backed by an affixed lustre of corrugated gold foils to enhance their shine were thought to protect the blood of the weapon's owner against infections contracted from wounds sustained in battle in a form of sympathetic magic. Silver was also reworked from old coins, but there was an indigenous supply from Derbyshire and the Mendip Hills. In the seventh century, Frankish gold coins, the nearest available supply, began to become debased by the addition of increased quantities of silver, affecting the lustre and quality. Garnets too were suddenly in short supply, and jewellers were forced to recut existing examples for wider use. Only exemplary and expensive examples continued to be imported, where instead of being used in large numbers in the kind of exquisite examples we see in the Staffordshire Hoard, they were used individually, to make pendants. Amethysts, glass and cowrie shells were also highly prized. We have seen how Aethelbert of Kent was strongly influenced by the kingdom of the Franks across the sea, and how he had converted to Christianity in order to introduce Frankish innovations into his kingdom. The decline in the quality and the availability of gold and precious jewels as imports diminished the power of Kent very considerably, and other localised port settlements grew up in Wessex, East Anglia and, probably, in Northumbria. This scarcity of the raw materials for luxury adornment of exemplary persons was a threat to the most elevated class in society. Status was defined by the display of what young people today call 'bling'. Scarcity also affected values and it is very possible that one of the motives behind the rape of Northumbria was to acquire some 'working capital', as the late Nicholas Brooks called it, for goldsmiths and manufacturers of elite jewellery. One of the theories that the research project for the Staffordshire Hoard are working on is based on the idea that what was discovered constituted a mass of material which was gathered together originally in order to be reworked into new works of art, but which was for some reason concealed and then forgotten about. At any rate, this was a time when these items were particularly rare and valuable and Penda would have been very mindful of that fact.

The unlikely and extraordinary alliance between Cadwallon and Penda had seemingly achieved its goals. The devastating defeat at Haethfelth caused the disintegration of the Northumbrian state. Penda's forces looted and ransacked the country at will, acquiring vast treasures, which were not only of Northumbrian origin. Edwin had looted Wessex, and his dowry from his second wife, Aethelburh, sister to King Eadbald of Kent, tributes from Eorpwald of East Anglia, as well as rich gifts from Rome, meant that the treasure consisted of artefacts derived from diverse sources.

The Northumbrian queen and her infant children fled to Kent for sanctuary, and the country split into its former component parts. However, Penda had now completed his part of the bargain, and the Mercian part of the army returned home with their spoils. Eanfrith, who had been driven into exile by Edwin, now returned to claim Bernicia, the northernmost part of Northumbria, while Osric, Edwin's cousin, claimed Deira. While these two remained, Cadwallon was compelled to stay on with his British/Welsh forces ensconced in the north country, far from their homeland in a hostile region among resentful natives, and moreover, his field force was now effectively halved. Having invaded in autumn, Cadwallon and his army were now forced to spend an uncomfortable winter in such quarters as they could improvise. They now foraged for food in desperate sallies, burning, pillaging and ravaging the stricken Northumbrian peasantry. Bede's comment that Cadwallon proved himself 'a barbarian crueller than any pagan' avenging himself on the whole population irrespective of age, sex or religion, is certainly true. These Welsh soldiers, whose country had been under the heel of Edwin's occupying army, were not the gallant Celtic knights of Arthurian myth. Ancient hatreds against the English emerged in the form of a race-war which raged unconstrained. It is true that ultimately this had all been Edwin's doing, through his policy of aggressive expansionism and his pretensions to imperialism. But none of this should excuse or obfuscate the terrible sufferings of the Northumbrian folk, as, not for the last time, their country was looted, burned and pillaged, and their poor people starved and were murdered by a callous, indifferent conqueror.

To compound these iniquities Cadwallon treacherously killed Eanfrith during peace negotiations, and Osric, fearing a similar fate, attempted to invest Cadwallon's fortified encampment. But Cadwallon sallied out with strong forces and wiped out the Deiran besiegers, killing Osric. The Northumbrian cause seemed irretrievably lost, but at the nadir of their fortunes, a Christian hero emerged to save the day. The two sons of Aethelfrith, Oswald and Oswy, had languished in exile since 617 under the protection of the king of Dal Riada. On the lonely tiny island of Iona they had been educated by monks steeped in the traditions of their founder Saint Columba. Both young men became devout and learned, and now came the time for them to return to their native land on a holy mission to deliver it from its oppressors. Unlike Edwin, their loyalties lay with the Celtic Church of Columba, not with Rome, and this appealed to those common folk whose blood was half-British, and whose faith was less ostentatious and politically loaded than Catholicism. Oswald gathered an army in Lothian, many of whom were from Dal Riada, and set out to confront Cadwallon. Cadwallon marched north from York to meet them, and just outside Hexham a bloody battle was fought in sight of Hadrian's Wall. Oswald was outnumbered but placed his faith in God. He had had a vision of St Columba assuring him of victory and drew up his forces beneath a raised wooden cross. The Welsh remember the battle as 'the strife at Catscaul', or the 'battle on the Wall', but the English called it 'Heavenfield', presumably because of its almost miraculous consequences. In a desperate struggle, the Welsh onslaught was contained and driven back before their whole army turned and fled. There would be no mercy for them after the depredations they had inflicted on Northumbria, and they were ruthlessly pursued until practically their entire army was wiped out. Cadwallon himself was trapped at a place called Denis Brook, now Rowley Burn, and killed. In one of those supreme ironies of history, he was slaughtered within miles of the country from which his illustrious ancestor Cunneda had marched south into North Wales to establish the kingdom of Gwynedd, and his adversaries included descendants of those very people who had been transplanted there all those years before. The great high king was dead, and with him died the hopes of Britain in the shadow of the ancient wall. All the bardic lore was set at naught by this stunning Northumbrian victory and Gwynedd relinquished its claims on English lands. Thereafter the free British became a new entity: the Cymry. The Prophesy of Myrddyn had been undone. Cadwallon would have done better to listen to the Prophesy of Taliesin:

> Their Lord they shall praise,
> Their speech they shall keep,
> Their land they shall lose,
> Except wild Wales ...

Oswald's victory had momentous consequences for the spiritual development of Northumbria. His Christian faith was very sincere and he immediately called in missionaries to evangelise backsliders and provide pastoral care to the desperately impoverished and psychologically bewildered population. Such folk were naturally reticent and the first attempt failed miserably, defeated by the 'indomitable barbarism' of the ordinary people. A young monk named Aedan remonstrated with the failed missionaries, commenting that perhaps what was needed was a more gradualist approach not predicated on the sophistries of theology but on 'the milk of milder doctrine'. Here was wisdom, and this young man was sent out to try his luck among the starving bereaved and beleaguered country people. By prodigious efforts and an example of self-abnegation, he won the hearts of the common folk, traversing the kingdom on foot. As soon as rich gifts of plate or money or fine clothes were given to him by the nobility, he gave them away to beggars, chastising the rich for their materialism and display. Monasteries proliferated and began the slow process of healing the devastated land. The glory of English Christianity, the monastery of Lindisfarne, became the base from which a dynamic cultural revival spread a synthesis of Irish creative energy and English diligence and method. Northumbria opened like a flower and its revival was all the more remarkable considering how close it had come to extinction. It was an enterprise involving the whole people, young and old, male and female. St Hild at Whitby was one of many abbesses whose authority was equal to their male counterparts. In time the monasteries of Jarrow, Monkwearmouth, Ripon and Hexham, and the great library at York, were to usher in a golden age of English Christianity whose influence was felt in the Germanic homelands across the seas. Oswald travelled by sea to St Oswald's Bay in Dorset in order to be present when King Cynegils of Wessex was baptised in 635, and Oswald's marriage to Cynegils' daughter sealed an alliance which presaged a renewal of hostilities with Mercia. It was an unfortunate fact that Penda still reigned supreme in the Midlands, resolutely pagan, more powerful than ever before. The time could not long be delayed for a showdown with him, and in 641 or 642 Oswald set out to destroy the heathen warlord once and for all. But Penda was still a force to be reckoned with, a man at the height of his powers. It would be no easy matter to defeat him.

Meanwhile, Penda had been preparing for the conflict which he knew must soon erupt. Oswald seems to have made overtures to Eowa, Penda's brother, with the object of suborning him into a potential rebellion against the latter. This, combined with the new alliance between Northumbria and Wessex, constituted the threat of a war on two fronts: north and south. The disaster at Heavenfield had eliminated Gwynedd as a serious military power, but there still remained another British ally who could supplement Mercian power. This was the kingdom of Powys and its subsidiary state-lets, Pengwern and Luitcoit. The ruler of this state was one Cynddylan ap Cyndrwyn, whose later exploits will be of some importance to my theory. His very existence has proven contentious, and this has come about because of a stubborn refusal by Anglo-centric historians to lend credence to a corpus of Welsh poetry which records his deeds. These have been treated as interpolations, inserted at a much later date in order to promote a national literature for the purpose of establishing a Welsh national consciousness. This is to profoundly misunderstand what these poems actually are, which is a synthesis of history and mythology. This is not a peculiarly Welsh phenomenon. English history is littered with exactly such instances of conflation between historical events and folk stories, pithy aphorisms which embody the essence of a situation, a time and place and a person; think of King Alfred of Wessex and his burning of the cakes, for instance. We cannot confirm that the story is true or untrue, but we do not thereby consign Alfred to the realms of myth and legend, denying his achievements. It is a prejudice of our literate culture to disparage and dismiss stories as if they are all mere fictions. Actually, illiterate societies preserved vast stores of complex information without recourse to writing; indeed, one of the reasons the druids underwent a training which could last up to twenty years, was so they could become proficient in the art of mnemonic prosody. They knew Greek and Latin but set nothing down in writing, precisely because they thought that to do so may have the effect of corrupting sacred lore. An analysis of these poems in the following chapter will unpick these issues, and as I will conjecture, the Staffordshire Hoard may provide crucial evidence of their veracity. For the moment, let us proceed on the basis that Cynddylan, ruling from his court at Llys Pengwern (perhaps near Baschurch outside modern Shrewsbury, perhaps from Caer Guricon or Wroxeter) did actually exist, and that when 'The Son of Pyd requested, he was so ready!'. The 'Son of Pyd', or Son of Danger, is none other than Penda, and Welsh annals state that this alliance was sealed by the marriage of Cynddylan's sister, Heledd, to Penda. At any rate, there now followed a very real war, recorded as faithfully in Welsh texts as in English, perhaps more so. The result was a disaster on a grand scale for Northumbria and Oswald.

That such an alliance between Penda and Cynddylan has a historical reality seems to be borne out by the trajectory of Oswald's attack. In the subsequent battle, Penda's brother Eowa was slain, but it is a moot point as to which side he fought on. If Eowa had indeed been suborned by Oswald then his army may have included a substantial contingent of Mercians fighting alongside the Northumbrians. Such heterogeneous armies were notoriously prone to last-minute defections, and perhaps Eowa switched his allegiance during the battle in this way, fighting and dying alongside his brother. Forces from Gwynedd and other Welsh kingdoms may also have swelled Penda's ranks, for Oswald's march led him to the Welsh border country. The battle was fought on 5 August 641 or 642, at a place called Maes Cogwy by the Welsh and Maserfelth by the English. The Northumbrians were subjected to a relentless onslaught by the Mercians and their British allies until Oswald, seeing that all was lost, knelt to say prayers for his doomed soldiery. Oswald's position was stormed by Penda and his body hacked in pieces. His head and limbs were set on poles and affixed to a tree as an offering to Woden for this greatest of Penda's long string of victories. Subsequently, the battlefield became known by the Welsh as Croesoswallt and a legend took hold that he had been crucified. Oswestry or 'Oswald's Tree' is said to have grown up around the spot, though this is contested. The pagan offering represented a rite long observed among pagan Germanic tribes. Bede and his countrymen thought that Penda had reverted to this barbarism in order to mock Oswald's piety and religion. Indeed, Penda's Welsh (and also Christian) allies seemed shocked by it, and in later annals they attributed Penda's victory to diabolical intervention. It was to be the last blood-rite of its kind until the coming of the Vikings, and even allowing for Bede's tendency to demonise pagans, its perpetration speaks of a savagery that looked backwards to the pure Wodenism of another age. Miracles were said to have occurred near the spot where Oswald fell and his brother Oswy retrieved the remains of his sainted sibling the next year. They were eventually laid to rest at Bardney in Lindsey, but, as we will see in a later chapter, the relics retained their magical power for hundreds of years, eventually being relocated to Mercia.

Penda was now the de facto Bretwalda whatever Bede might have thought, and his influence was massively enhanced. In 644 he invaded Northumbria in a reprisal raid and once again devastated and looted that country, besieging Oswy, Oswald's brother and successor, at Bamburgh. The town was set alight by Mercian marauders but the flames were said to have been extinguished by a prayer offered up from Aedan, who from the island of Inner Farne could see Penda's army stacking faggots against the walls of the fortress. 'Lord, see what evil Penda does', Aedan is said to have exclaimed, at which point the western wind, which had threatened to immolate the entire town, turned, saving the Northumbrians from disaster. This may be a later legend, but it conveys the sense of fear and doom the Mercian king brought in his wake. Penda was only bought off by yet another tribute of great treasure. The Mercian rampage continued when Cenwalh, king of Wessex, put away Penda's sister who he had taken, presumably reluctantly, as his bride. Wessex was promptly invaded and Cenwalh driven into exile for three years in East Anglia. That kingdom was invaded in turn, not once but twice, and its king driven out, no doubt after much of his royal treasure had been carried off. Penda was becoming a personification of the warrior dynasts and semi-divine heroes of *Beowulf* and the likes, and as Frank Stenton postulated, he must have become the subject of some similar saga himself. As he grew older, more avaricious and more assured of his own invincibility, the temptation must have grown to crown this reputation with one last unquestionable victory over his arch-enemy Northumbria, and if he was as truly demonic as Bede portrayed him, perhaps he also yearned to purge all England of the Christ-God. However, such a view is almost certainly incorrect. Penda tolerated Christian missionaries inside Mercia and is said to have remarked that the most despicable people in his eyes were those who having converted and received baptism then went on to become apostate. Far from being a monster, he seems rather to have been someone who knew his own mind, expected loyalty and constancy and respect for the hallowed traditions of his ancestors, and who despised the fickle and faint-hearted who changed their beliefs with any wind which blew. All his life he had led from the front, personally killing many enemies in battle; not for nothing was he called the 'Son of Danger'. It is fitting that he died as he had lived, sure in his heathen faith to the last. But for a brief interlude, it seemed that this hoary old warlord had abandoned conflict and chosen instead the path of peace.

The incentive for a diplomatic political settlement was probably concern for the fate of his sons. The two rival kings concluded marriages between their children. Peada, Penda's heir apparent, was married to Aelfleada, Oswy's daughter, and Oswy's son Alchfrith was married to Penda's daughter Cyneburh. Peada had perforce to convert to Christianity, and he allowed Christian missionaries to evangelise his own sub-kingdom of the Middle-Angles. It was this complex arrangement which, I believe, may unlock the secrets of the Staffordshire Hoard. It was an uneasy truce, predicated on marriages which must have been intolerable to all parties concerned. Why Penda decided to abrogate the treaty we just do not know. Perhaps he had recourse to consultations with pagan practitioners, rune-readers who warned him of treachery, but more likely he had calculated that a man in his late fifties, perhaps even older as he now was, had better strike his blow before he was overtaken by infirmity. There must be a strong suspicion too, that peace and miserable ease were anathema to this most constant of warriors. War had been the making of him and in the absence of a campaign he was simply bored. So, in 655 Penda assembled a gigantic host, composed of contingents from thirty different English and British peoples: a vast horde intent on plunder. This very diversity was to be Penda's ultimate undoing.

Once again, Penda's forces were unleashed on a hapless Northumbria, marching far into the north country, leaving a burning wasteland in their wake. Oswy had no choice but to adopt the strategy of Fabius Maximus, avoiding battle and leaving his countrymen to suffer the depredations of the Mercians and their allies. Once again, Oswy sued for peace. As well as the usual offerings of gold and precious treasures, he gave up his own son, Ecgfrith, as a guarantee of his good faith. Penda appeared to have triumphed yet again, and late in the campaigning season he was content to turn for home, leading his heterogeneous forces south. On 15 November 655, Oswy caught up with him near Leeds during a heavy rainstorm. The location of the battle is unclear. It was known in Welsh as Maes Gai, or Gaius Field, and in English by the name of the swollen river on which it was fought: Winwaed, which some experts think is the little River Cock near Leeds (near a housing estate called Pendas Fields). Penda's undoing proved to be the diversity and unreliability of his disparate forces. Cadfael ap Cynfeddw of Gwynedd, leading Penda's Welsh allies, left the latter to his fate, for which he was ever after calumniated as 'Cadomedd' or 'the battle-shirker' by his countrymen. Aethelwald of Deira, son of Oswald, whose body had been gibbetted on a tree by Penda, could perhaps be excused for abandoning the old man as he stood at bay in the mud and rain, and only Aethelhere, king of the East Angles, remained loyal to face Oswy's onslaught. Even so, Oswy must have approached the battle with the utmost trepidation, for before him stood the indomitable warrior who had bestrode the whole country of England for over twenty years. On the night before battle, Oswy prayed earnestly, promising that if he gained the victory he would offer up his daughter as a nun and build a dozen monasteries. There was no escape for Penda, and as the River Winwaed rose in spate, he turned to face his enemies for the last time. Indeed, we must doubt if there could have been any other choice for such a man, and as his army was overwhelmed in the lashing rain, he bravely resisted to the end, until, finally, the Northumbrian vanguard reached him to hack his head from his body; so ended the life of the last pagan king of the Mercians. At last, Oswy could truly be called Bretwalda. The battle marked the conclusion of a bitter and relentless war, which had exhausted both Mercia and Northumbria. Now Oswy was the undisputed victor, and for the Mercians dark days lay ahead. It was in these dark days that I believe a consignment of treasure came to be buried in an obscure field in the Staffordshire countryside.

5

ANCIENT VOICES

Oswy's victory at Winwaed was a disaster not only for Mercia but also for its Welsh allies. Northern Mercia was annexed, but Peada, Penda's son and Oswy's son-in-law, was suffered to remain as a puppet king of the Middle-Angles. This was conditional upon his accepting Northumbrian missionaries and Church appointees selected by Oswy, and Peada's submission to Northumbrian governors north of the Trent. To ensure his complicity in the programme, Aelfleada, Oswy's daughter and Peada's wife, kept her husband under constant surveillance to ensure he did not become reprobate. Within months, Peada had begun to renege on the arrangements, and Aelfleada arranged for Peada to be murdered. Such tender matrimonial behaviour was unfortunately the most ready expedient of the political manoeuvring of these times, as was the elimination by assassination of rivals and the extermination of collateral kinsfolk. To read Bede's *Historia*, one would think that the Northumbrian missions were entirely congenial embassies whose only aim was to spread the love of Christ to benighted barbarians, but we should bear in mind that behind the monks stood hard men, ready to wield the knife.

The mission to the Middle-Angles had come about as a result of Peada's marriage in 653, and it had been at his request that four monks from Lindisfarne had come into his kingdom. Three were English, Adda, Betti and Cedd, the other, Diuma, either Irish or Scots. Their reception was friendly and they met with at least superficial success. However, it may well have been their meddling that had precipitated the war of 655. Penda had been content to tolerate the mission in his son's sub-kingdom, but when Diuma was consecrated as bishop by Finan of Iona and a potential see had been found for him at Repton, the old pagan demurred. As we have seen, Penda had miscalculated, and now Oswy (according to Bede), 'having cut off the wicked king's head, converted the Mercians and the adjacent provinces to the grace of the Christian faith'. For all his piety, Oswy was above all a shrewd politician whose aim was to emasculate Mercia and eliminate any future potential for resurgence in the Midlands. Peada's brother, Wulfhere, had been spirited away and kept in hiding by Mercian nobles who remained stubbornly loyal to the old ways, suspecting, rightly as it turned out, that Peada's reign would be short. Now that Penda was dead, it was above all necessary for Oswy to have Peada establish a see from which Diuma could exert ecclesiastical control, and now Repton seemed too far east. Ideally he needed a centre close to the heart of the Mercian aristocracy in Tamworth and also close to the British state-lets which formed a salient into Mercian territory; Bede's 'adjacent provinces', for whom Finan's project of a network of Church organisation dominated from Iona, was a threat to their own clerical authority. The place selected, innocuous enough from Oswy's point of view, but extremely contentious for those on the ground, was Lichfield. There may well have been method in this, for by exhorting Peada to enforce this decision, Oswy knew that he was setting the old allies of Mercia and Pengwern against each other. Morfael ap Glast, who exercised authority from Caer Luitcoit, only a few miles from Lichfield, must have been very disturbed by these developments, to say the least, and his kinsman Cynddylan of Pengwern even more so. The writing was on the wall. Northumbria could now use Mercia as a tool to eliminate the British east of the Severn, and the time had come for war.

There was another reason why Caer Luitcoit was an especially sensitive area for the free British. Stephen J. Yeates in his *The Tribe of Witches* points out that it was a significant shrine, hallowed for centuries: 'There is a major shrine on the northern edge of the forest at Wall, in Staffordshire, just outside the study area'. There is a theory that this shrine was sacred to Brigit, a saint whose personality had developed from an ancient Celtic goddess and that Hammerwich was the site of one of King Arthur's twelve legendary battles, Bassa. Now, whatever the truth of the legends, the important thing is that there is growing evidence that the character of 'Arthur the Soldier' as a mythical Celtic messiah was probably already established by this time among the British. It may well be that the 'Canu Heledd', one of the poems under consideration in this chapter, contains a very early reference to him, for she calls her brothers 'the whelps of Arthur'. The etymology of the passage is disputed but it does not stand alone. Another early reference to Arthur occurs in the 'Gereint fab Erbin' contained in the *Llyfr Coch Rhydderch*. At a place called Llongborth (possibly Portsmouth or Longport in Somerset), Gereint or Gerontius is a companion of Arthur:

> In Llongborth I saw Arthur's heroes who cut with steel
> The Emperor ruler of our labour.
> In Llongborth Gereint was slain, heroes of the land of Dyfneint
> Before they were slain they slew ...

Now, the point of this digression is not to churn over the debate about the case for a 'historical' Arthur, but to introduce the idea that by this time such a hero figure had emerged into the British/Welsh consciousness, representing resistance and eventual redemption. It is noteworthy that Powys, the territory under examination in this chapter, may well have been the epicentre of this original legendary lore. Near Llanfair Caereinion lay the seat of the princes of Powys, called Mathrafal which has been thought to have been an early prototype for Camelot. In the Shropshire Hills near Priestweston, an early legend identifies Mitchell's Fold stone circle as the site where Arthur drew the sword from the stone, and the River Camladd nearby there is claimed as Camlann. As the most exposed of all the Celtic kingdoms these lands were highly militarised. Indeed, the resident tribe which had occupied the area for hundreds of years, the Cornovii were the only British tribe known to have supplied recruits for the Roman army (they served on Hadrian's Wall). A tradition exists that they had supplied auxiliary troops for the defence of the south-west against Irish raiders, and that Cornwall is named after them. These strong military traditions permeated the elite ruling class especially and we have seen that Cynddylan had been a faithful ally of Penda, fighting alongside him at Maes Cogwy. He almost certainly accompanied Penda's invasion of 644 and was probably present during the ill-fated invasion of 655. Cadfael ap Cynfeddw, the so called 'battle shirker', had deserted Penda as we have seen, and he was Cynddylan's technical overlord, so it is likely that the war bands of Pengwern were among the Welsh contingents which escaped the slaughter at Winwaed. Cynddylan's own sister, Heledd, may have been widowed when Penda had fallen and so he would have been very aware of the danger looming on his eastern and northern frontiers. His response was to attack, in a large, mounted raid like that at Catraeth mentioned earlier. Pressure, must have been building at Caer Luitcoit of a military nature, and news of this would have been swiftly conveyed to him by Morfael along the still-serviceable Roman road of Watling Street. The system of defence devised by Pengwern (or Dogfeiling) was predicated upon rapid support to each of the three strongholds ruled by sub-kings. These were Caer Guricon (Wroxeter), Caer Magnis (Kenchester) and finally Caer Luitcoit (Wall). The poems mention that the size of Cynddylan's war band was 700, and these would have been cavalry, the favoured arm of the British. This may not sound like an exceptionally large force, but the element of shock and surprise could quickly demoralise and overwhelm infantry forces if they were unprepared. One of the scenarios posited for the deposition of the Staffordshire Hoard is that it was buried sometime in the mid-seventh century in order to conceal it from raiders. Here was just such a raid at exactly this time, within two miles of the burial site, commemorated by poetry which specifically mentions the seizure of 1,500 cattle, eighty horses and much booty taken from monks; is this a coincidence? However, this is only one among several possibilities, though it does seem intriguing.

It seems to me that the case for considering the connections between the raid on Caer Luitcoit, Peada's difficult political predicament, his eventual sudden death and the Staffordshire Hoard are so compelling as to be ineluctable. So, let us now consider the possibilities in detail. The most important distinguishing feature of the Staffordshire Hoard is its essentially military nature. It is almost exclusively comprised of war gear. So far, pommel-caps and hilt decorations of up to 150 swords have been identified. We have seen that swords were the weapon of choice of the military elite, lavishly decorated by expert metal-smiths using incredibly intricate filigree cloisonné work and animal designs. The painstaking process of forging pattern-welded sword blades was revered as a kind of magic. Swords were given individualised names such as 'Brain-biter' and were thought to possess personalities and fates. No sword blades were deposited in the hoard. They were valuable gifts to bestow on valorous and distinguished warriors for services rendered; they were prestigious items with only one practical use. Captured swords from fallen warriors on the field of battle would have been gathered up and offered to the victorious king. Valuable precious decoration would have been removed and set aside for the royal goldsmith, who would have been a resident in the king's household. So many swords, and fragments of even rarer helmets, indicate that these weapons were once personal possessions of a king, taken on the field of battle from fallen enemies, or offered in tribute to him. Was my father correct in his epiphany that the king in question was Penda? It certainly seems possible, even probable. As we have seen, Penda looted Northumbria on three separate occasions, had invaded Wessex and East Anglia several times and had every opportunity to acquire a stock of precious treasures from all over the country over a period of more than two decades. It is noteworthy that virtually no items of Celtic derivation or design are in the hoard. As Penda's allies, they were immune from his depredations. It has even been suggested that following the catastrophe of Winwaed, the treasures may have been buried as some kind of ritualistic or votive offering associated with Penda's demise. Presumably the king's body (certainly his head) could not have been extricated after the battle, and considering Penda's treatment of Oswy's brother's body, he would have been extremely reluctant to relinquish any remains. No body was found at the Hammerwich site, but the possibility exists that some heathen ritual, perhaps modelled on *Beowulf* may have been performed despite the absence of his mortal remains. I do not believe this was likely. Royal or princely funerary rites such as those at Taplow or Sutton Hoo were incredibly elaborate and considered affairs. The forty coins found at the latter site were included as payment for the oarsmen of the boat, for instance. The Staffordshire Hoard was not laid out in any such way and gives every appearance of having been gathered together into some sort of bundle or sack and simply stashed away in hopes of later recovery – but who stashed it away intending to recover it?

My theory on this, and it is provisional until the research project reports in due course, is that it was buried by one of Penda's sons. My favourite suspect of the three potential candidates is Peada. He would have certainly received a share in the spoils of Penda's innumerable wars and was a reigning sub-king in his own right. His situation was very delicate, as we have seen. He was now a dependant king whose survival was conditional upon obedience to his father-in-law, who, it will be recalled, had very recently beheaded his own father. His court was now infiltrated not only by his treacherous wife, who eventually compassed his murder, but by churchmen utterly loyal to Oswy as well as Northumbrian diplomats acting as spies in the royal household. He must have feared for his life, and if indeed he possessed a share of Penda's treasures he had every reason to. We have seen how swords, helmets and personal effects of elite warriors were personalised to them specifically. As such they were extremely incriminating, because in the closed world of the military elites, kinsmen of men who had died in battle were obliged to revenge themselves on those who had killed their relatives. This is a very important point to consider. Richard A. Fletcher in his excellent study *Bloodfeud: Murder and Revenge in Anglo-Saxon England* analyses the complex codes of honour and interplay of kinship retaliation which motivated Anglo-Saxon warrior elites. Royal status was no protection against these savage vendettas. King Edmund was killed in a vain bid to defend his steward against an enraged kinsman at Pucklechurch in Gloucestershire, centuries later when more civilised manners had supervened. In the times we are considering, Peada must have known he was living on borrowed time. His brother, Wulfhere, was in hiding, and the thought of escape must have crossed his mind on an almost daily basis. The most obvious sanctuaries were his former Celtic allies, Pengwern, Powys or Gwynedd and possibly even Ireland. Any such egress had to be by one crucial route-way, Watling Street, the highway to North Wales. I am convinced that the positioning of the hoard site was no accident. It was on a prominent ridge just 100 yards or so off the Watling Street, perhaps marked by some then-significant marker such as a large tree, visible from the road and easily accessible from it. It could have been easily arranged for a hawking or hunting party to divert and bury the treasure there, where it could have remained in readiness for the time when Peada made his escape bid. It was a substantial enough stash to keep him in comfort for a long time: eleven pounds weight of gold and over three pounds weight in silver. Of course, he never did return; his wife, Aelflaeda, saw to that. This is one scenario involving Peada, but there is another, even more intriguing.

Peada's eventual murder, through the agency of Oswy's daughter, Aelflaeda, is a powerful indicator of how precarious his position was. Oswy could well have devised some 'loyalty test' which involved his cooperation in the project of establishing a diocesan centre in the debatable area near Lichfield. This was the context for Cynddylan's retaliatory raid, but what do we actually know about this? There are two key texts, both of them ancient Welsh poems. I am not alone in positing a connection; a local archaeologist, Johnny Whitteridge, has also noted the possibility, but so far as I am aware, no one else has sought corroborative evidence from the writings themselves. Now, Bede tells us in his *Historia* that Peada had been baptised 'at Wall'. Bede is full of praise for the young Christian convert and is apologetic about his contrived murder during Easter 656. Bede is not a contemporary witness, but wrote many years later. He says that Wall 'belonged to the king', but he may not be correct. Caer Luitcoit may still have been (at least precariously) British. Clearly, though, something had happened there involving the Church and Peada, and I believe this was an incursion by Peada into contested territory, sponsored by Oswy. This can only have been attempted using armed force and could not be ignored by the princes of Luitcoit and Pengwern, and we have a powerful poetic record of what followed.

One of the most fatal practices among the British royal houses was partition of kingdoms among all eligible heirs, including bastard sons. This fatally weakened British resistance to external enemies and led to brutal wars between neighbouring kingdoms. Cynddylan was technically the king of one of these state-lets known as Dogfeiling, named after the Dogfeilion, the name of the dynasty. This means something like 'servants of the Dagda'. The Dagda was originally an Irish and Pictish deity and the patron god of the tribe. Cynddylan's family was large – consisting of eleven other brothers and nine sisters – and although this has been interpreted as a mythical intrusion, such large families were entirely possible in these times. Cynddylan attempted to intrude one of his brothers, Elwyn, as king of neighbouring Powys, whose royal dynasty was not related. Heledd was sister to Cynddylan, and a Welsh tradition states that she was married to Penda at some point. Large royal families gave many opportunities for sealing alliances with other kingdoms, and indeed this was the principal means of achieving these. The pathos of the poem known as the 'Canu Heledd', or 'the lament of Heledd', comes about because it describes the death not only of her nation, but also of the British struggle as a whole, and as well as these, the death of all her royal siblings, including Cynddylan, a deeply personal tragedy.

Heledd (or at least a poet writing from the perspective of Heledd) says that her brothers, imbued with Arthurian bravado, departed to attack Wall.

> My heart is aflame like a firebrand ...
> Brothers I had, better it was when they lived,
> The whelps of Arthur, our mighty fortress.
> Before Caer Luitcoit they triumphed;
> There was blood strewn for the ravens, fierce attack;
> They shattered lime-shields the sons of Cyndrwyn.
> Till I am in my resting place
> My heart will grieve for Cynddylan, the full famed lord.
> Glory in battle, great plunder,
> Outside Caer Luitcoit, Morfael took it.
> Fifteen hundred cattle and five stewards,
> Four score horses and splendid armour,
> Each bishop rushing to the four corners,
> Hugging their books could not save the monks ...

The reference to bishops may indicate that Diuma was in the process of taking up his episcopal residence in the presence of his peers, and this would have been the main provocation. Note that the poet says the battle took place 'before Caer Luitcoit' and 'outside Caer Luitcoit', and this perfectly describes the position where the hoard was discovered, less than two miles from Wall. The sudden British onslaught had clearly caught the English unawares and the area was plundered of livestock, horses and even the monks' books which they clutched to their breasts in the chaos. If Peada was present, as seems very likely, it could well be that among his baggage was his royal treasury, now extremely vulnerable to raiders whose main thoroughfare would have been the Watling Street. Could it be that fearing for his safety he ordered it to be buried quickly in sight of the road before he was overrun? Evidently he was defeated, in spectacular style, and this was the last British victory east of the Severn. It served as Peada's death warrant. Oswy could not tolerate the botching of his most important political project and orders would have been conveyed to his daughter to eliminate him. That Oswy was this ruthless will become evident from the remainder of the poem, to which we will shortly return.

The arrangement by which tributes were paid to Penda by Caer Luitcoit in exchange for limited autonomy could not continue now that Oswy was the de facto ruler of Mercia. Cynddylan may even have been sheltering Wulfhere, Peada's brother, in hopes of precipitating a Mercian rebellion against Northumbrian rule. The possibility that Wulfhere may have buried the treasure while he was being concealed is remote, for he survived and would surely have returned to claim it. However, his royal residence at Bury Bank or the Rings at Darlaston near Stone in Staffordshire was not far away. The final candidate of the three sons of Penda is Aethelred. He must have been too young to have been deeply involved in the political manoeuvres in 656 but there is a possible link to him if the hoard is actually from a later date than I postulate. There are some pieces in the hoard, especially the Christian crosses and the 'gold strip', which may argue for a later date than the 650s. A new type of design, known as the Insular Style, was developing at this time, the impetus for which came from the Lindisfarne Gospels. It was a fusion of Teutonic and Celtic motifs and soon began to influence designers of elite jewellery, especially Christian objects. The presence of these objects may indicate that they could not have been produced until the fashion was in full swing, probably at about the time Aethelred came to the throne of Mercia in 675. The gold strip is a particularly valuable artefact from an archaeological point of view because it contains a (faulty) Latin inscription which may also provide clues. Three Christian crosses have been folded and bent, either in order to degrade or destroy their inherent magical power or just to pack them into the most convenient space for transporting them. Clearly whoever did this did not revere the Christian God. The gold strip looks like it could have formed one arm of a cross. It is inscribed, highlighted in niello, on both sides, with words from the Book of Numbers 10:35: 'Rise up, O Lord, and may thy enemies be dispersed and those who hate thee flee from thy face'. If the strip was from a cross or a reliquary, there may be a reason why this particular phrase was used. It was thought to contain magical powers. We have seen that the British were capable of using a form of psychological warfare against their English foes by evoking land spirits and spectres of dead ancestors, casting curses and spells. Saint Guthlac used a very similar prayer to that used on the gold strip to exorcise British 'ghosts' and if the protective prayer used was the one popularised by him it must date from between 673 and 714, contemporary with Aethelred's reign. This then begs the question of how Aethelred could have acquired such a treasure. We do know that Aethelred smashed a Northumbrian army on the River Trent in Lindsey in 679, so there would have been every opportunity to strip the dead, but if he did so the question then remains as to why he subsequently buried it so far away in Staffordshire and never returned for it afterwards. I include these other theories because they could be correct, but as yet we have little evidence to support them. The late Nicholas Brooks seemed to have strongly supported the idea of the treasure as 'the working capital of a royal armoury near Lichfield' and this is still a popular view. But there is no evidence of any metal working or occupation in the area, which must have been desolate and remote, except for the telling presence nearby of the Roman road. What is also in question is the extent to which this area was actually part of Mercia at all at this time, and whether Lichfield yet existed. The diocese was finally established by St Chad in 669, so if the hoard was buried after that date then maybe it did, but not if it was deposited before. It is this tricky question which has inspired me to make these speculations, for as we have seen time and again, Mercian history has often been misinterpreted. It would be unfortunate if this were to be the case yet again.

My own theory, in a nutshell, is that the hoard comprises elements from the booty seized by Penda during his campaigns or received as tribute following them. I think it was buried by one of his sons, most likely Peada, for his sudden death rendered him unable to return for it. There is as much evidence for it as any other theory, and as little. I concede that I may be wildly inaccurate in this view, and I would be happy to relinquish it if someone else can provide a more convincing and well-evidenced scenario. In all probability we will never have a definitive answer, but the Staffordshire Hoard is still one of the most important, almost talismanic finds ever discovered, for these 4,000 objects represent a unique time which defined England and Wales as we know them. Northumbria had triumphed in the long war, and Mercia was a defeated vassal; a rump state. The final expulsion of the British into what we now know as Wales was achieved as a direct result of the conflict at Wall-by-Lichfield. The heart-rending lamentations of the 'Canu Heledd' and the 'Marwnad Cynddylan' marked the end of a 200-year conflict between Celt and Teuton, at least in this phase. Mercia had yet to see its greatest days, and within a few years it was to embrace Christ at last. Northumbria had survived and was soon to enjoy the calm and ease of more peaceful times amid which its astonishing culture flourished. Whoever buried the hoard, they did so at a time of profound cultural moment. Beyond this I am not prepared to go.

Cynddylan's success at Caer Luitcoit was a gift for the bards and established him as a Celtic folk-hero, 'the bright buttress of the borderlands' but the realpolitik was otherwise. A desultory raid by a few hundred men was not going to stop Oswy. In 659 a Northumbrian counter-raid caught the Dogfeilion royal family off guard at Cynddylan's royal hall Llys Pengwern, somewhere in the Tern Valley. The entire family were in attendance save for Heledd. The hall was stormed and burned and all within slaughtered without mercy. The heart of the little kingdom had been eviscerated at a blow, leaving the common folk bewildered and bereft. Their grief was inconsolable and they immediately knew that their land was lost. In our democratic age we can only dimly empathise with such desperate emotions as those expressed in Heledd's poem, because we cannot fully appreciate the culture of veneration of exemplary persons. A great king or prince was felt to be almost god-like, yet at the same time interconnected with his subjects in a profound union. We see such occasional outpourings of emotional energy in exceptional circumstances even in our own times (such as the death of Diana, Princess of Wales). Female poets were a rarity in those times and some have doubted that Heledd's lament was actually written by her. Yet she alone had survived as the last living link to the mythic times, when Britain had been one with Rome and civilized, powerful and wealthy. Who better than this lonely widow to write the bitter epitaph of a doomed people?

> The hall of Cynddylan is dark tonight
> Without fire, without light,
> And what a silence surrounds it!
> The hall of Cynddylan is dark-panelled,
> It shelters no laughing company now,
> Woe to him who comes to a sad end!
> The hall of Cynddylan has lost its splendour
> Now that his shield is in the grave.
> Once this roof was not open to the stars...
> The hall of Cynddylan is dark-ceilinged
> Now that the English have killed
> Cynddylan and Elwyn of Powys...
> The eagle of Eli screams loud.
> He is wet with men's blood,
> With the heart's blood of Cynddylan the fair.

The eagle of Eli guards the seas,
The fishes no longer swim in the currents
He howls to see the blood of men.
The eagle of Eli wanders lonely in the forest.
At first light he feeds
From the victims of his tricks.
The grey-beaked eagle of Pengwern
Cries most piercingly,
Greedy for the flesh of him I love
The Eagle of Pengwern called afar tonight,
He can be seen in the blood of men.
Tren is too well named the deserted city.
The churches of Basa are in mourning tonight
As they hold the remains of the pillar of battle,
Of the heart of the men of Argoed ...
The churches of Basa are in flames tonight,
Very little remains of them ...
The churches of Basa are silent tonight,
And I too am sad ... my grief is too great.

The loss of Pengwern left an aching void, a yawning emptiness in the hearts of the Welshry, the leaderless remnants of the British race left to fend for themselves in the forests and hills of Lloegr. Another poet, A. E. Housman, captured the sense of this psychical wilderness in his *The Welsh Marches*:

When Severn down to Buildwas ran
Coloured with the death of man
Couched upon her brother's grave
The Saxon got me on the slave.

The sound of fight is silent long
That began the ancient wrong;
Long the voice of tears is still
That wept of old the endless ill.

In my heart it has not died,
The war that sleeps on Severn side;
They cease not fighting, east and west,
On the marches of my breast ...

The defeat was final, irrevocable. The British retired into Wales to create a new mountain nation, with only their language and their religion and the tales of the bards to comfort them in their shadowed valleys. Across the border, Mercia encroached into their former territory under a new king, Wulfhere, and from his desolate hiding place he emerged to rebuild his stricken nation, with an indomitable will and a new faith.

6

THE MERCIAN SUPREMACY

The Mercian confederation was predicated upon consensual agreement to put their separate tribes under rulers they had accepted in folk moots. To accept an overlord from outside their folk groupings was intolerable to them, and Peada's death gave them the chance to re-assert their independence in the shape of Wulfhere, Penda's second son, who was in hiding where he could not be controlled by the Northumbrian governors or clergy. The opportunity to emerge and seize power was not long in coming. Oswy was on campaign against the Pictish king Talorgan in Scotland, and in 658 three Mercian nobles, Eafa, Immin and Eadbert, proclaimed Wulfhere as the new king of Mercia, slew or drove out the Northumbrian governors and raised large forces. Oswy was compelled to accept a restored Mercian independence and thenceforth his energies were concentrated on his northern frontiers and in settling the disputation between 'Celtic' and 'Roman' parties within the church. Hunted from place to place for three years, Wulfhere had developed cunning, guile and intelligence in plenty and now put these to good use as he reconstructed and extended Mercian power. Unlike his father, he came to terms with

Northumbria and instead concentrated his efforts on building a southern hegemony. He was wise enough to realise that this could not be achieved unless he had the legitimacy of the Church behind him, and so he converted to Christianity, not under compulsion but by his own freely given oath.

A strange legend is associated with Wulfhere's conversion, which probably came about to explain his divergence from the Mercian folk religion of his father. In a hagiography of St Chad, a story is related of how Wulfhere slew his own sons, Wulphad and Ruffius, because they had been converted by St Chad (or in other versions a solitary holy man). The boys were supposed to have been buried beneath stones near the eponymous town called Stone in Staffordshire, and in contrition for this brutal act Wulfhere converted to the faith himself. St Peter's church at Kinver in Staffordshire was said to have been dedicated in memory of his murdered sons, but these tales of saints and their doings often coalesced around some innocent youth who had been eliminated as a result of political intrigues. A similar story (and one with as little proof behind it) is told of St Kenelm who was decapitated in the Clent Hills during a hunting expedition. We cannot know the truth of the legend, but we do know that Ceollach, second Bishop of Mercia, retired to Iona, to be succeeded by Trumhere, who was Wulfhere's preferred candidate. It became crucial at this time for Mercia to assert its own religious identity, because Oswy had become conflicted between his personal political ambitions and his religious apparatus. By inviting Irish/Scots influence from Iona into Lindisfarne, and establishing a solid bloc in north-central England whose religious life was dominated from these centres, Oswy naturally assumed that political and administrative control would follow. These Celtic holy men, and their austere English protégés, were too other-worldly, too spiritual, to comport themselves to the demands of high politics, but there were other churchmen who were only too willing to sub-serve the will of the king. The Synod of Whitby in 663 or 664 was the result of this contention. Oswy used as his expedient the long-standing divergence of the

Irish from the universal Church in the matter of the calculation of the date of Easter. His queen was Catholic, and so even within the confines of the royal hall her attendants and clergy would still be observing lent while he and his warriors were feasting. The same abstinence applied in the area of sexual relations and the irritated king convened the synod to resolve these delicate matters and other anomalies such as which tonsure was correct. The Irish and their acolytes wore theirs bare from ear to ear, after the manner of the ancient druids, but the Romans wore theirs in a coronal fringe, to represent Christ's thorn crown. Both parties could not be right. The case for the Irish was simply put by Colman, Bishop of Lindisfarne. Surely the king, who had been schooled and offered sanctuary on Iona, must know that these were the ways of St Columba and therefore sacrosanct? Wilfred, a young and intelligent advocate for the Roman ways, was dismissive of the Irish tradition, and his discourse seemed almost contemptuous of these holy men from the west, and of Columba and his 'rustic simplicity'. Wilfred's closing speech offered a stark choice for Oswy: would he adhere to the church of Columba and his monks, dwelling at the edge of the world in their windswept monasteries, or to that of 'the most blessed prince of the apostles', St Peter? Oswy's sardonic smile to Colman made clear which party he would support. Jokingly he said he did not wish to get to the gates of heaven and find himself disbarred because he had offended him who kept the keys. The very people who had saved Oswy's life, guarded him, fed him, educated him and who had devoted all their energies into converting his stricken realm, were to be cast aside. Oswy had applied a corrective to the anomalies of the Irish church, but he did not make Edwin's error of aligning himself exclusively to Rome. Wilfred was triumphant, but his project to recapture Northumbria for Rome foundered and he was eventually exiled. The dissension Whitby caused within the Church could not be resolved by the partisans of either faction, and it was left to a more neutral mind to redirect its energies in the shape of one of the most influential and extraordinary men of the Anglo-Saxon age. He was neither English nor Irish, but a native of the country now called Turkey, an elderly Greek named Theodore, and he immediately grasped that the centre of religious and political gravity in England had moved south, to Mercia.

The principal royal exponents of the Roman party in England were Oswy of Northumbria and Egbert of Kent. Their nominee for the vacant post of Archbishop of Canterbury, Wigheard, had died immediately after arriving to meet Pope Vitalian in Rome. Vitalian offered the vacant post to Hadrian, a Berber refugee from North Africa who had become abbot of a monastery near Naples at the age of just thirty, but he refused. After considering other candidates, the position was finally accepted by Theodore of Tarsus, who, at the age of sixty-five, was asked to make the arduous journey to England. Vitalian specified that Hadrian should keep company with him on the long journey since he had travelled in France before and had contacts there. Bede thought that the Pope had sent Hadrian to ensure that the elderly Greek did not introduce ideas from the Eastern Church into England. It took over a year before the duo arrived, but they set to work with method and determination. Theodore's first concern was that Chad (brother to Cedd who had been invited as a missionary to the Middle-Angles by Peada), now Bishop of York, had been consecrated in an irregular fashion. He upbraided Chad about this to receive the reply from the humble monk that he was willing to resign immediately, considering himself unworthy of such high office. Theodore was impressed by such humility and re-considered. He instead sent Chad to be Bishop of Mercia, and the vacant See of York was given to Wilfred. Meanwhile, Wulfhere had established Mercian dominance over large parts of southern England. By astute political manoeuvring and military intimidation he was able to secure an alliance with Sussex which converted the last pagan area in England, the Isle of Wight, to Christianity and transferred its allegiance to Sussex. His marriage to the daughter of the king of Kent gave him traction with Theodore in Canterbury and he also gained overlordship of Essex. His nominee became

Bishop of London, and by the time Theodore convoked the Synod of Hertford in 673, the man whose father who had been a notorious pagan was the most powerful man in England south of the Humber, respected by the most influential figure in the early English Church. It was an incredible achievement, for in one man's lifetime Mercia had been transfigured from dark-age barbarism into a civilised and influential power of national and international significance. Moreover, this transformation was quite genuine, for Wulfhere was pious, open-minded and generous. Wilfred's biographer, Stephen of Ripon, explicitly states that the king invited Wilfred into Mercia and granted him large estates where he founded many monasteries. Unfortunately, the old enmity between Northumbria and Mercia flared up again in a dispute about the province of Lindsey. Kent rebelled against Wulfhere's control and he suddenly died in 675. He had travelled far, from being a hunted fugitive to the most powerful king in England, but the question now was, could this recovery last?

King Ecgfrith, the new king of Northumbria, calculated that it could not. His invasion of Lindsey had provoked Wulfhere into a counter-invasion which had had the effect of promoting an insurrection in Kent against Mercian overlordship in support of Hlothere, brother to Eadric, the former king of Kent. Aethelred, Wulfhere's brother and successor, soon showed that he had inherited his father's rapidity and ruthlessness. He marched on Kent in 676 and burned Rochester, including its cathedral, driving its bishop into exile. Theodore must have greatly feared that the ancient enmity between Northumbria and Mercia was about to engulf the whole country of England. Aethelred then marched north, and in 679 on the banks of the River Trent a huge battle was fought in which Ecgfrith's younger brother was killed and the Northumbrian forces routed. We have already seen how kinship retaliation in blood feuds had the effect of prolonging and intensifying hostilities, and Bede comments, 'There was now reason to expect a more bloody war, and most lasting enmity between those kings and their fierce nations.' What saved England from yet another conflagration was the intercession of Theodore. Aethelred agreed to pay compensation for the slain prince and to agree to the installation of Putta, the bishop who had been forced to flee from Rochester to become a teacher of music, as Bishop of Hereford. In exchange for these concessions Aethelred was given Lindsey. This tricky compromise was ultimately to Mercian advantage, because with Northumbrian power restrained on its northern frontiers, Aethelred could consolidate Wulfhere's former control of Kent, Essex and Sussex. Theodore created three new episcopal sees in Mercia, and Aethelred interred the remains of St Oswald of Northumbria in a new monastery at Bardney in Lindsey, which territory he now indisputably controlled. It is difficult to conceive that Theodore's arbitration could have been viewed as anything other than partiality in Mercia's favour. He greatly reduced Wilfred's diocese of York and the infuriated bishop set off to Rome to complain to the Pope in person. Wilfred was ultimately vindicated, but Northumbrian influence had been curtailed to the advantage of Mercia, and this came about through Theodore's preference. Eventually Theodore died in 690 at the (then) very great age of eighty-eight. Aethelred was content to refrain from further military adventurism, and when his beloved wife was killed as a result of a blood feud at the new foundation of Bardney, he became increasingly withdrawn from the world of high politics, finally retiring to the monastery himself in 704 and giving up his throne. By the time of his abdication, Mercia was the greatest power in England and a bastion of the Christian Church. The sons of Penda, Wulfhere and Aethelred, had rescued Mercia and transformed its fortunes, but even greater days were to come.

The devotion and discipline Theodore and Hadrian had brought to their task had completely transformed the English Church. Theodore's pupil Aldhelm became the tutor of the great Mercian king Aethelbald. No longer were the English the unsophisticated pupils of Irish missionaries but the intellectual and spiritual equals of any country in Europe; their own missions to their ancestral homelands would ultimately convert the pagan Germans. London had become a Mercian city and its crucial trade was now under the direct control of the Mercian monarchs. This effective suzerainty over the most economically important part of England and the wise governance of educated churchmen serving powerful monarchs laid the foundations for the modern English state. However, Aethelred's sudden abdication in favour of his nephew, Ceonred, left a temporary uncertainty about the future of the realm. In his turn, Ceonred abdicated to go on a pilgrimage to Rome, and five years after Ceonred became king, Aethelred's own son, Ceolred, succeeded him. Tradition has ascribed an evil reputation to Ceolred, who may have been insane as well as drunken and debauched. He forced his cousin Aethelbald into exile in the fenlands with St Guthlac at Crowland, and he is described as a violator of nuns and ecclesiastical privileges. A monk of Wenlock had a vision that the king was bound for the infernal regions, and in 716 he died at a feast cursing the clergy, either intoxicated or in the grip of some sort of psychosis. After a brief interregnum, Aethelbald, a descendant of Penda's brother Eowa, returned to claim the throne. His reign was long (forty-one years), and by its end Mercia was unquestionably the supreme power in England. Under two mighty and long-reigning kings, Aethelbald and Offa, a new concept of 'Engla-lond', a unified state of all English peoples, was born, and it was conceived in Mercia.

Aethelbald describes himself in the Ismere Diploma of 736 (a grant of land at Stour-in-Ismere on the borders of Worcestershire and Staffordshire) as 'King of all the southern English'. This was not an idle boast. He was the acknowledged overlord of Wessex, East Anglia and Essex, and punitive military expeditions into the West Country and his seizure of the region around modern Berkshire confirmed his military might and his authority over the crucial trading port of London. By 746 he had elevated his status when witnessing charters to 'King of the English' and the implication is clearly that all other sub-kings should owe tribute to him, in just the same way that the sub-kings of Mercia had once acknowledged Penda's authority. The impetus for this radical change in national consciousness had come about as a result of Theodore's reform of the Church, and in particular the Synod of Hertford, which was, as William Stubbs described it, 'The first constitutional measure of the collective English race.' To Aethelbald it must have seemed that if the various dioceses of all the English kingdoms could be compelled to accept the authority of one archbishop in England by their freely given consent, then it must follow that the rulers of the lesser realms could choose to acknowledge him as an over-king. Ultimately, Mercia's dominance was predicated upon military force, but this was now used sparingly, and then only if its supremacy was challenged by rebellions. However, at this stage, the other kingdoms were still very far from submitting to a Mercian imperial project.

Despite his de facto overlordship and his pretensions to an English empire, there was one area where Aethelbald's authority had no force. This was Wales, and especially in Powys, where the Welsh kings were beginning to re-assert themselves, raiding over the border, carrying off livestock, burning villages and generally being a nuisance. For all his putative power, Aethelbald was never able to entirely subdue these guerrilla incursions and the border became a chronic problem. Towards the end of his long reign, the idea of a fixed border defence patrolled by troops in rotation was made a reality in the shape of Wat's Dyke. From this structure, Offa was to develop the idea for his much larger dyke. Aethelbald was, however, powerful enough to pillage York in the 740s and his power within England was unchallenged. Yet his reputation is somewhat unsavoury. St Boniface, the English missionary to the Germans, sent a letter upbraiding him, sneering at his imperial pretensions and criticising his seizure of church property. Boniface particularly reproached him for his lustful lifestyle, entreating him to marry and to abstain from the sins of the flesh. There is a story that Aethelbald killed the kinsman of an abbess and there is a general impression of a man corrupted by wealth and power, haughty and proud, insincere in his Christian devotions. Despite Boniface's exhortations, he remained unmarried and left no children. Perhaps his immorality, especially the violation of nuns, was the reason for his ultimate demise. In 757 he was murdered at Seckington near Tamworth by his own bodyguards while he slept. The motive is unknown but he was briefly succeeded by a usurper, Beornred, who may have instigated the assassination but who was deposed and driven into exile immediately by Offa, Aethelbald's cousin and another descendant of Eowa. Unlike most of the Mercian kings, his name has endured down the centuries. He was to become Mercia's greatest king, internationally renowned, and along with Alfred the Great and Athelstan one of the founding fathers of England as we know it.

In chapter two we saw how Offa's succession was viewed as being of dubious legitimacy, and how he had sought to ameliorate this by stressing his own descent from Eowa and therefore from Offa of Angeln. Beornred's claim to the throne must have had some (perhaps stronger) evidence to back it and so Offa made strenuous efforts to eliminate this from the historical Church records, denouncing him as a '*tyrannus*', or illegitimate usurper. The difficulties about this were initially a great handicap to Offa. The satellite kingdoms that owed tribute to Mercia were seething with resentment at the best of times, but any question pertaining to Offa's right to rule incentivised the client rulers into bolder action, even rebellion. This was the background to Offa's early years as king; he felt it necessary to prove himself equal to and even to exceed the eminence of his predecessors, but it was no easy task. To make up for the perceived deficit in his bona fides, Offa had to prove that he was a charismatic king, wielding unquestioned power within his own realm. The traditional means of doing so was, of course, war. His first opportunity to assert himself was in the Welsh border country, where in 760 he repelled a large Welsh raiding party near Hereford, demonstrating to his own people that their security from attack was paramount for him. From the outset, Offa asserted the status Aethelbald had claimed before him, 'King of the English', but as well as this he went further. The component sub-kingdoms of Mercia such as Middle-Anglia and the kingdoms of the Hwicce and Magonsaetan had long since ceased to have even nominally independent rulers. Instead these had been demoted to the status of 'ealdorman' or 'duces', a lower rank of nobility considerably inferior to the king. Offa now replicated this process in the satellite kingdom of Sussex and seems to have had a similar plan in mind for Kent and perhaps even Wessex. This recalled the absolutism and imperialism that had undone Edwin of Northumbria in his day and was similarly resented. This was not merely a question of prestige. The huge tributes demanded by Offa meant that the lesser kings found it increasingly difficult to render them and maintain their own elite households and estates, whose noblemen and clergy they were obliged to wine and dine on a grand scale. Feasts were not the delicate dinner parties of our own times but vast community gatherings in gigantic timber halls where one night's consumption might consist of 300 loaves (flat breads which served as a rude platter), forty-two casks of ale, ten jars of honey, a cask of butter, ten cheeses, 100 eels, five salmon, twenty chickens and ten geese. Other delicacies might include ducks, pigeons, venison, pike and even porpoises. The large numbers of retainers seated on the mead-benches expected the nobility, especially kings, to provide all these comestibles as their right. As a peripatetic ruler, Offa moved around his kingdom to various estates to spread the burden, but the lesser kings were obliged to render up vast quantities of luxury foodstuffs, ale and wine. Ultimately, all this came from the labour of the rural peasantry, whose diet was barely sufficient to maintain themselves at the best of times. These food renders were known as the *feorm* from which we derive our modern word 'farm', for to provide such a continuous supply required organisation under the supervision of kings' stewards. The diminution in status of the lesser kings rankled, as did Offa's habit of overlooking them when issuing and confirming charters and land grants, and indeed rebuking them if he perceived that they had exceeded their authority. Egbert of Kent had such a charter revoked by Offa for having 'presumed to place land, which his lord has given him, under the authority of another without his lord's consent'. The Church often found itself in similar disputes with Offa. The monastery at Stour-in-Ismere had been given by its abbot to Worcester Cathedral but Offa demurred. There is a hint of what is called today 'micro-management' about Offa's monarchic style, and the impression is confirmed by his creation of an innovative standardised currency he introduced based on Frankish coins, which he clearly intended to circulate not just in Mercia but throughout England. Where Aethelbald had pretended to an English empire, Offa seemed determined to establish it as a reality.

However, foodstuffs were the least of the worries of the lesser kings. When they were summoned to meet him at one of his estates, such as Sutton Walls outside Hereford, he expected lavish and expensive gifts to be presented to him and his queen of gold and silver coins, herds of cattle, exquisite weapons (such as Charlemagne's gift of an Avar sword) fine clothes, hunting hounds, rare falcons and the likes. To displease the king could be dangerous. One of his guests at Sutton Walls, King Aethelberht of East Anglia was murdered on Offa's orders there in May 794. Offa was ruthless and cunning and could be cruel. In 764 he devastated Kent. In 771 he invaded and subdued West Sussex, and in 776 Kent again, though in a battle at Otford he was repelled. These exploits did not go unnoticed on the Continent, to which some exiled rebels fled for protection from his implacable revenge. Offa's model of monarchy seems to have made a strong impression on Charlemagne who had chosen Alcuin of York and the Irishman Dicuil to administer his vast empire. The gift of the Avar sabre was not the only transaction between the two men. Charlemagne described Offa as his 'faithful friend' and mutually advantageous trade agreements were concluded. This sometimes brought complaints from the mighty emperor, who exhorted Offa to ensure that English woollen cloaks and blankets, which were highly prized in Europe and Ireland, should be delivered in a standardised size. Offa obliged, but added a caveat in his reply, asking Charlemagne to ensure the prompt delivery of 'black stones', presumably stones for milling. This may seem to us rather quaint, but this correspondence reveals something very important. Offa is (diplomatically) saying that he considers himself the equal of the emperor, a man to be reckoned with on the world stage.

Such a man clearly intended to leave behind him a legacy, a monument to his achievements and his power. The most obvious expression of this is the great dyke along the Welsh border which exists to this day. The Welsh problem was a running sore and in 783 Offa decided to attend to it once and for all. In the summer of that year he struck deep into Deheubarth, a kingdom in South Wales whose seat lay at Dinefwr on the River Tywi. Welsh annals state that the 'Mercian incendiaries' inflicted a 'devastation of Britain', burning and looting the whole area of south-central Wales. This was the prelude to Offa's supreme project, the construction of a 150-mile-long dyke from Basingwerk near Prestatyn to Sedbury on the Severn Estuary. Along much of its length stood a thirty-foot-high earthen bank, possibly surmounted by a palisade, and incorporating gateways to control ingress and egress. In front a ditch was dug, six feet deep by twelve feet wide. It is more than twice as long as Hadrian's Wall, and it may be that it was inspired by the latter. Beacons along its extent could easily alert contingents of troops stationed at regular intervals to any incursions. The Welsh called it then as now *glawd Offa*, and even today it inspires awe. This was his intention, for the labour required for the task demanded a level of authority and organisational skill not seen in these islands since Roman times. It was Offa's right to summon his subjects to provide *burhbot*, the construction of forts and the repair of roads and bridges. Contingents from all over England duly arrived, where they would be allocated a section of the dyke to complete, marked out by posts. Gangs of labourers working in this way in rotation, numbering many thousands in total, probably completed the work within a year or so. From then on drovers and traders could enter England at specific points under close supervision, but raiders found an obstacle which made their enterprises extremely risky. Now Offa had emulated his namesake,

Offa of Angeln, who had 'fixed the boundary', but more than that he had surpassed Charlemagne, whose project to excavate a canal between the Danube and the Rhine had been abandoned. He was not content with this, however. The royal capital at Tamworth was reorganised and rebuilt, incorporating a revolutionary watermill and a massive timber-aisled palace over 100 feet in length, decorated with exquisite tapestries. This was enclosed by sturdy defences, palisades and a deep ditch. Hereford was similarly rebuilt according to a plan, with timber houses and shops fronting onto wide streets to enable carts to pass. By 785 Offa had regained control of Kent after deposing its king. The man who could organise the immense labour entailed in the construction of Offa's Dyke could dispose of armies which no desultory rebellion could hope to challenge. Personally controlling the lucrative trade of London, Offa's wealth was staggering, and now this energetic king turned his attention to other important matters such as the drafting of new law codes and, perhaps most important of all, the standardisation of the coinage.

The impetus for upgrading and standardising coinage came from Francia. The *denier*, a large, thin, silver coin was standard there, and as trade at London and other ports grew it was felt necessary to model a new English coin on this. The result was a silver penny, versions of which remained as the bedrock of the British currency until decimalisation in the late twentieth century. The first versions circulated in Kent but Offa soon appropriated them as his model. Very large quantities were struck, bearing his name and image, ensuring his fame spread along the network of trade routes within Charlemagne's empire and beyond into Spain and the Arab World, the Byzantine Empire and even Russia. In these places he was known as 'King of England' without a doubt. The number of mints was trebled. This sudden wealth did not go unnoticed in Scandinavia. However, within 'Engla-lond' itself, Offa's power was still resented. It may have been the fact that Aethelberht of East Anglia had issued his own silver pennies, bearing his own image, which caused Offa to have him murdered. It was the act of an ageing mobster, not of a great king, and it shocked the people, who made Aethelberht into a saint. Offa had grown avaricious and cruel and paranoid; above all he felt the need to secure his dynasty, to ensure the destiny of his scion, Ecgfrith. With this in mind, and to mark his thirtieth year on the throne, not only were special silver pennies minted bearing his queen's image as well as his own, but his son was to be crowned and anointed king in Offa's own lifetime by his new archbishop. After ingratiating himself with the Pope, Offa had been given permission to establish Lichfield as a new archbishopric. Great new stone churches were rising in Mercia, for Offa enriched the Church as well as his own coffers. Thirty years was a significant jubilee indeed, but even for Offa, his star was fading.

By now Offa had intruded Beorhtric, whose bona fides were as dubious as his own, as king of Wessex. The defeated candidate, Egbert, was forced into exile with Charlemagne and relations between Francia and Mercia soured. This was the last thing Offa wanted, and to soothe relations he proposed a marriage alliance. Charlemagne was content to accept one of Offa's daughters as a bride for his son. Offa's real aim was to marry Ecgfrith to Bertha, Charlemagne's eligible daughter and favourite. Offa's presumption and arrogance, to consider his family as equal to that of the emperor, was the last straw. Charlemagne cut off the English trade; it was no mere diplomatic snub but what we would call today 'sanctions'. No doubt the main reason for Charlemagne's wrath was the presence at his court of English rebel exiles, some of whom calumniated and diminished Offa, depicting him as a greedy, ruthless tyrant of dubious descent. Offa used intelligent Church contacts and generous endowment of Frankish monasteries to enable reconciliation between the two rulers. Alcuin, an Englishman, was the emperor's chief statesman. Trade was becoming too important to jeopardise. There was one last great divide in England which had endured since the first Anglo-Saxon settlements: the split between 'south-Anglia' and 'north-Anglia'. In 792 this divide was, at last, bridged. Offa's daughter, Aelflaed, was married to King Aethelred of Northumbria. Two years later East Anglia was invaded and its king killed. The great project was complete. Offa was now supreme in England, and the Mercian king was overlord of all the English. 'Engla-lond' was a fact.

Like any new idea, a new state takes a while to consolidate. Offa did not have such time, and neither did his precious son. Offa died at the end of July 796 at Offley in Hertfordshire. His dream rapidly died with him. Ecgfrith succeeded but was dead within months. The satellite kingdoms immediately rebelled and attempted to shake off Mercian domination. The monk Eadberht Praen set himself up as independent king of Kent, but Mercian power was still ruthless and irresistible and he was taken to Mercia in chains where he was savagely mutilated by being blinded and having his hands chopped off. Amazingly he survived and ended his life as a monk at Winchcombe in Gloucestershire some years later. Coenwulf, a cousin of Offa, succeeded to the Mercian throne. He had caught the imperial bug from his predecessors, styling himself 'Emperor of Britain' in emulation of Charlemagne. The Anglo-Saxons had come full circle. Now, the rude pagan barbarians were themselves ruled by 'emperors', living in a society dominated by trade, luxury, wealth and rudimentary but prospering towns, spending coins with the image of an imperial ruler on them. Although they were nowhere near as sophisticated as the Romans, the *idea* of a civilisation like theirs was within their grasp, and all this had come from the Mercian kings. Mercia's power did not immediately wane, but shortly before Offa died a small but shocking incident had taken place far in the north of England which was to spell the end of Mercia, and which was an omen for all the English. Lindisfarne had been raided by Northmen from across the sea. They had sacked the sacred place, killed its monks and carried off its treasures. They were pagan Vikings from Scandinavia. The great scholar Alcuin, the foremost Englishman of his time, the wisest man in Europe, summed up the danger perfectly:

An immense threat hangs over this island and its people. It is a novelty without precedent that pirate raids of a heathen people can regularly waste our shores. Yet the English people are divided, and king fights against king. Saddest of all, scarcely any heir of the ancient royal houses survives, and the origin of kings is as dubious as their courage ... Study Gildas, the wisest of the British, and examine the reasons why the ancestors of the British lost their kingdom and fatherland; then look upon yourselves, and you will find among you almost identical causes.

This theme, of a national decline ordained by God and visited upon the nation in the form of barbaric invasion, is one which will recur again and again in the Anglo-Saxon story.

Mercia reverted to its old struggles against the Welsh. Coenwulf invaded and wasted Gwynedd Dyfed Powys and Brycheiniog in the 820s leaving Wales a famine stricken wasteland. Lichfield was no longer an archbishopric. Coenwulf had suggested a compromise to Pope Leo III by which the Mercian archbishopric would be moved to London, but this was rejected in a signal from Rome that Mercia was losing its pre-eminence. How did this mighty kingdom end? The answer is, of course, the coming of the Vikings, but Mercia lingered on in a diminished form until 918. It still had a crucial role to play in English survival and recovery in the years ahead. Often it is not the histories of a people which tell their story, but their legends. The saddest tales are those which tell of the end of kings and their realms, conveying the atmosphere of the times most tellingly of all. Such is the case in Mercia, where in the Clent Hills they still tell the story of Saint Coenhelm or St Kenelm. His famous well, at Romsley near Halesowen in Worcestershire, is still venerated, and 'cloutie rags' are hung for healing there to this day. The tale says that Coenwulf's son Kenelm was hunting there in Offmore Wood in the Clent Hills with his aunt Quendrida's huntsman (and secret lover) Askoberht. She had contrived to have the boy murdered, and this was duly done. His head was smitten from his body beneath a thorn bush, and on that spot a spring burst forth in a miraculous flow. A sacred white dove conveyed the news to the Pope whose legates discovered the boy's hidden grave with the help of a sacred white cow. In the Clent Hills the rhyme is still sung.

> In Clent by cowbatch
> Under a thorn,
> Lieth Kenelm, king-born
> His head off-shorn ...

The evil aunt, at least in legend, got her just reward. In reality, Kenelm probably died fighting the Welsh, but the legend tells much about the last days of the Mercian empire. Plotting and murder now sat uneasily with a godly, sentimental Mercian people who immediately made the place into a centre of national pilgrimage and repentance, Kenelmstowe, now sadly disappeared. The mighty kings of olden times had been replaced by people less worthy to rule, corrupt and wicked. They were no longer the living gods of the old days, except when they had been sanctified by being cruelly assassinated, their saintliness revealed by holy animals. This was a new world where faith comforted the people and gave them hope that an evil world could be redeemed. Soon, they were to need this faith, for they were about to enter upon a grim time of trial, a battle for their very survival.

7

THE STORM FROM THE NORTH

The decline of Mercian power began as soon as Offa died. In 801 the Northumbrians were emboldened to attempt an invasion of Mercia which was followed by a counter-invasion by Mercia of Northumbria. The following year, Egbert of Wessex, who had been in exile at Charlemagne's court, returned to claim his throne. Ceonwulf had his hands full in the north and the Mercian army he sent to expel Egbert was led by a mere ealdorman, Aethelmund, whose army was defeated by the levies of Wiltshire. By the time of Ceonwulf's death in 821, Egbert was strong enough to contend on equal terms. The death of Kenelm, Ceonwulf's son, whether by foul play as in legend or by other means, left a distant kinsman Ceolwulf as the only practical successor. He sought to gain legitimacy and show charisma by the traditional method of plundering Wales but failed to impress and was soon afterwards set aside by the Mercian nobles. There then followed a procession of dubious kings, elevated amid the bitter factionalism of civil wars. A scribe who had witnessed the synod of Clofesho in 803, at which the archbishopric of Lichfield had been downgraded, summed up the national decline neatly: 'after the death of Ceonwulf, King of the Mercians, many quarrels and innumerable disputes had arisen between important men and ministers of God's churches ... concerning a multitude of secular affairs.' In 829 Egbert invaded Mercia and drove its king Wiglaf into exile, becoming its overlord, and renewed dissension there rapidly turned into civil war. Such squabbling blinded men of power to the Viking raiders – a larger threat that was looming across the seas which Alcuin had warned of – who had been pillaging in Francia as far inland as Paris which they sacked in 845 under a Danish leader named Ragnar. At first they came as raiders, sea pirates who came on hit-and-run missions for plunder, but Alcuin's exhortation of the English to look to Gildas and his warning from history of the fate of divided peoples under weak rulers was ignored. In 825 Iona suffered the same fate as Lindisfarne in 793 and the monks there were slaughtered. Ireland was heavily assaulted with over thirty raids recorded in the Irish annals. Who were these heathen raiders? In essence they were not so very different from their Anglo-Saxon predecessors. It is true that the Norwegian element among them was more distinctive, but most of them headed to the Isles of Scotland and to the Norse colonies in Ireland. The Vikings who carried out the first raids were Norwegians, but the later invasions consisted mainly of Danes, and DNA sampling has been unable to distinguish their modern ancestors in England from the Anglo-Saxon strains which preceded them. Their homelands were just north of the original Anglo-Saxon ancestral lands. In speech, although they spoke a broad dialect, they could be understood by English people quite easily. They had retained Norse pagan deities such as Woden (called by them Odin) though there may have been some Christians among them too. They set sail for exactly the same reasons as the Anglo-Saxons centuries before: raiding and plunder, then settlement. Savage clan wars, a lack of good farmland and over-population all provided an impetus to construct clinker-built, shallow-draught longships and *knorrs*, the wide-bellied storage vessels, and set out for new lands with better prospects. They were superb seamen, confident in their ability to cross the stormiest of seas, even (eventually) reaching North America. They were incredibly tough and hardy and could live off the land in the harshest environments on the most meagre of diets. Completely oblivious of Christian ethics, at least until later on, they were vicious, cruel and almost demonic terrorists, who spared no one, regardless of age or sex, except if they were pretty enough or strong enough to be taken as slaves. Women were particularly valuable as a commodity in these times because death during childbirth was commonplace and feminine labour for domestic and agricultural tasks was at a premium. They learned to ride and use weapons as soon as they could stand and were proficient warriors, fighting alongside their shipmates in disciplined formations with high morale and fearsome weapons. Indeed, they were fanatical about war and were the ancient equivalent of modern suicide attackers. It was counted among them as an honour to die in battle and thereby be entitled to enter Valhalla where they would feast and drink sweet mead forever with the pagan gods. At Trelleborg in Denmark, Jomsborg on the Baltic coast and similar places, they trained in huge enclosed encampments with barracks for 1,000 men, or concentrated their vast fleets for large-scale offensive campaigns. It has become fashionable to stress the positive contribution they made to European culture in the last few decades, and I would certainly not wish to diminish their extraordinary skills and achievements, but the whole impression we get from reading accounts of their onset from contemporaries who witnessed it is one of terror, fear and hatred for these barbarians who seemed like a scourge from God. It is possible that their sudden emergence in large numbers, and their contempt for Christian culture, was due to the ravages of Charlemagne, whose fanatical war against the pagan Saxons and southern Danes had forced Scandinavians into a coalition bent on revenge for massacres the emperor had inflicted upon them. This would go some way to explaining why it was that specifically Christian sites were so ill-used by them. Their ruthlessness and audacity proved almost sufficient to overwhelm western civilisation completely, and of all countries in Europe none was more exposed to their ferocity than England. With the devil's own luck they arrived at a time when the separate Anglo-Saxon kingdoms were divided and weak, an opportunity they exploited to the full.

The raids increased exponentially over three decades until in 865 the *micel here* or 'Great Army' arrived. Hundreds of ships conveyed a force of some thousands to the East Anglian coast under *jarls* or commanders, and kings called Ivar and Halfdan, the sons of a chief called Ragnar Lothbrok. Its objective was nothing less than the rapid conquest of the Anglo-Saxon realms. We may wonder how it was that once-mighty English kingdoms with ancient martial traditions went down so swiftly in face of the Viking onslaught. The answer to this is that they had the immense advantages of mobility and surprise, and their far-off homelands across the sea were immune to retaliation. They deliberately targeted the kings and their royal retinues, and once they were captured the Anglo-Saxon monarchs were faced with a stark choice, either to do their bidding or suffer the grim fate of the 'blood eagle', a gory ritual whereby the king's body was cut open while he was still alive and his lungs splayed out like an eagle's wings. The Vikings cunningly exploited the political in-fighting within the Anglo-Saxon kingdoms, and in 867 they drove out Osbert of Northumbria and installed their own man, Aella, who they later deposed, subjecting him to the sacrifice of the 'blood eagle'. Another puppet, Egbert, replaced him, but wisely fled into exile in Mercia lest he meet a similar fate, to be succeeded by Ricsige, yet another tool of the Great Army. In 869 the invaders turned on East Anglia whose king Edmund had no choice but to resist. In November 869 he fought the Norsemen near Thetford and was soundly beaten. He escaped to a wood called Haeglesdune near Hoxne. Later legend has obscured the facts somewhat, but the broad outline is clear. Until 1848 a huge oak known as St Edmund's Oak stood at the scene of the latter's martyrdom. When it collapsed an iron arrowhead was found in its heart about five feet from the ground. This confirms the story recounted by his armour bearer that when the king was captured he was sacrificed to Odin. Ivar 'the Boneless', his captor, had a sinister reputation as a Nordic shaman or warlock, and there is no reason to doubt that Edmund's end was as gory as legend relates. He was tied to the tree, whipped and then used as target practice for archers, so that arrows protruded from his body 'like the spines of a hedge-hog'. He was then either subjected to the 'blood eagle' or impaled on a stake, before being beheaded to preclude Christian burial. In legend, the head was thrown into a thicket where it was guarded by a miraculous white wolf (the symbol of the East Anglian royal house). The head cried out to monks sent to search for it and it was miraculously reunited with the body, ensuring Edmund's sanctification. Like Oswald of Northumbria before him, he was seen as a sacrificial victim, like Christ bound to a tree to be slaughtered by heathens. He became the national saint of the whole English people until the Norman Conquest, and the story tells us much about the psychological trauma the Great Army had inflicted upon them. Northumbria and East Anglia had gone down. Now it was the turn of Mercia.

The Mercians were not slow to appreciate the danger that confronted them. What we would call today 'joint military manoeuvres' had been initiated with Wessex as early as 853 when the Mercian King Burgred and King Aethelwulf of Wessex joined forces to invade and subjugate Wales. Burgred married Aethelwulf's daughter, Aethelswyth, to consolidate the alliance. Thus began a relationship between the two countries which would eventually bring about a united English nation. Economic relations were put on a similar basis of uniformity and the two countries adopted a virtually identical currency. Unfortunately, none of this proved sufficient to ensure Mercian survival. In 853 a Viking force under the command of a captain called Orm raided Anglesey and then moved on to Powys whose king fled to Rome. They then intruded into Shropshire as far inland as the Wrekin. Burgred tried to invoke the new alliance with the West Saxons but King Aethelwulf was abroad on a pilgrimage to Rome. Fortunately, the Welsh rallied and destroyed the Vikings, killing their leader. However, the arrival of the *micel here* posed a threat much more serious. In 867 the Vikings took Nottingham, right at the heart of Mercia, and Burgred immediately asked for West Saxon aid. King Aethelred of Wessex, with his younger brother Alfred, arrived to lay siege to the Norsemen who had walled themselves up in the old city around St Mary's church. The Vikings were masters of defensive warfare and the English allies could make no progress, rapidly running out of supplies. This failure led to recriminations between the two monarchs which soured the new alliance. Eventually, after payment of a considerable tribute, the Vikings moved off in 869. When they emerged in Berkshire, the next year Burgred failed to reciprocate the aid the West Saxons had given him, probably in hopes that the Great Army would move on into the West Saxon heartland. The attack on Wessex developed during 870 and 871, when Alfred bought them off, and they moved to London, in Mercia. The reason for this itinerancy was twofold: to obtain supplies and the horses which they needed for mobility, and also to blackmail the various kings in rotation. By exposing the limitations of mutual support, they also undermined the alliance. Eventually, in the winter of 873 the invaders moved to the heart of Mercia and encamped at Repton. Burgred fled to Rome where he died in ignominy, and a Viking puppet Ceolwulf II was set up in West Mercia. East Mercia was taken by the Vikings. A large number of Viking skeletons have been found at Repton, including one which may be that of their leader, Ivar 'the Boneless'. The context for the bones is a mystery but there may well have been dissent in the Viking camp for they were said to have left in two separate groups. The 'foolish king's thegn' Ceolwulf who had been granted West Mercia as a rump kingdom was entirely the tool of the Great Army, and he had no choice but to stand by as Guthrum, its new leader, prepared an invasion of Wessex. Ceolwulf was the last king of Mercia, an ignominious end to this once-mighty realm, but it was to have one last glorious rally under one of the most famous women in English history. With Mercia out of the way, only one English kingdom remained – Wessex – and the Vikings must have been supremely confident that it too would soon fall.

In late 870 the Viking host encamped at a place between the Thames and the Kennet just outside Reading. When their foraging parties ventured out for supplies they were confronted by a West Saxon ealdorman, Aethelwulf, and a skirmish took place at Englefield which forced the Vikings to retire behind their fortifications. Within the week, King Aethelred and Alfred, his younger brother, came up with large forces and besieged the Viking camp with the same result as at Nottingham some years before. As soon as the West Saxon forces had been repulsed and had retired, the Vikings sallied out in early January 871, and marched along the ancient Ridgeway to a place called Ashdown. Now began one of the most dramatic confrontations of the Anglo-Saxon age, which was to bring to the fore England's most esteemed and beloved national hero, Alfred the Great. However, at this stage, Alfred was not yet king, and the army was commanded by his elder brother King Aethelred. When the Danes came in sight, Aethelred was deep in prayer, refusing to leave his tent until mass had been concluded. Alfred was wise enough to see that this could prove a fatal error and promptly led the army into the attack before the Danes could gain the initiative. Leading a furious charge 'like a wild boar' he led the Englishmen uphill and smashed into the Vikings near a stunted thorn tree, near which the Danish leaders and their elite warriors were gathered. Overlooked by the effigy of a white horse which had been cut into the chalk in Iron Age times, a tremendous struggle raged all morning. The Danes were now fighting in the open, probably outnumbered, and were disconcerted by the ferocity of the English attack. Five *jarls* and a Danish king were killed before finally Aethelred came up with his own household troops. At this the Danes turned and ran, leaving the whole ridge covered with dead and wounded men. Alfred pressed the pursuit and slew many more Vikings before the battered stragglers reached their fort at Reading. Ashdown was a great victory against the Viking marauders, and showed they could be beaten by determined and well-led forces. Unfortunately this success turned to failure almost instantly. Within the month the Danes emerged again and fought with Aethelred and Alfred at Basing near Reading. This proved a major setback for the West Saxons, who suffered heavy losses. In early spring at Merantun, the brothers tried again and the battle seemed evenly matched. The Vikings appeared to have retired but at a given signal returned to the fight and overwhelmed the English. At this low point in their fortunes, King Aethelred died in April, and as his sons were still in their infancy, the crown passed to Alfred. On him now fell the heavy burden of continuing the war, and while he was attending his brother's funeral, news came that the Danes had destroyed part of the West Saxon army near to their encampment. At Wilton the Danes were again victorious and nine battles were fought with them in the first year of his reign. Such a sustained effort exhausted Wessex and eventually Alfred came to terms with them, effectively paying them to leave his realm. They went only so far as London, in Mercia, having won a costly victory, but the suspension of hostilities was recognised by both sides for what it was – a temporary armistice. Wessex had struggled manfully and had survived, and Alfred prepared for a resumption of the war. There must have been many among his own subjects, as well as the Danes, who wondered if he could prove equal to the task, for this greatest of all Englishmen, 'England's darling' as Layamon dubbed him, did not at first sight seem the stuff from which heroes are made. He was disabled by a chronic illness, a sort of neurasthenia or palsy, from which he suffered all through his life. Like many such great men, his debility masked hidden strength, and under pressures of unprecedented intensity this emerged in the form of almost superhuman gifts, as we will see.

Asser, the Welshman who became the great man's biographer and confidante, tells a tale which reveals something about the personality that could overcome such challenges, and his precocious predilection for literary matters. As children, the royal siblings had been gathered together by their mother, who promised an illuminated compendium of English poetry to the child who memorised it first. Despite being the youngest, Alfred won the prize, having patiently listened to it being read out by his tutor until he knew it perfectly. This diligence and concentrated effort was his particular strength, but for the time being all Alfred's energies were directed to the task of defending his realm against the barbarians. By 874 Mercia had been effectively conquered or brought under vassalage. The *micel here* had been in England for nine years and must have been continually reinforced by new recruits from Denmark which kept up its numbers. Many of the old campaigners were content to take their share of the plunder and become farmers in Northumbria, but the younger men, under new chiefs called Guthrum, Anwend and Oskytel, were keen to resume the fight. These three occupied Cambridge and in 876 they marched through the heart of Wessex to the Dorset coast. Alfred shadowed their movements and attempted to buy them off as he had done before, but in the night they slipped away and rode into Devon, where they shut themselves up in Exeter. Here they were besieged and entered into treaty negotiations again, eventually agreeing to leave the kingdom and return to southern Mercia. The next place they occupied was Gloucester, where they arrived in late summer. Alfred's army, or the main bulk of it, were busy getting the harvest home. Alfred must have calculated that they would not prove dangerous during the winter months, but this was a major miscalculation. It may well be that the Danes had some sort of espionage network in England by this stage, for Guthrum now struck a blow that appears to have been based upon intelligence as to Alfred's whereabouts. The king had spent Christmas at Chippenham with his family and a few trusted retainers. Unfortunately, that town is not far distant from Gloucester for a mounted force, and Guthrum suddenly appeared with a large war band 'after Twelfth Night'. By a miracle the king escaped, but he was forced to take refuge in the Somerset marshes while the Danes ravaged Wessex, billeting themselves on the hapless yeomen, abusing their womenfolk and eating up their precious winter supplies. Many nobles, in order to preserve their treasures as well as their wives' honour, fled by sea, perhaps as far as France.

By stealth and cunning the Danes had finally brought Wessex low, but they had failed to achieve their main objective. Alfred still lived, as they learned to their cost. In daring hit-and-run raids, he attacked and slew their foraging parties, as well as venturing out to punish collaborators. In a miserable winter he encamped at a place well known to him, Athelney, where a low hill protruded above the impassable marshes which could only be accessed by small boats. With no more than 200 men under his command, it must have seemed as if his days were numbered. The Danes knew roughly where he was and an attempt by twenty-three shiploads of them to land on the coast of north Devon, and capture or kill him, was observed by the men of Devon, who attacked and slew 800 of the Vikings and captured their famous banner, 'the Raven', which was thought to possess magical powers that rendered those who marched under it invulnerable. This small (and costly) success was a major turning point from a psychological perspective. The Viking depredations, their humiliation of the English and liberties taken with their women had sown seeds of hatred during winter, and news of the slaughter of the raiders in Devon spread after church services. Spring was coming and Alfred was still in hiding. All men waited for the summons to arms, but where was the king?

Legendary lore, written down many centuries later gives us some clues as to the answer, but there is reason to suspect that these tales may be based on anecdotal stories whose author was no one less than the king himself. William of Malmesbury, writing in the 1120s, tells us the most famous tale, of how Alfred sought shelter in the cottage of a humble cowherd. While the man of the house was at his duties,

> The woman of the house, the cowherd's wife, was preparing to bake some scone cakes. While the king sat by the hearth, busy tending his bow and arrows and other weapons of war, the cakes began to scorch: seeing this, the wretched woman ran quickly in and snatched them from the fire, scolding the indomitable king and saying, 'Hey fellow, can't you see the cakes are burning? Why didn't

you turn them over? You'll be quick enough to swallow them when they're ready.' The miserable woman little thought she was speaking to the famous King Alfred, who had fought so many battles against the pagans and gained so many victories over them.

Other stories tell of how the king stole out into a Danish encampment and entertained them by playing the harp around the campfire, but perhaps even for the mighty Alfred this would have been a little too impetuous. The tales give us a picture of a man travelling incognito in a country ground down by poverty, anxiety and war, and of a king reduced to finding shelter with the meanest sort of people, sharing with them the daily grind of provisioning themselves in a world where a 'scone cake' may have been the only meal of the day, and the irritation of a peasant woman who was not prepared to have her meal ruined by a military interloper. The thoughts in the disguised king's mind were probably of a gravitas the poor woman would have struggled to comprehend, even had she known his identity. He could not hide forever and needed to take the immense gamble of emerging from obscurity, showing himself to the people and staking all on one last showdown with the Danes. In early May 878 he sent out his messengers, telling the men (that is the fighting men) of Wiltshire, Hampshire and Dorset to meet with him at a well-known meeting place, Egbert's Stone. The hosting was well attended, but there must have been many who had doubts he would arrive for the rendezvous. When he did arrive they were jubilant and immediately they marched towards Chippenham, the Danish fort, to Iley Oak by Warminster. At dawn the following day, having scouted out the Viking position, they marched onto Salisbury Plain to meet the Danish army at Edington then called Ethandun. Thanks to Alfred's biographer, the Welshman Asser, we have a description of the battle which must have issued from Alfred's own mouth:

(There) he attacked the whole pagan army, fighting ferociously in dense battle-order, and by the divine will eventually won the victory, made a great slaughter among them, and pursued them to their fortress. Everything left outside the fortress, men, horses and cattle he seized, killing the men, and encamped outside the gates. After fourteen days the pagans were brought to the extreme depths of despair by hunger, cold and fear, and they sought peace.

It had been a stunning victory, won by a man who a few weeks before had been burning cakes in a peasant hovel. The Danes knew that they could never impose themselves on the abused people of Wessex again, or hope to prevail against a people united and militant under a powerful, ruthless and intelligent leader. They also knew that to buy their lives they had no choice now but to submit to terms that amounted to abject surrender.

The treaty terms were uncompromising. Guthrum was required to convert to Christianity, along with all his chief men. At Aller, near to Alfred's former base at Athelney, he duly arrived and was baptised along with thirty of his followers. Alfred stood as godfather to him and Guthrum received the baptismal name of Athelstan. Asser recounts the ceremony and its aftermath:

> Guthrum, their king, promised to accept Christianity and to receive baptism at King Alfred's hand; all of which he and his men fulfilled … three weeks later the king of the pagans, with thirty of the best men from his army, came to King Alfred at a place called Aller … King Alfred raised him from the holy font of baptism, receiving him as his own son; the unbinding of the chrisom on the eighth day took place at the royal estate called Wedmore. Guthrum remained with the king for twelve nights after he had been baptised, and the king freely bestowed many excellent treasures on him and all his men.

This was a psychological demonstration of his dominance not, as is often portrayed, an act of saintliness and virtue. It seems to have worked too, for Guthrum meekly led his army out of Wiltshire into Gloucestershire where they set up camp at Cirencester, then in Mercia. A year later, Guthrum and the army moved to East

Anglia, where, by the terms of the treaty, they were permitted to settle. Alfred knew that total victory over the Vikings could not come about in his lifetime, and therefore Danish settlement was accepted in a territorial partition whereby their predominance and customs would prevail north of 'the Thames and up the Lea, then along the Lea to its source, then in a straight line to Bedford, then up the Ouse to Watling Street'. The area of Danish preponderance, the so-called 'Danelaw', was a tacit admission that Alfred had accepted accommodation with the Scandinavians, but this did not imply that he accepted them as equals. Rather it was an astute move, which forced all free Englishmen, wherever they may be, to look to him as their national leader. This was of exceeding importance in the formation of a united English kingdom. Also, it forced the Danes to conform to ideas which were previously alien to them, such as the submission to legally binding treaties. Even if Guthrum or his successors became apostate, they had crossed a Rubicon. Certainly Guthrum minted coins in East Anglia bearing his baptismal name and suffered the Christian shrines in his new kingdom to remain. Thus began the process whereby the Vikings were civilised and tamed and eventually incorporated into 'Engla-lond', but this lay well in the future.

Wessex had come through the fire of war but had suffered all the depredations of foreign occupation. It was not enough to have prevailed in war, as Alfred well knew. The *modus operandi* of the Vikings was now known, and what exacerbated the situation was that they were now ensconced permanently in England with a land border from which fresh assaults could supervene. To prevent this, Alfred set about a complete reorganization of his kingdom, whereby defended towns called *burhs* would provide regional refuges in times of danger. These were garrisoned and depots were set up within them to enable them to withstand siege. They served a dual purpose, for the increase of mercantile trade depended largely on security from the threat of banditry. So within the *burhs*, mints were set up and taxes levied on a new class of urban dwellers which enabled investment in a standing-army or militia – the *fyrd* – which, serving in periodic rotation, meant that large forces could be deployed in times of threat. Alfred was also alert to the threat from the sea, and in his reign he personally supervised the construction of revolutionary new warships which could challenge the Vikings even before they made landfall. These innovations, driven forward by the power of his personality and inventiveness, showed a capacity for forward planning and orientation to a larger goal. That goal, once the dream of the Mercian kings, was a united English kingdom under one ruler, not one enforced as under Aethelbald or Offa, but as the expression of popular loyalty and identity. Although he could not bring this about in his lifetime, his son, daughter and ultimately his grandson took up the idea and made it into a reality. All these astonishing achievements in war and peace merit in themselves the appellation 'Alfred the Great', but he did not win this reputation for them alone. This extraordinary man won that accolade for another reason, when, during middle age, he became literate and turned his talents to yet another project.

There had been a time when the English kingdoms had exported knowledge and learning to the rest of Europe, and Alcuin of York had been the epitome of scholarship and statecraft, but the Viking assault had changed all that. As Alfred himself wrote,

> So general had been the decay (of learning) in England that there were very few this side of the Humber who could understand their rituals in English or translate a letter from Latin into English; and I believe there were not many beyond the Humber. There were so few that I cannot remember a single one south of the Thames when I came to the throne.

A lesser man than he was would perhaps have imported scholars to reinvigorate the culture, but Alfred took it upon himself. Under the guidance of trusted churchmen, he translated some books into English whose contents were 'most needful for men to know'. These were Gregory the Great's *Pastoral Care*, Bede's

Ecclesiastical History of the English People, the *Soliloquies* of St Augustine and the *Consolations of Philosophy* by Boethius. The boy who had memorised Anglo-Saxon verses to win the prize of an illuminated book had in middle age learned to write, to translate and to publish, for these works were presented to bishops for the elucidation of their clergy, who he hoped would convey their message to their illiterate flocks. However, the peace could not last forever. In 878 Viking raiders moored in London, which probably still had a Danish garrison. This was tolerated but in 884 a landing took place in Kent and Rochester was put under siege until Alfred arrived to drive them off. In 886 Alfred dispensed with diplomatic formalities and drove the Danes from London and occupied it, despite it being technically a Mercian city. This shows that the old rivalry between the two kingdoms had now been subsumed by the common desire to provide a united front against the Vikings. This common purpose was not the work of Alfred alone. A charter of 883 endorsed by Alfred recognises an ealdorman of Mercia, Aethelred, as a sub-king of West Mercia. This little-known personage was to become one of the most important men in Anglo-Saxon history. In effect, he had agreed to become a viceroy of what remained of Mercia on Alfred's behalf. He probably originated from the nobility of the ancient Hwicce around Gloucestershire, and as a sign of his importance he was given Alfred's daughter Aethelflaed in marriage. This daughter, who was the eldest of Alfred's children, was to become a figure of legend in her own right, one of the most esteemed women of her age. Meanwhile, Alfred had restored the ancient Roman walls of London, repopulated the city with new settlers, rebuilt the quay and defended the only bridge that spanned the Thames. As soon as the work was completed, Alfred restored London to Aethelred, cementing the new English alliance by this generous act, as well as by the marriage of his daughter.

This new English alliance was soon to be tested. In 892 a fleet of over 300 Viking ships crossed the sea from France to Kent. They split into two squadrons before Alfred and his eldest son, Edward, engaged them. Edward destroyed the larger force at Farnham, but the smaller (but still very substantial) part of it encamped at Benfleet in Essex. Its leader, a notorious pirate called Haesten, had sallied out to seek provisions, horses and booty in Mercia, but while he was away the Viking camp was attacked by a coalition of various English forces and its ships seized and the women and children taken as prisoners. Haesten called for reinforcements from the Vikings from the Danelaw and rampaged all across the Midlands until they were finally cornered on an island in the River Severn at Buttington by Aethelred of Mercia, who may have called on Welsh aid to ensure they could not escape. After a very long siege, during which the Vikings were forced to eat their horses, they broke through the ring and made for Shoebury on the other side of England. This tells us much about the sheer toughness and endurance of these folk, whose indomitable spirit is still the stuff of legend. When they emerged again the English were forced into a scorched-earth policy whereby all livestock and corn was destroyed, depriving them of any means of sustenance. Instead, Haesten led his army into Wales, mercilessly ravaging it for the best part of a year before returning via Northumbria to the Thames estuary. All this was done while the mighty King Alfred looked on, and it had fallen to his son and his deputy in Mercia, Aethelred, to do most of the hardest fighting. However, in 895 Alfred supervised an attack on the Viking fortified encampment on Mersea Island in Essex. This, like so many similar attempts to storm Viking forts, failed miserably. The Vikings then advanced into Hertfordshire, about the River Lea, and constructed a new base. By now it was harvest time, and to prevent the labourers being slaughtered and the corn seized, Alfred posted a constant watch on their camp. The Vikings intended to escape by ship via the River Lea to the Thames and thence out to sea, but Alfred prevented this by blockading the river with a boom. Seeing that there could be no escape by that route, Haesten led his men out, smashed through the English encircling forces and force-marched his army across the breadth of England once again, this time to Quatt, near Bridgnorth in Shropshire, where his encampment is still called 'the Danery'. Aethelred stationed them there all through the winter and into early summer 896, before at last they were force-marched into Northumbria and East Anglia where they dispersed, with little to show for several years of unrelenting piracy. This episode shows us two crucial themes which were to dominate in the coming generations. The first was the incredible hardihood, enterprise and audacity of the Vikings, who now roamed at will, appearing first in one realm, then in another, constructing impenetrable defences, seemingly unconcerned by adversaries, even men of the quality of Alfred. The second thing it shows is that the English had learned to live with this plague, had devised measures to contain it and were prepared to cooperate as never before in order to resist it, and it is at this stage in our story, perhaps, that we can discern a people who now thought of themselves no longer as Mercians, West Saxons or East Saxons etc., but as 'Englishmen'. That, ultimately, was Alfred's lasting achievement.

Alfred died in late October 899 as the old century passed. His people, the *English* people as a whole, not just the West Saxons, mourned him and made him a figure of legend. Even the catastrophe of the Norman Conquest could not obliterate his fame. William of Malmesbury, writing many centuries later, recounts stories of farm labourers who still told of his famous deeds: of how in his reign golden arm-rings had been hung at the crossroads, none daring to violate his peace and of how St Cuthbert had appeared to him in a vision in the dark days, when he had fled into the marshlands of Somerset. Folk tell such tales of the giants among their people, men who have channelled divine forces into this sorry world. Some people may say that these are just that, mere tales, exaggerations for effect, and perhaps they are. They were certainly not how this complex and driven man saw himself:

What I set out to do was to virtuously and justly administer the authority given me. I desired the exercise of power so that my talents and my power might not be forgotten. But every natural gift and every capacity in us soon grows old and is forgotten if wisdom is not in it. Without wisdom no faculty can be fully brought out ... to be brief, I may say that it has always been my wish to live honourably, and after my death to leave to those who come after me my memory in good works.

Who can say that he did not?

1. Wroxeter, the Roman baths. Wroxeter still functioned as a thriving city well into the sixth century. (Photograph courtesy of Etrusia, Flickr CC2.0)

2. Liddington Castle. One of the sites suggested for the crucial Battle of Mount Badon. (Photograph courtesy of Feeling my age, Flickr CC2.0)

3. Wall-by-Lichfield, the Roman baths. Wall was a crucial way station on Watling Street and became the centre of a British principality, Caer Luitcoit. (Photograph courtesy of Alun Salt, Flickr CC2.0)

4. Wall-by-Lichfield as it is today. (Photograph by the author)

5. Watling Street, the ancient Roman Road which was still in use in the seventh century, with the modern A5 looking from Wall towards nearby Hammerwich. (Photograph by the author)

6. Priestholm, the tiny island from which Cadwallon escaped to find refuge in Ireland. (Photograph courtesy of Smabs Sputzer CC2.0)

7. The Six Ashes Inn between Bridgnorth and Kinver, anciently Onnenau Meigion, a sacred Celtic sanctuary. (Photograph by the author)

8. The way back. View west from Six Ashes, where the Mercian/British alliance commenced the campaign to liberate Gwynedd. (Photograph by the author)

9. St Thomas' church, Wednesfield, 'Woden's-field', originally a sacred pagan sanctuary. (Photograph by the author)

10. The Edward the Elder Primary School, Wednesfield. The memorial plaque commemorates the millennium of the Battle of Tettenhall, reputedly fought at Wednesfield. Edward the Elder was not likely to have been present, however. (Photograph by the author)

11. The Woden Inn at Wednesbury, 'Woden's fortress'; the cult of Woden was strong among the pagan Mercians. (Photograph by the author)

12. The view from Barracks Lane, Hammerwich, where the Staffordshire Hoard was discovered, looking towards nearby Wall-by-Lichfield. (Photograph by the author)

13. Barracks Lane near Hammerwich. Note the incline once represented by the ridge where the Staffordshire Hoard was buried. (Photograph by the author)

14. Modern junction signing on Barracks Lane. Note the proximity of the Roman Road of Watling Street. (Photograph by the author)

15. The mysterious Wychbury hill fort near Stourbridge, a possible candidate for a cult grove of the *Hwicce* tribe as postulated by Stephen J. Yeates. (Photograph by the author)

16. St Kenelm depicted on the church gate at Romsley, Worcestershire. (Photograph by the author)

17. The spot where St Kenelm was reputedly murdered, and where a sacred spring burst forth. (Photograph by the author)

18. St Peter's church, Kinver, Staffordshire, originally dedicated to the memory of King Wulfhere's murdered sons. (Photograph by the author)

Left: 19. Lichfield Cathedral. The siting of the see was the possible cause of the dispute between Peada, Oswy and Cynddylan. (Photograph courtesy of Snake3yes, Flickr)

Below: 20. Offa's Dyke. (Photograph courtesy of Freddie Phillips, Flickr)

Left: 21. The King Alfred Statue in Winchester, by Thorneycroft. Even Winston Churchill regarded him as the greatest of all Englishmen. (Photograph courtesy of Ewen Roberts, Flickr)

Right: 22. The Lady of the Mercians. This statue at Tamworth Castle depicts Aethelflaed/Ethelfleda with the young Athelstan, whom she fostered. (Photograph courtesy of Elliot Brown, Flickr)

23. The 'Danery' near Bridgnorth, Shropshire, where Haesten's Viking marauders encamped during the winter of 895/96. (Photograph by the author)

24. The extremely ruined Bridgnorth Castle, which stood on the site of one of Lady Aethelflaed's extensive network of *burhs*. (Photograph by the author)

25. Corfe Castle in Dorset. Here King Edward 'the Martyr' was cruelly murdered. (Photograph courtesy of Chris Parker)

26. Eamont Bridge, Cumbria, where Athelstan received the submission of subservient kings. (Photograph courtesy of Ashley Van Haeften)

27. View over the battlefield of Assandun, now Ashingdon in Essex. Cnut built the church of St Andrew as a memorial to all those who died. (Photograph courtesy of W. J. Prior)

28. The Priory of St Mary's, Deerhurst, Gloucestershire. Here Edmund 'Ironside' and Cnut met to divide England between them. (Photograph courtesy of Hugh Llewelyn)

29. A view of Battle Abbey across the Hastings battlefield. Harold was reputedly slain where the abbey was built. Note the sharp incline which would have been steeper in those days. The Anglo-Danish army would have lined up atop the ridge. (Photograph courtesy of Jim Linwood)

30. Battle of Senlac (Hastings) mural in Battle, East Sussex. (Photograph courtesy of Jim Linwood. Mural by Anthony Palmer)

31. The Stiperstones, Shropshire. Here Edric 'the Wild' passed from history and into legend. When England goes to war he emerges to lead the 'Wild Hunt' across the land. (Photograph courtesy of Jonathan Stonehouse)

32. Arley Redstone, Worcestershire, where the poet Layamon retired to write his *Brut* in English, preserving Anglo-Saxon culture for posterity. (Photograph by the author)

33. A silver coin from the reign of Offa of Mercia. (Courtesy of the Portable Antiquities Scheme)

34. A silver coin from the reign of Alfred of Wessex. (Courtesy of the Portable Antiquities Scheme)

35. A silver coin from the reign of Athelstan. (Courtesy of the Portable Antiquities Scheme)

36. A silver coin from the reign of Edgar 'the Peaceful'. (Courtesy of the Portable Antiquities Scheme)

37. A silver coin from the reign of Cnut. (Courtesy of the Portable Antiquities Scheme)

38. A silver coin from the reign of Harold Godwinson. (Courtesy of the Portable Antiquities Scheme)

39. A silver coin from the reign of William the Conqueror. (Courtesy of the Portable Antiquities Scheme)

8

THE LADY OF THE MERCIANS

The special circumstances that had caused the sons of King Aethelred of Wessex to be overlooked and set aside in favour of Alfred in 871 brought about a succession crisis immediately following his death. Two candidates for the throne of Wessex emerged. The first and obvious choice was Edward, Alfred's eldest son (though not the eldest of his children). The other contender was Aethelwold, eldest son of the former King Aethelred, Alfred's brother, whose claim was therefore strong. Of the two cousins, Edward had the immense advantage of having led the West Saxon army and having proven himself as an able commander. It was known that Alfred had indicated that his wish was for him to succeed to the throne, and this endorsement by the greatest Englishman of the age, the saviour of the Anglo-Saxon race, meant that the leading churchmen and nobles were enthusiastic in his support. Aethelwold would not accept this consensus, and at a time when Wessex needed to consolidate the works of Alfred, the country was instead riven by internecine strife. The petulant Aethelwold used his own personal troops to fortify his royal estates against Edward, who immediately blockaded them.

Foolishly, Aethelwold fled into the territory of the Northumbrian Danes, whose support he canvassed against his cousin. The Vikings of York were of course eager to exploit this division and accepted him as their king for a time and put considerable resources at his disposal. In 902 he intrigued with the Danes of East Anglia and persuaded them to attack West Mercia and Wessex. A more foolish strategy could hardly have been devised because Alfred's old ally Aethelred, Lord of Mercia and Edward's brother-in-law, was thereby converted into an enemy. Edward retaliated and invaded East Anglia reaching the Fenlands, an impassable obstacle for any army. Edward was content to return home, but the Kentish part of his army failed to respond to his command, probably because they sought more plunder. The Danes cut off this section of the English and badly mauled them, but during the battle Aethelwold was killed. This removed any doubts about Edward's legitimacy and enabled him to take up his father's project of establishing a united English nation as undisputed king.

The episode was a trenchant reminder for Edward of the power the Danes could exert over English politics. Aethelwold's scheming, though directed in the main to destabilising and deposing Edward, also extended to intrigues against Aethelred of Mercia. He had recruited to his cause a landless Mercian noble, Beorhtsige, who he hoped to install as his own Mercian viceroy. The battle between the men of Kent and the Danes in East Anglia in 902 left Aethelwold and Beorhtsige dead, as well as the king of the East Anglian Danes, but a new threat to Mercia had developed. Norse Vikings from Dublin, under a commander called Ingimund, were driven from Ireland into Anglesey, but the king of Gwynedd foiled their attempt to disembark there. Instead they moved on to the Wirral peninsula. Aethelred was forced to contain this new Viking influx by fortifying Shrewsbury, but fortunately for him the arrival of Ingimund was greeted with as much anxiety among the Danes as among the Mercians. The Norse were at this stage enemies of the kings of York, and, their numbers being not very great, they contented themselves with the occupation of a base around

Hoylake on the Wirral, which became a small but irritating colony from Aethelred's point of view. It proved necessary to fortify Chester against them in 907 but this must have been a severe drain on Aethelred's limited resources. Meanwhile, Edward had been inactive on the military front for some time, instead encouraging English nobles to purchase lands from the Danes on the borders of the Danelaw as an expedient for re-establishing English control without further expenditure of his own treasure or the lives of his soldiery. This may have been a cunning strategy designed to lull the Danes into a false sense of security, because quietly Edward was planning a joint assault with Aethelred into Lindsey which was heavily settled by the Danes. In 909 the attack went in and the whole area was brutally devastated for over a month. Aethelred removed the sacred remains of St Oswald of Northumbria from Bardney Abbey, the foundation of his illustrious namesake Aethelred I of Mercia, and took them with him to Gloucester to be reinterred in his own regional capital. This provocation by the English allies had the effect of goading the Danes into offensive action of their own, and their target for revenge was Aethelred and his rump sub-kingdom of West Mercia.

This preamble brings us to yet another contentious period in Mercian history, which has until recently been misunderstood. Now that the West Saxons had become the dominant political power among the English, the entries in the *Chronicle* increasingly reflected their point of view, just as in his time Bede's *Historia* had reflected a Northumbrian perspective. Once again it was Mercia whose contribution was obfuscated and to some extent distorted, but the reasons for this were quite different. It was true that Wessex had become the leader among the various English peoples, and that the rump sub-kingdom of Mercia was now much reduced in size, influence and power. It was not, however, a vassal state of Wessex. Lord Aethelred was a man of honour, who was prepared to cooperate fully with Edward, as he had once done with Alfred. This was demonstrated by his participation in the devastation of Lindsey in 909. His family connection,

through his wife Aethelflaed, Edward's elder sister, ensured that relations with Wessex were so close as to imply a virtually united English kingdom of Wessex and West Mercia, and this is how some versions of the *Chronicle* portrayed subsequent events, with Edward as the predominant English leader, ably assisted by Aethelred, and then after his death by Lady Aethelflaed. The *Mercian Register*, an independent chronicle compiled within the region, appears to contradict this view. The counter-invasion of Mercia by the Northumbrian Danes in the summer of 910 was the point at which the history of the Anglo-Danish struggle becomes confused, and I believe this was due to a retrospective diminution of the Mercian contribution in the war that followed. The reason for this was down to something more than the bias of West Saxon chroniclers. Edward is called 'the Elder' in our history books in order to distinguish him from Edward 'the Confessor' some generations later. It is true that he was Alfred's eldest son, but his eldest child was Aethelflaed, Aethelred of Mercia's widow. It seems rather strange to me in these days of feminist re-evaluation of the positive role of women in ancient societies that she has largely escaped a revised analysis of her distinguished role in the defeat of the Northumbrian Vikings. This would be justified in response to the anti-female bias of the West Saxon version of the *Chronicle* abetted by understandable silence from the Viking sources and the misogynistic attitudes of the Church. My opinion is that she was a dynamic English war leader, at least the equivalent of Edward, and perhaps as significant as her esteemed father, the so called 'Lady of the Mercians'. Her story is one that ought to be told with pride by all English men and women, and she is one of the unsung exemplars of the Anglo-Saxon age.

The blow which fell on West Mercia in the summer of 910 was (perhaps deservedly) cruel, well planned and designed as an act of vengeance for the intrusion into Danish Lindsey the previous year. King Edward was, conveniently, in far-off Kent where he was preoccupied in gathering a fleet. Therefore, Aethelred was left to cope with the invasion unaided and the Danes under two kings,

called Halfdan and Eowils, easily progressed through the Mercian heartland destroying everything in their wake. They eventually reached the River Avon, not far from Aethelred's stronghold of Gloucester, to which we must presume he retreated while frantic messages were sent to Edward. The Danes then made a fatal error. They crossed the Severn at some point and harried the Severn Valley area until they reached the crossing called Danesford near Bridgnorth in Shropshire, at exactly the place where Haesten had encamped in the winter of 895. Aethelred had garrisons at several *burhs* in the south Mercian heartland and a hard core of fighting men drawn from the royal estates around Winchcombe. It is unclear whether he was assisted by West Saxon ealdormen on his borders who reinforced him, or by Edward himself, as is often claimed, but there is no mention of his presence in the *Chronicle*, which states only that he 'sent his army both from Wessex and Mercia'. It seems likely that the West Saxon element were levies from Wiltshire and Somerset which conjoined with Aethelred, who was actually in overall command of the combined English force. On 5 August the English fell on the surprised Danes from the rear after a rapid forced march, and the latter, laden down with booty, were overwhelmed in a ferocious assault. The site of the battlefield was identified as Tootenhall, now called Tettenhall, a suburb of Wolverhampton, but the candidates for it have always aroused fierce controversy. Tettenhall is a possibility that cannot be simply dismissed, and folk traditions identified the place as the battlefield. Unfortunately these traditions may well be later interpolations. Battlefield Hill near Wombourne in Staffordshire also claims to be the 'field of slaughter' but with as little evidence. Aethelweard, a descendant of the West Saxon King Aethelred, was said to have become a hermit at Bridgnorth where he retired to write an extensive history of the Anglo-Saxon era in the late tenth century. He claimed that the actual battlefield was at Wednesfield, or 'Woden's Field', to the east of Wolverhampton. Given that he was privy to local information and was an exceptionally gifted historian, we may perhaps concur, but in fact there is no convincing evidence for any of the sites mentioned above and perhaps there were separate but related engagements with the Danes at several locations. The outcome was not in doubt, however. The Danes were surrounded and utterly overwhelmed, with hardly any of their number able to make good their escape. Even men of the highest rank were slaughtered, as the *Chronicle* says, 'There fell King Eowils, and King Halfdan; Earls Other and Scurf; Governors Agmund, Othulf, and Benesing; Anlaf the Swarthy, and Governor Thunferth; Osferth the collector, and Governor Guthferth.' When we consider that it was the Viking tradition to stand by their lords until death, and then to defend their bodies, and that each of the above named men must have had large personal retinues with them, the carnage at Tettenhall must have been truly horrific. It was Aethelred's victory, almost certainly, and his subsequent obscurity in conventional histories is to be regretted. It may well be that the ageing commander paid for it with his own life, for within six months he died, possibly from wounds received in the fight. It had so weakened the Viking kingdom of York that they never regained their former power, becoming instead a target for Ragnall, king of the Norse Vikings of Dublin, and for Aethelflaed, Aethelred's widow, who immediately took over as the Mercian leader, 'the Lady of the Mercians'. As I hope to show, it was through her offensive operations in the Midlands that the Danes were subjugated, eventually suing for peace from this redoubtable woman. The victory over the Danes was a joint effort, but her part in the campaigns has been so poorly attested in mainstream historical sources that it seems remiss not to give an account of it.

Although she was a West Saxon, her mother had been Mercian and she had arrived in Mercia as a young bride in 886 or thereabouts. The bridal party had been attacked by the Danes and she had been forced to take refuge in an old fortress, until relieving forces arrived. Her husband was very much older than she was and the couple had only one child, a daughter, Aelfwynn. There is a tradition that Aethelflaed abstained from sexual relations after the birth, perhaps due to a painful childbirth, though legend has ascribed the decision to her religious purity. As Aethelred became older he seems to have been troubled by illness, perhaps old war wounds which incapacitated him. Aethelflaed had deputed for him on these occasions and had been found more than competent. After all, she was the eldest child of the most famous Englishman of the age, and given Alfred's obsession with learning she must have been educated by the finest tutors available. Such a woman must have keenly felt the exclusion from kingship due to her gender and may have resented it. Daughter to a powerful king and ally of Mercia, Alfred, she was also the sister of Edward, the new king of Wessex, and the alliance was the only security for what remained of English Mercia. As soon as her husband died, she was acclaimed as its new ruler by the most powerful nobles and churchmen in the region. This was in itself extraordinary in these times, but what makes her unique is that she was not content to deputise military command to her chief warriors. Instead she took personal charge of the army and led it on campaign, and her wars were ultimately successful, bringing the Vikings to heel. However, the traditional dress rehearsal for Mercian rulers was an invasion of Wales. Aethelflaed was quick to demonstrate her power to any Welsh ruler who dared challenge her. Most of the Welsh rulers had already submitted to Edward so as to gain his protection from their traditional Mercian enemies. Their calculation was that Edward was now de facto overlord of Mercia, and while the status of women in Celtic society was more elevated than in England the idea of a female ruler may have caused them to become reckless.

She began her reign by making a very significant concession to her brother. Two of the most important cities in Mercia, London and Oxford, were given away to Edward. This must have been bitterly resented by those nobles affected but it came about out of political and military necessity. Aethelflaed seems to have decided at an early stage that she would fight an offensive war. First she had to build strong new *burhs* in the north and west to contain any Viking probes. Once this was done she could concentrate all her forces on the frontiers of the Danelaw and reduce their fortresses one by one. London in particular needed a large garrison and this detracted from the forces available for her northern spearhead. She must have known her brother constituted a threat, for had he wished he could have simply annexed Mercia, but this would have been costly in military and political terms for him. London was what he prized, and by sacrificing it, Aethelflaed guaranteed her security on the throne of Mercia. It was an astute move. In 912 the building of new *burhs* at Scergeat (a place we cannot yet identify) and Bridgnorth were completed. The river crossing at the latter had been targeted by the Danes in 895 and again in 910, and this was now denied to them. The plan seems to have been agreed with her brother for he built one that same year at Hertford. The following year, forward operations against the Danes began. Edward built a new *burh* at Witham to cover Essex, while Aethelflaed built another at Stafford and refortified an existing fort at Tamworth, which had fallen into a dilapidated state. The Danes must have still been too weak after Tettenhall to challenge these English operations, but in 914 there was a new emergency. Two Viking captains, Ottar and Harold, had been raiding in Brittany when a plague spread there. They immediately headed for Cornwall, the Bristol Channel and the Severn Estuary, which they entered, plundering far inland. They captured a Welsh bishop and sacked South Wales before entering Arkenfield on the Herefordshire borders. Unlike the Welsh, the Mercians had a long-established system of *burhs*, and their garrisons, probably alerted by a system of beacons, were quickly deployed to intercept the Vikings:

> The men from Hereford and Gloucester and the nearest *burhs* met them and fought against them and put them to flight and killed earl Harold and a greater part of the army and drove them into an enclosure and besieged them there until they gave them hostages promising that they would leave the king's dominion.

The *Chronicle* account implies that Edward had coordinated operations throughout South Wales, Wessex and Mercia and this demonstrated what could be achieved by such joint operations. Aethelflaed quickly returned to fortress construction at Eddisbury, Warwick, Weardbyrig (probably around Chester), Runcorn, Bremesbyrig (Bromsberrow outside Ledbury) and Chirbury on the border of Powys. This constant construction work, or *burhbot* as it was known, was a very effective way of instilling military discipline and obedience into the ranks of the *fyrd* or militia. This meant that when they were finally deployed in offensive operations they would be at the peak of physical fitness and military cohesion. Patiently over a three-year period the Mercian war machine had been brought to a state of battle-readiness. The time had come to test it in action and the testing ground was, of course, Wales.

It is not clear if the general submission of the Welsh to Edward had caused them to relax their recognition of Aethelflaed, or if their perceived impudence was down to her sex, but all that was needed was a convenient provocation from her point of view. This was provided when Abbot Egbert, who had attested charters bearing her own name and who carried papers about him conferring her protection upon him and his companions, was murdered in Brycheiniog in South Wales, probably by Welsh malcontents who blamed the English for their sloth in responding to the Viking raids the previous year. As soon as the news carried to her, Aethelflaed ordered an immediate concentration on the South Wales border and within three days she invaded the territory of Tewdr, the king of the region, who withdrew to his fortified Crannog on a man-made island in Lake Llangorse, a place then called Brecananmere near modern Brecon. Tewdr escaped by boat, but his royal village was destroyed, and his court, including his queen were taken as hostages into Mercia. The whole territory was subjected to the traditional burning and wasting which was an inevitable consequence of medieval wars. Tewdr eventually capitulated and attested charters witnessed by her successors, so it seems obvious that the Welsh had learned their lesson. This was a woman to respect. The reason for this savage reaction may have been that she could not afford small incidents on the

Welsh border to distract from her planned offensive against the Danes. As it happened, the war in England had taken a new turn. The Danes had long feared Edward's potential to attack their Midland colonies, and at last they coordinated a general assault on the areas held by him. Unfortunately for them, their old *elan* had deserted them, and they probably lacked sufficient numbers. Moreover, instead of concentrating their blow, they advanced in three separate columns which were easily defeated in detail. The Viking power had for the time being spent itself. Viking myth told stories of how at Ragnarok, the end times, their warriors would be vanquished by an invincible warrior woman, at whose onset their courage would fail them. For the Danes in the five boroughs, Derby, Nottingham, Leicester, Stamford and Lincoln, their fortified strongholds across the waist of England, it must have seemed that the relentless advance of Alfred's son and daughter was irresistible.

It was at this point that brother and sister launched an all-out offensive which rained hammerblows on the Midlands and East Anglian Danes. Edward had compelled the Danes of Bedford to depart his kingdom into Normandy without a fight. After building new *burhs* he defeated three separate Viking attacks and advanced to Tempsford. Aethelflaed quickly observed the Viking deployment to the east and took advantage of it. In summer 917, while the Vikings were pre-occupied fighting Edward, she launched a heavy and ferocious attack on Derby, a key Danish stronghold. Despite a presumably weakened garrison, the siege was costly, as *The Mercian Register* relates: '(the) lady of the Mercians, with the help of God ... obtained the borough of Derby, with all that belongs to it; and, there also four of her thegns, who were dear to her, were killed within the gates'. There may be a hint here of the emotional and psychological cost for this woman, who relied on devoted *thegns* personally loyal to her who had ensured her secure succession and rule. Derby was sacked in revenge for this high expenditure in Mercian blood.

By a strange twist of fate, the initiative of the English effort had now passed to Aethelflaed. Edward attacked the Danish fort at Tempsford and carried it by storm and then took their fortress at Colchester, killing the Danish king of East Anglia. By now it was autumn and the country around the Cambridgeshire Fens and several powerful Danish boroughs such as Northampton, Cambridge and Stamford stood in his way. Aethelflaed now struck the killing blow. Leicester was the centre of a solid Danish *bloc*, a colony which had always thought itself invulnerable to English attack, but early in 918 the Lady of the Mercians harried the countryside and besieged the city. It seems likely that the fate of their compatriots in Derby the year before was much in the minds of the Viking garrison, and they chose to capitulate to her. In legend she progressed into the city bestowing alms on the poor folk as a sign of her mercy. Edward was now free to advance upon Stamford, which refused to yield, but meanwhile frantic negotiations were taking place. The Danes knew that the screen of boroughs in the Midlands which had protected their northern heartland around York were now in shreds. Her mercy at Leicester was a sign to them that if they surrendered to Aethelflaed they may obtain terms which would be relatively advantageous, and so it seems emissaries were dispatched offering a negotiated peace with her. The reason for this had to do with a fascinating piece of internal Viking politics.

The catastrophe at Tettenhall had decimated the Viking nobility of York and into the vacuum a Norse king from Dublin, Ragnall, had intruded. The York Danes were by now Christians, but Ragnall was an old-fashioned, unregenerate pagan. His various expeditions against other enemies gave the opportunity for potential negotiations with Aethelflaed, and through her, Edward. Therefore, in summer 918 they promised to swear oaths of allegiance to her, knowing that an advance into Yorkshire by Edward must first contend with the mighty fortress of Nottingham, 'the key to the North', and Lincoln, before he constituted a major threat. What happened next was a spectacular turning point in history, for on 12 June 918 Aethelflaed suddenly died. She was on the brink of causing a major political upheaval. If the Danes had duly surrendered to her there would have been nothing to stop her forces marching on York and receiving the submission of all the Northumbrian Danes. Her death was recorded internationally, in Wales, Wessex, Ireland, but most poignantly in her own realm of Mercia where she soon acquired the reputation as a warrior saint, very much like Jeanne d'Arc in later times. Was there anything suspicious about her death at such a crucial juncture? Unfortunately we will never know, but there was something most unsavoury about the fate of her young daughter, Aelfwynn. It was the decision of the Mercian nobles to honour the written will of the lady and her husband Aethelred before her. West Mercia was to pass to their daughter, who would become thereby Lady Aelfwynn. This was not to be, however. Edward left the siege of Stamford and arrived at Tamworth where he deposed his niece and had Aelfwynn conveyed to a monastery at Shaftesbury in Dorset, far from the people she had once briefly ruled. Nothing is heard of her again. Edward, by this cruel expedient, had achieved something which had been in the minds of English monarchs for generations. He was now king, not of Wessex alone, but of the consolidated kingdom of Wessex and West Mercia, and it must have seemed to him that all England south of the Humber must soon be his. At last there was a 'King of England'.

Before he could rest on his laurels, Edward first had to complete the business of mopping up the remaining Danish garrisons in the Midlands. The toughest nut to crack was Nottingham which he besieged in late 918 with a new combined English army of Mercians and West Saxons. However this was achieved he had obtained submission from the Danish garrison within months, and he required their prisoners to construct a new *burh* on the south bank of the Trent, either at Wilford or West Bridgford, and a bridge to be built, somewhere near the same spot where the modern Trent Bridge spans the river today. Edward shrewdly spared the Viking garrison and arranged that the city would be held by a joint command of Danish and English troops in future, and we must presume that this was a signal to York that he was prepared to be a magnanimous conqueror. The following year he obtained submission from the folk of the Peak District and built a *burh* at Bakewell, driving a wedge into Danish-held territory, and then exerted his authority around Chester, building a new *burh* at Thelwall and refurbishing the dilapidated defences of Manchester. These military demonstrations were designed to warn off Norse and Scots interlopers who may have been encouraged to take advantage of the plight of the Northumbrian Danes. The most dangerous of these was Ragnall, the heathen Viking who aspired to the kingship of York. Events had played into Edward's hands when Ragnall had sailed to Dublin to assist his brother in regaining the throne there. He hurried to York to salvage the situation but by then a consensus had developed which committed all the kingdoms of the north to tacit submission of Edward as their overlord. Edward had finally realised an ancient English dream, of expelling the Vikings and securing the English realm from the Mersey to the Humber. The contribution of Aethelflaed was important and has often been played down, but there is no denying that the final victory belonged to Edward. He had struggled all through his adult life to achieve this outcome, and we should not be surprised that he died while patrolling the northern frontier at Farndon-on-Dee in July 924. Alfred had been a hard act to follow, but he had risen to the challenge and in concert with his bellicose sister he had finally overcome the Vikings. They had not disappeared, however. The Dublin Vikings under their ruler Sihtric had never submitted to him and it was their growing power over the kingdom of York which promised a future Norse revival. All that was needed was a change in the political wind, a succession crisis, or best of all a weak English king to encourage their legendary capacity for resilience and resurgence.

Initially their prospects looked good. Athelstan, Edward's eldest son, was illegitimate. Therefore, Edward had indicated that the throne of Wessex should pass to Alfweard, his legitimate son by his second wife, and Mercia would go to Athelstan who had been brought up at the Mercian court and schooled in the monastery at Worcester by Aethelflaed, his esteemed sister. This division of the hard-won, unified English kingdom, which was Edward's life's work, was not to Athelstan's taste. He had been the favourite grandchild of the worthy Alfred, who had given him gifts of a military cloak, a sword and shield when he was a mere child, a 'flaxen-haired *aetheling*' as he is described. The seething resentment of a man steeped in political in-fighting and war since boyhood did not promise well for England, but fortunately for the English Aelfweard died only weeks after Edward, in August 924. Alfweard's younger brother immediately claimed the throne but Athelstan was not to be denied. In 925 he was crowned as king of the West Saxons at Kingston-on-Thames, but he would not rest content with this. The grandson of Alfred had in mind a greater kingdom, indeed an empire of the English which would subordinate the Vikings, Welsh, Cornish and Scots under his rule.

9

THE EMPEROR OF BRITAIN

In 925, the year of Athelstan's succession, it had been sixty years since the arrival of the 'Great Army'. By this time it was no longer accurate to describe the people of the Danelaw as Danes, rather some were the descendants of Danes who had settled in northern and eastern England, many of whom had interbred with English womenfolk, whose culture owed more to their common experience of living in England than to their remote Scandinavian ancestry. While they probably formed a regional warrior aristocracy which had been granted land when East Anglia, Northumbria and the region of the five boroughs of the Midlands had been divided out among the Viking armies, their numbers were comparatively small. The land they had seized had been won in the teeth of continuous resistance and they had not had an opportunity for massive folk movements such as had taken place during the Anglo-Saxon period. It was not their ethnic background which made them dominant in the Danelaw, but their superior social status. For the peasants who tilled their fields in the areas where they held their domains, they were simply lords and it may have been that they enjoyed more rights under the Danes than they had previously known under

English masters. Just as in more recent times, lords had more in common with each other than with the lower orders, whose existence was at this time only a little more important to them than livestock. Their toil was essential, of course, and from them the food rents and *burhbot* and the levies for their armies were drawn. Anglo-Saxon nobles had always had reciprocal duties to the peasantry and slaves. At Christmas, for example, a slave might receive the dung of the animals for the duration of the feast or at Easter the first milk from the flock for a week. So when we speak of a divided England in the tenth century, it is perhaps more accurate to speak of different regions with different cultural traditions, some of which may have been derived from a Scandinavian origin, rather than a strict ethnic divide. As the Norsemen converted to Christianity and adopted the model of Anglo-Saxon monarchy and government as their own, there was probably little to choose between daily life for ordinary folk whether they dwelt north or south of Watling Street, the de facto border.

In essence, this was the problem for the Scandinavians. Their settlements were military bases, with adjacent colonies where they were sometimes in the majority, but islanded in the fragmented remnants of the former English kingdoms they had overwhelmed. However, the Vikings were also settled throughout the country in small farmsteads or *tofts* where they toiled alongside people whose ancestors were English, or British, in the rural areas, and they plied their trades and handicrafts in urban centres all over the north and east, and as time went on in the south as well. In the areas which were under Danish or Norse control, their laws and customs prevailed, and they may have preserved their own dialect, but their preponderance, although it was more rooted in the native culture than the later Norman Conquest, had more to do with economic and political circumstances than purely military subjugation. The conflict with Athelstan was not a struggle between Englishmen and Danes as such, but was more to do with the fight to keep their way of life and their traditions, and this was also true for the nations at the Celtic margins. We have seen previously how the Viking kingdoms were not homogeneous as a bloc, united against the English enemy, but were often involved in deadly vendettas against one another. By the time of Athelstan's succession they had lost the military initiative and were probably intimidated by the growing power of the West Saxons. Their overtures to Aethelflaed and subsequent submission to Edward, prove that they had accepted the realpolitik of the times, but their difficulty lay in persuading Ragnall, the Norse interloper from Dublin, of the wisdom of this course of action. Fortunately for them, Ragnall died in 921, but he was immediately succeeded by yet another Dublin Viking, Ragnall's brother Sihtric 'Caoch' who enforced himself on the York Danes, installing a powerful garrison. Clearly then, the politics of the Danelaw were complex and unpredictable and military intervention was as likely to produce negative consequences as otherwise. Athelstan was wise enough to attempt a more subtle approach, and in January 926 he invited Sihtric to Tamworth where the latter did homage to him, promised to become a Christian and was betrothed to Athelstan's sister, who he subsequently married. This eminently reasonable settlement broke down almost immediately.

Athelstan's augmented kingdom of Mercia and Wessex had been won with some difficulty. Alfweard's younger brother Edwin must have had strong support from powerful nobles in the West Saxon aristocracy, for it took Athelstan a year before he was finally crowned king. His power base was in Mercia, his adopted homeland, and ironically it was his undisputed status there which was to prove the key to his subsequent success. Edward's deposition of Aelfwynn was an act of cynical aggression which must have humiliated the Mercian nobility. His rule was preferable to the Scandinavian alternative, but he ruled in Mercia by virtue of armed force, not consent. In Athelstan's case things were different. He was a known quantity, for he had been schooled at Worcester under the protection of the sainted Lady of the Mercians, and like her he had become an honorary Mercian. Indeed, to the Mercians he must have seemed like the son Aethelflaed had never had, rather than Edward's scion. This enabled him to rely on a consolidated kingdom in the Midlands and the south from which he could finally overawe the Viking kingdom of York. Sihtric, Athelstan's brother-in-law, died in 927 without being baptised. He was succeeded by yet another brother, Guthfrith, of the Clan Ivar, a congeries of pirates and slave traders from Dublin. Ostensibly he came to York as protector of Anlaf, Sihtric's young son, but the reality was that the Clan Ivar coveted the rich trade routes between York and Dublin which snaked over the Pennines. Athelstan mobilised his considerable forces immediately and marched on York. This was one of the most significant turning points in all English history. The folk of the north country, what had been Northumbria, had never before submitted to a southern king, but now this had to be endured. Athelstan ostentatiously demolished the ancient defences but was merciful to his antagonists, and although much property was seized, the churches were spared and there was no 'ethnic cleansing'. The mere fact of a southern English king in York was sufficient to demonstrate the new political reality. In his *Mercia and the Making of England*, Ian W. Walker suggests that Guthfrith had been expelled and had taken refuge in Strathclyde, a semi-autonomous kingdom which acknowledged the overlordship of Constantine, king of the Scots. Strathclyde coveted the Celtic principality of Cumbria, whose king, Owain, suddenly found his Lakeland redoubt the centre of events of considerable political gravitas. Athelstan's mighty army was ensconced at York and the initiative lay with him. As a demonstration of his power, an issue of coins was minted at York where he styled himself *rex to(tius) Brit(anniae)*, or 'King of all Britain'. On 12 July 927 the kings of the Scots, Strathclyde, Aealdred the English ruler of Bamburgh and Welsh kings attended a ceremony at Eamont Bridge south of Carlisle. Here all of them submitted to Athelstan and gave sacred oaths to keep peace with him. They gave up their kingdoms and were instead reappointed as his liege men. They undertook to 'renounce all idolatry', by which was meant that they would refrain from relations with pagan Norsemen from Dublin such as Guthfrith, and Athelstan stood as sponsor to Constantine's son at his baptism. This elaborate and impressive show actually masked an inherent weakness in the English position. Athelstan could not maintain a huge army in the north on a permanent basis, and the submissive kings knew that at some point he would withdraw. His rivals in Wessex must have been constantly in his thoughts and as soon as the conference at Eamont Bridge was concluded he turned south with his army to subdue those recalcitrant Welsh who still refused to yield to him. He must have known that the pledges and oaths he had received at Eamont Bridge would soon be broken.

The renegade leader of the anti-English party in Wales was Idwal Foel King of Gwynedd. Hywel Dda of Deheubarth and Owain of Gwent had attended the ceremonial submission in Cumbria and so were presumably in Athelstan's retinue when he rode south. Utilising their local knowledge, Idwal was winkled out of his stronghold of Snowdonia and five Welsh kings were summoned to Hereford where yet another ritual submission took place. Because of Idwal's rebellion, the Welsh were forced to pay an excruciating annual tribute of twenty pounds of gold, 300 pounds of silver, 25,000 oxen, hunting dogs and falcons, and to agree to be his liege men. The frontier in the south was fixed at the River Wye. This humiliation did not pass without notice in Cornwall where the Celts rose in rebellion. Athelstan marched swiftly to put the rising down, expelling Celtic speakers from Exeter and fixing the boundary with Cornwall on the River Tamar. A powerful message was being sent out to all the minorities within Britain. Athelstan intended to establish English hegemony by robust treaties, which if they were broken would attract savage reprisals. However, in Cornwall, Athelstan established a see at St Germans and endowed the Church with lavish gifts and estates. This procession of English might bred a seething resentment among his humiliated inferiors, however, and this was to erupt into serious conflict later on.

The consolidation of English power involved acts of ruthlessness. Athelstan's rival, Edwin, was drowned at sea, allegedly on Athelstan's orders. A large tract of the Midlands and East Anglia was granted to a loyal subordinate of the king, another Athelstan, nicknamed 'Half-king', who acted as a viceroy on his behalf. With internal matters seemingly settled, the king turned his attention to international statesmanship and the arrangement of prestige marriages for his sisters to various European monarchs and nobles. Like Offa, he fancied himself a contender on the international stage. In order to inculcate a patriotic and loyalist spirit, Athelstan commanded that every free-born lad in England was to swear their allegiance to him: 'In the first place, all shall swear in the name of the Lord, before every holy thing, that they will be faithful to the king'. This may sound like a medieval form of the Hitler Youth to us, but we need to recall the context. The English had been involved in a life-and-death struggle for sixty years. War had made them hard, militaristic and brutal. Every boy was needed for military duty, so much so that Athelstan enacted another measure. Henceforth, no boy under the age of fifteen was to be executed. Manpower was too precious a resource to waste in this way. The comparisons with Nazi Germany or the Soviet Union may not be so far-fetched. Family members were expected to inform on backsliders: 'No one shall conceal the breach of it on the part of a brother or a family relation, any more than in a stranger'.

The system of *burhs* begun by Alfred, and later extended by Edward and Aethelflaed, was strengthened further, and in the towns Athelstan permitted mints to be set up which were strongly regulated and controlled by him, with strict rules about the weight of coins, enforced by ruthless penalties for any infractions. We have an impression, then, of a man who was resolute that his will should be done in all matters, more than ready to crush any opposition, and in 934 this was demonstrated by a campaign against the king of the Scots which showed English superiority by land and sea.

At the end of May 934, Athelstan gathered his army at Winchester and in less than ten days had progressed to Nottingham where the armies of Mercia and his new Welsh vassals conjoined with him. The immense force, perhaps over 15,000 strong, pushed on northwards to Dunnottar and a fleet sailed to Caithness in the far north of Scotland. Athelstan visited the shrine of St Cuthbert, the saint who had appeared to his grandfather in a vision, at Chester-le-Street, but in truth no divine assistance was required. As the vast host progressed through Scotland, all livestock was seized as punishment for the non-payment of tribute. Constantine had no choice but to surrender. His son was taken as a hostage and Constantine was taken as a virtual prisoner back into England to be paraded before the king's subjects. In 935 at Cirencester another act of ritual submission was arranged, and five kings bowed before Athelstan, Constantine of Scotland, Hywel of Deheubarth, Owain of Cumbria, Morgan of Gwent and Idwal of Gwynedd. Cirencester, formerly Caer Cerin, had once been the second largest Roman city in Britain and it was almost within sight of South Wales. It must have galled the Welsh kings as they saw their drovers arriving with fat herds from their own lands to be marked off on the tally-sticks of English stewards. They were for the moment powerless, but Celtic resentment is a dangerous force to meddle with. Athelstan had made powerful enemies whose only hope of prevailing against him lay in uniting their forces, and such thoughts must have been in all their minds as they returned home as humiliated vassals of an Englishman who styled himself, unashamedly, as an emperor.

The glorious climax of the entire Anglo-Saxon age now commenced. King Olaf Guthfrithson of Dublin was astute enough to see an opportunity in the humiliation of the Scots and Welsh. He made secret overtures to all the defeated kings, especially Constantine, promising large aid from Dublin, the Isle of Man and the Western Isles in a joint operation to eject the English from the north of England and re-establish the Norse kingdom of York with himself as its ruler. This daring plan was the only way to concentrate sufficiently large forces against the mighty English army and it would be a battle the likes of which Britain had never seen before and which until the Wars of the Roses it would not see again. Constantine was persuaded, and in Wales the bards resorted to that ancient propaganda which we have noted in a previous chapter. The Welsh clergy encouraged the common people into supporting the rebellion, with hopeful prophesies of coming liberation from English oppression, and poets wrote celebratory lines on the victory before the battle had even been joined:

> There will be reconciliation between the Cymry and the men of Dublin,
> The Irish of Ireland and Anglesey and Scotland,
> The men of Cornwall and of Strathclyde will be made welcome among us, the Men of the North will have the place of honour,
> The stewards of Cirencester will weep bitter tears when for their taxes, we give them death.

Such were the inflated hopes of the author of *Armes Prydein*, a reworking of an ancient prophesy of Taliesin. The poet had entered a trance state known as Awenyddion, in which his inspired consciousness had become so elevated that he claimed clairvoyance. There was a political sub-text to this resurgence of Celtic panegyrics. Hywel Dda, the king of Deheubarth, had been forced to pass on the crippling taxation, levied on him by the English, to the poor farmers of Wales and the Welsh Church and there was despondency about this – to put it mildly. The propaganda was aimed at persuading Hywel to join the alliance, for if he did so then all the Welsh kings would surely follow his lead. Hywel was having none of this, however, and resisted the blandishments of both Olaf and his own beleaguered countrymen. The Welsh would stay true to their oaths and this involved passing on intelligence to Athelstan about the forthcoming invasion. By this means the English had time to prepare and the only question was, where would the blow fall?

The alliance was now down to three constituent elements: the Norse from Ireland and Man, Strathclyde and the Scots. There is a good deal of contentiousness about where the battle, known to history as Brunanburh, was actually fought. Some experts have favoured a site in South Yorkshire, either at Brinkley Wood or at Burghwallis just off the Great North Road. The latter was simply called 'Burgh' until the thirteenth century, when a family named Wallis acquired it, so it does not mean 'the fortress of the Welsh' as some people claim. The idea behind a battle in this region is that the Norse had sailed around Scotland to land in the Humber Estuary, where they would then have conjoined with the Scots and Strathclyde Welsh and is inspired by a much later chronicler, John of Worcester, who thought the Viking fleet landed in the Humber. In my opinion there is a much better candidate for the battlefield, namely Bromborough on the Wirral near Birkenhead. Its original name was Brunanburh, and the place name Dingesmere, which is mentioned in the Anglo-Saxon poem commemorating the battle, seems to mean 'the sea into which the Dee flows'. Professor Stephen Harding and Professor Judith Jesch from the department of Viking Studies at the University of Nottingham have written a convincing theory which strongly supports a site on the Wirral. It would have been an obvious place for the Norse landing for it had a long-standing Norse colony which would have greeted Olaf as a liberator. The Strathclyde Welsh and Scots army could have marched into England without hindrance to meet Olaf, and it is possible that Hywel and other Welsh kings had hedged their bets, promising support for Olaf at a place near their own borders. The allies fortified a hill called Wendun and drew up their immense army, perhaps 15,000 strong, to await the English assault. Athelstan had bided his time, gathering an even larger army from Wessex and Mercia, so large that he was forced to deploy it in two columns, one of them led by his dashing young brother Edmund 'the Magnificent'. There is no reason to doubt that sheer weight of numbers was the key to English success, and there may have been a truly national army of 20,000 battle-hardened and well-disciplined troops under the king's command. Sometime in the autumn the English commanders, grandsons of Alfred, arrived to meet their destiny.

What followed was known to the English simply as 'the Great Battle' and it was the climax of 500 years of almost continuous conflict. The men of Wessex took on the Scots and Strathclyde Welsh and the Mercians careered into the Vikings in an early morning attack. The result was a savage carnage. Irish chroniclers record a battle which was 'immense, lamentable and horrible, desperately fought'. All day long the struggle went on until the early twilight of that cruel autumn day gave the allies, or what remained of them, an opportunity to run to their ships, but Athelstan and Edmund were relentless in the pursuit, and the Vikings were hunted down and slain in thousands all through the night. Among the heaps of corpses around Wendun lay five kings, seven *jarls* and Constantine's son. Constantine somehow escaped, probably overland. Olaf came back home to Dublin with 'only a few' ships. The English had taken a severe beating too, with bishops and earls and many *thegns* numbered among the dead. It had been a hard fight but its outcome was a vindication of Athelstan and the idea of an English imperial power, so glorious that a panegyric poem in the *Chronicle* departs from the usual dry tone of the annals to celebrate it in terms which have more in common with the ancient poetry of *Beowulf* and the likes:

> In this year King Athelstan, lord of warriors,
> Ring-giver of men, with his brother, prince Edmund,
> Won undying glory with the edges of swords,
> In warfare around Brunanburh,
> With their hammered blades, the sons of Edward,
> Clove the shield-wall and hacked the linden bucklers,
> As was instinctive in them from their ancestry ...

The implication is clear that the West Saxon royal line of Alfred is a bloodline which is destined to prevail against all enemies of England, and now there is a country which can proudly call itself by that name, whether Mercians or West Saxons:

> All through the day the West Saxons in troops
> Pressed on in pursuit of the hostile peoples,
> Fiercely, with swords whetted on grindstone,
> They cut down the fugitives as they fled.
> Nor did the Mercians refuse hard fighting

To any of Olaf's warriors, who invaded
Our land across the tossing waters,
In the ship's bosom, to meet their doom
In the fight. Five young kings,
Stretched lifeless by the swords,
Lay on the field, likewise seven
Of Olaf's jarls, and a countless host
Of seamen and Scots. There the prince
Of Norsemen, compelled by necessity,
Was forced to flee to the prow of his ship
With a handful of men. In haste the ship
Was launched, and the king fled hence,
Over the waters grey, to save his life.

The fate of the 'hoary-headed traitor' Constantine was similar:

No cause
Had he to exult in that clash of swords,
Bereaved of his kinsmen, robbed of his friends
On the field of battle, by violence deprived
Of them in the struggle. On the place of slaughter
He left his young son, mangled by wounds
Received in the fight ...

Finally, and poignantly, the poem eulogises the sons of Edward, and the so called 'A version' of the *Chronicle*, which is the most partisan of all the versions in favour of Wessex, stresses the 'Manifest Destiny' of the English under the descendants of Cerdic:

Likewise the English king and the prince,
Brothers triumphant in war, together
Returned to their home, the land of Wessex.
To enjoy the carnage, they left behind
The horn-beaked raven with dusky plumage,
And the hungry hawk of battle, the dun-coated

> Eagle, who with white-tipped tail shared
> The feast with the wolf, grey beast of the forest.
> Never before in this island, as the books
> Of ancient historians tell us, was an army
> Put to greater slaughter by the sword
> Since the time when the Angles and Saxons landed,
> Invading Britain from across the wide seas
> From the east, when warriors eager for fame,
> Proud forgers of war, the Welsh overcame,
> And won for themselves a kingdom.

Had it not been for the Norman Conquest and its destruction of the English national culture, it is very probable that this epic poem would still be recounted to our schoolchildren as *the* high point in the English national story, but sadly it is of the Battle of Hastings and 1066 that they learn, not of the 'Great Battle' of Brunanburh in 937. Indeed, the obscurity of the battle in the English memory is a cypher for the later suppression of English culture. It was impossible to eradicate Alfred from folk-memory but Athelstan's exploits were of a particularly military nature, which had the potential to inspire Englishmen to dream of a glorious future as well as a glorious past. The poem explicitly states that the culmination of the entire Anglo-Saxon age has come at Brunanburh, vindicating 500 years of toil and conflict. So, the strange thing is that the high point of English history and the illustrious English emperor who achieved it have been almost excised from the popular imagination, the province now of academics and specialist enthusiasts, and almost forgotten. It is a salutary lesson on the uses of history.

The victory at Brunanburh established Athelstan as an exemplar among Christian monarchs in Europe. It is a little-known fact that he anticipated Henry Plantagenet by intervening in Continental affairs, and, utilising his new sea power, assisted Louis IV of France in his war against dissident nobles within his own court. Brittany was also given assurances of military aid, with the intention of denying harbours to Viking fleets in future. The English seem to have lost their skills in seamanship over the centuries but Athelstan revived them, with every intention of extending his power even as far as Scandinavia itself. The exiled son of King Harald of Norway, Hakon, was fostered by Athelstan, and provided with ships with which to invade his native land and regain his kingdom. Despite his curious obscurity in the eyes of modern Englishmen at the time, he was respected and beloved by his people, a superstar of his day. William of Malmesbury describes him as 'of medium height, slender in body, his hair flaxen, beautifully mingled with golden threads'. This personal appraisal, and William of Malmesbury's almost sycophantic exposition of the king's virtues, probably came about because Athelstan chose to be buried in that town, on the borders between Wessex, the home of his ancestors, and Mercia, where he had been raised by his sainted aunt. He died at Gloucester two years after the great victory at Brunanburh of some unspecified sickness. It was a John F. Kennedy moment. The Irish annals lamented the passing of 'the pillar of dignity of the western world'. Despite his good looks and evident virility, he never married and left no children. In all probability there was some pact between him and his younger brother Edmund that he should abstain from fathering children so that his brother should succeed him in a seamless transition, with no civil war. If so, this was a particularly personal sacrifice for the benefit of his people, which has been little remarked upon. The English had lost their hero, but for those folk who had been trampled underfoot by his might there was jubilation. York immediately rose in revolt and the Danelaw reasserted its independence, for Edmund was a mere teenager, and although he had fought in the Great Battle he was as yet untried. Incredibly, Olaf Guthfrithson, the Viking who had fled in terror over the sea after Brunanburh now returned and claimed the throne of York with the complicity of Archbishop Wulfstan. Olaf then marched into the five boroughs and even besieged Northampton, but the English garrison held out against him. He then turned north, to assault the old Mercian capital of Tamworth which finally fell after a tough fight. The *burh* was ransacked and Lady Wulfrun, an eminent local landowner and noblewoman after whom Wolverhampton is probably named, was taken as a hostage for ransom. Edmund seems to have dithered during this Viking resurgence, but finally he did act and pursued the Viking army into Leicester where Olaf and the treacherous Wulfstan took refuge. Despite being closely besieged, the latter two managed to escape and fled north, leaving their army behind them. Edmund had lost the initiative and resorted to diplomacy. Olaf was recognised as king of York and the Danelaw, while Edmund retained English Mercia. Olaf married the daughter of Orm, the chief man of the confederation of the five boroughs.

This unexpected Viking comeback must have come as a nasty surprise to the English. All Athelstan's achievements were put in jeopardy and Edmund seemed impotent to deal with the Viking threat. Fortunately Olaf overextended himself. He invaded the lands of Ealdorman Oswulf, the English ruler of Bernicia, the northernmost part of the former Northumbria. Olaf was killed during the campaign, allegedly as divine retribution for his desecration of churches and monasteries. A kinsman of Olaf with the same name was proclaimed king in York, but he was weak and vacillating, unable to act with his cousin's energy and decisiveness. Now the initiative lay with Edmund, and in 942 he launched a bold counter-offensive which recovered the five boroughs. The men of York reacted by trying to depose their weakling king, but he managed to survive a coup by yet another cousin, Ragnall. This political infighting enabled Edmund to reassert his authority over York, and eventually the warring cousins were forced to make peace with him. Edmund exploited his new power base in the north to invade and punish Strathclyde; the sons of Donald, the king of that region, had their eyes put out on Edmund's order. After reconciling himself to Archbishop Wulfstan, who had assisted in the deposition of the Viking cousins, he ceded Strathclyde to Malcolm, the Scots king. The emergency had passed, and English authority had been re-established by this youthful (he was no more than twenty-one) king. Now, England was to experience something that it had long forgotten, a condition strange, almost outlandish: peace.

10

THE ENGLISH SUPREMACY

More peaceful times were indeed coming, but in Northumbria there was one last spasm of violence. King Edmund died violently in 946 as the *Chronicle* relates: 'This year King Edmund died, on St Augustine's day. That was widely known how he ended his days; that Leof stabbed him at Pucklechurch'. There are varying accounts of this incident and no absolute agreement as to the venue. Some say that Leof was a returned exile whom Edmund had banished six years previously for pillaging, and that recognising him in his presence on the holy feast day of St Augustine, which the Anglo-Saxons held sacrosanct for obvious reasons, the king flew at him and pulled him down by the hair, at which Leof drew his knife and committed regicide. Others say that Leof was in a state of blood feud with the king's cup-bearer and the two began a fight in the king's presence. Edmund interposed himself to protect his servant and died defending him. It could just have been a drunken brawl. The English were notorious for their heavy drinking, especially on feast days. However it came about, Edmund's sons were too young to succeed him and so the crown passed to his brother Edred. The period of confusion following Edmund's death led to a rebellion in Northumbria. The Archbishop of York, Wulfstan, and the chief nobles of York had given oaths of loyalty to Edred, but within months they invited a Viking freebooter, Eric 'Bloodaxe', to rule there. He was of royal Norwegian blood but had been driven out of that country because of his tempestuous and vicious nature, yet this did not appear to have given Wulfstan pause for thought. The extraordinary thing was that a Christian English clergyman in the north preferred the rule of a man of this type to that of the southern English king, and this came about because of the deep political faultline which had existed between northern and southern England since the earliest times. For a long time Northumbria had been a virtual annexe of Scandinavia, while southern England was coming increasingly within the orbit of Continental Europe. Ultimately the country had to fall entirely within one sphere of influence or the other, and the remainder of this story will be largely taken up with the out-workings of this geo-political dilemma. Immediately, however, Edred was justifiably infuriated and lost no time in visiting revenge on the northerners.

Eric was baptised as soon as he took up residence in York, then the second city of England, with a bustling population numbering in the tens of thousands and thriving trades. In effect it was a sort of city state with its own ecclesiastical and political elite whose wealth and security depended upon the armed force a man like Eric could project. The attraction of York was that it was a centre of international trade and had a multiplicity of handicrafts for merchants and manufacturers from all over northern Europe. Even in the time of Offa of Mercia, Alcuin of York could write of it: 'This beautiful, healthy place, of noble setting was destined to attract many settlers by its richness. To York from diverse peoples and kingdoms all over the world they come in hope of gain, seeking wealth from the rich land, a home, a fortune, and hearth-stone for themselves.' By the mid-tenth century, York was a dynamic hub with a resident population of 25,000 people or more and thousands of visitors and traders. This may not sound much by modern standards, but in the context of a national population of just 2 million it was a grand metropolis.

Edred invaded with a large army in 948; 'This year King Edred overran all Northumberland; because they had taken Eric for their king; and in pursuit of plunder was that large minster at Ripon set on fire, which St Wilfred built'. Oda, Archbishop of Canterbury, confiscated the bones of St Wilfred, the intention being to deprive the Northumbrians of a focus for their particularism. The destruction of this vast church, one of the finest in all Europe, was a massive psychological blow to the northerners, and this desecration of so holy a shrine confirmed their view that the folk of the south were barbarians and iconoclasts. While the main English army ranged at will, wasting the land and destroying the rebels' means of sustenance, a smaller force had been detached to guard the crossing of the River Aire at Castleford, but it was intercepted by Eric and wiped out. Edred suffered from some sort of debilitating sickness which made him irritable at the best of times but the news so infuriated him that he declared he would utterly destroy Northumbria once and for all. Seeing that their investments and 'hearth-stones' were in dire jeopardy, the magnates and clergy of York immediately deposed Eric and made a humiliating submission to Edred, including compensation for those killed at Castleford. Edred was soothed by this and withdrew, but once again Wulfstan intrigued to bring in yet another Viking from Dublin, Olaf Sihtricson, as the new king of York. Edred must have been exasperated by this development, but perhaps because it was out of the campaigning season acceded to Olaf's rule in York if he would give undertakings to repel any further adventurism from Eric. However, in 952 Olaf was evicted and Eric was called in yet again, with the active connivance of Wulfstan. The eminent churchman relied on the sanctity of his cloth for protection but his scheming against the English king had condemned him in the latter's eyes and he was seized and imprisoned at a place called Iudanbyrig, while Edred plotted Eric's downfall.

Eric appears to have defeated a combined army of Bernicians

and Scots shortly after his return. As his grim nickname testifies, this Norse warrior would be no pushover, but in 954 he was ambushed at Stainmore in the Eden Valley and killed alongside his brother and his son. Edred lived only a year after him, to be succeeded by Edwy, the eldest of Edmund's sons. He was a mere youth, handsome and highly sexed. At his coronation banquet he was discovered by Dunstan, the esteemed Abbot of Glastonbury, cavorting with Aelfgifu his betrothed and her mother, with the crown casually discarded while the threesome romped. Dunstan was furious and dragged the youth from the unseemly scene, severely admonishing him, but in doing his duty he had succeeded in alienating Aelfgifu who demanded Dunstan should be exiled from court as soon as they were married. To comment further on the matter would be prurient, but suffice to say that a more peaceful era had dawned, where such decadence could be indulged.

Edwy's reign was short. His alienation of key courtiers included powerful nobles such as Athelstan 'Half-king' and his own grandmother, as well as Dunstan and his supporters, whose project to revive the monastic tradition was anathema to him. Soon a plot was hatched to depose Edwy and replace him with his younger brother Edgar as ruler of Mercia and Northumbria. Seeing which way the wind blew, Edwy put away his wife on the pretext that they were cousins. He remarried to a more respectable lady but suddenly died shortly afterwards. Despite being just sixteen, Edgar had keen political instincts and immediately elevated those nobles and churchmen who had been deprived of offices through his brother's caprice. Edgar's reign became a legendary golden age for the Anglo-Saxons, and he was eulogised as 'Edgar the Peaceful' in the *Chronicle* because of the comparative absence of conflict while he was on the throne. War had been a way of life for so long that these few decades of peace seemed almost heaven-sent, but what was peace like for the Anglo-Saxons?

The overriding concern of all people, whether Anglo-Saxons, Danes or Celts, was agriculture. More than nine out of ten people lived in tiny rural communities with strong bonds of kinship, scratching a living from the fields and rearing livestock such as geese and pigs, which lived in their homesteads alongside them. They held their land from more powerful folk and were required to labour for them and to render up food-rents. This was why the destruction of peasant villages by invading armies was prosecuted with such ruthlessness, because by depriving the nobility of their adversaries of labour and rent, they were striking at the heart of their economy. War was a curse on the poorest folk who lived in constant fear of invading armies or Viking raids in which their homes and means of sustenance would be destroyed, resulting in famines so severe that there are recorded instances of entire communities gathering atop sea-cliffs, holding hands and then hurling themselves onto the jagged rocks below rather than endure the slow, agonising death of starvation. Their lives were anyway brief. Few lived to be forty years or more and disease and pestilence and cattle murrain wiped out entire villages and devastated large towns. The year after Edgar died, 976, came 'the great famine in England'. Again, in 1005, 'this year was the great famine in England, so severe that no man ere remembered such.' There are numerous similar entries in the *Chronicle* which demonstrate just how precarious the existence of ordinary people was, even in a time of peace.

The work was continuous, back-breaking and took up every hour of daylight. A contemporary dialogue involving an imaginary character called 'Ploughman' tells us something about the daily routine:

> I go out at daybreak driving the oxen to the field, and yoke them to the plough; for fear of my lord, there is no winter so severe that I dare hide at home; but the oxen having been yoked and the share and coulter fastened to the plough, I must plough a full acre or more every day ... I have to fill the oxen's bins with hay, and water them, and carry them outside ... it is hard work, sir, because I am not free.

The slaves who laboured on Anglo-Saxon farms consisted of

poor people captured in the innumerable wars and also of people who had been accused of petty offences who were partially scalped to identify them as malefactors whose punishment was bond-slavery. Those who were 'simple minded' or mentally ill were often impressed in this way also. Women laboured at the incessant domestic chores, but also at the vital task of weaving in small sheds with sunken floors, known to modern archaeologists as Grubenhauser, where female infants would watch the process, learn and then assist until they became competent. The very word 'weave' derives from *wif* the Old English word for a woman. Clothing was all handmade but the rich pastures of lowland England were abundant in sheep and the fulling, production and export of woollen stuffs was a source of wealth in Anglo-Saxon England from the earliest times. There were other commodities for export too. One of the most important was salt, which was produced in salt-pans in places invariably called Wich, such as Droitwich and Nantwich. At Droitwich local rulers charged a levy of a shilling a cartload of salt and a penny for every pack-pony. Lead production was also lucrative because the huge expansion of church buildings created a ready market for church roofs lined with lead. These desirable commodities and products could be traded with foreign merchants for essentials such as quernstones from the Frankish Empire. Pottery was handmade, probably by women, and tanning and leatherworking were vital in an age when leather was the equivalent of modern plastics. Smiths and metal workers must have been ubiquitous, but finds of their actual workshops are still quite rare, though evidence of slag appears regularly. So we have an impression of a busy way of life where everyone had some productive purpose in tight-knit communities, where everyone's business was known to everyone else. Just as they worked together and fought together, they also worshipped together, and by Edgar's reign every community in England would have been Christian. The consolations of religion included 'holy days' or feast days when everyone joined in joyful and uproarious celebrations involving that traditional English pastime, heavy drinking.

However, Dunstan's reinstatement presaged a new mood in the English Church. Edgar had chosen him to be his new Archbishop of Canterbury and he was not slow to stamp his authority, emulating Benedictine monastic reforms which had been underway in Europe for many years. Thirty new monasteries were founded and six convents. Secular canons were replaced by monks and celibacy became standard. Aethelwold, one of Dunstan's protégés, was made bishop of the capital, Winchester, and he expelled married clergymen there, replacing them with monks from Abingdon. These reforms were not universally popular. The secular nobility resented the growing power and influence of the Church and the rural peasantry were conservative and nostalgic for the more easy-going Christianity of their forebears, especially resenting the marginalisation of women. Dunstan's innovations seemed to them like the imposition of foreign ways rather than the organic expression of their native faith. Aethelwold admonished Edith of Wilton for wearing unbefitting apparel even though she was of royal stock. This proto-puritanism grated with the common folk, whose grasp of theology was minimal but whose devotion to folk traditions, customs and superstitions was absolute. The interlude from the Viking menace brought about a spiritual revolution as churches and monasteries were rebuilt or established anew and learning was revived. Since the *Chronicle* accounts were written by monks, it is scarcely surprising that they heap lavish praise on Edgar, whose patronage allowed this transformation to proceed. The crowning glory of Edgar's reign came in 973 when he held a second coronation and anointment ceremony at Bath at which the faithful Dunstan officiated. His queen was crowned with him, but on this occasion Edgar was called 'King of the English', the first time the title had been used in a coronation. The ceremony formed the basis for the coronation of every subsequent monarch, including our current Queen Elizabeth II in June 1953.

There then followed an expression of might and power to equal that of Athelstan: 'Soon after this the king led all his marine force to Chester; and there came to meet him six kings; and they all covenanted with him, that they would be his allies by sea and land.' A story took hold that Edgar obliged the subject kings to row him in a barge upon the Dee Estuary as a sign of his absolute dominance. The imagery of 'marine force' and boats may be legendary but signifies another astonishing achievement of the English during Edgar's reign. They had finally taken control of the sea, and the coasts were patrolled by state-of-the-art warships numbered in many hundreds. It was this sea power which had (for the time being) contained the Viking threat, and this mighty fleet was capable of offensive as well as defensive action. At long last the Vikings were vulnerable to English retaliation if they dared to raid Edgar's realm, and the pirate kings of Dublin and Man knew this. Edgar was not a completely uncontroversial king, however. He married twice, and his second wife Elfrida (who was crowned with him at Bath) was the cause of considerable scandal. She was said to have been the fairest woman in all England and Edgar had sent one of his noblemen, Aethelwold, to assess her charms, with a view to marrying her. Aethelwold was said to have immediately fallen in love with her and married her himself. The story goes that Edgar killed Aethelwold while out hunting in order to take Elfrida to wife. Legend this may well be, but Elfrida produced two sons, one of which, Edmund, died in infancy. The surviving son, Ethelred, proved to be one of the most controversial and notorious kings of the whole Anglo-Saxon age, and his ill-repute may have caused later chroniclers to calumniate his mother. Although Edgar was probably the most powerful ruler in Western Europe, he was physically undistinguished and may have suffered poor health. He died in July 975 at Winchester to be succeeded by his son by his first marriage, Edward, a mere youth. Shortly afterwards, during the gathering of the harvest, a comet was observed, which apparition was always dreaded by the Anglo-Saxons as an ill-omen. On this occasion their superstition was well founded for with Edgar's demise, Anglo-Saxon England began a slow but sure disintegration from within, which made it vulnerable once more to enemies from overseas. Small wonder that this last period of

English greatness seemed to them to have been embodied in their dear departed king:

> Here ended
> His earthly dreams
> Edgar of Angles king;
> Chose him the other light,
> Serene and lovely,
> Spurning this frail abode,
> A life that mortals
> Here call lean
> He quitted with disdain ...

The poet has an intimation of forthcoming evil days, however:

> Then too was seen,
> High in the heavens, the star on his station,
> That far and wide
> Wise men call ... cometa by name.
> Widely was spread
> God's vengeance then
> Throughout the land,
> And famine scour'd the hills.
> May heaven's guardian,
> The glory of angels,
> Avert these ills,
> And give us bliss again;
> That bliss to all
> Abundance yields,
> From earth's choice fruits
> Throughout this happy isle.

It was not clear which of Edgar's sons would succeed him and two parties coalesced around the potential candidates. Edward was the eldest son by his first marriage, aged around fifteen. There were rumours that Edgar had seduced a nun at Wilton who had given birth to Edward out of wedlock, but these were almost certainly interpolated at a later date. William of Malmesbury thought his mother was a noblewoman by the name of Aetheflaed, but it may well be that Edward had been born out of wedlock. Ethelred, Edward's half-brother, cannot have been more than seven or eight years old when Edgar died. However, this made him an attractive candidate for powerful nobles who hoped to become regents until he came to maturity. The tensions that had built up because of Dunstan's project of reviving the monasteries now played out around the candidates with Dunstan and his ally Oswald, the principal churchmen, favouring Edward, and powerful nobles who had lost land and influence to the Church as a result of the policy, such as Aelfhere of Mercia, supporting Ethelred. Edward's party won the day and he was crowned in July 975, but the resentment of his opponents intensified as a great famine gripped the nation. Those secular nobles who had been the canons which Dunstan had expelled now returned and expelled the monks. Rioting and destruction of Church property took place, encouraged by nobles such as Aethelwine of East Anglia who took Hatfield from the monks of Ely. This turbulence came as a shock after such a long period of peace and the superstitious Anglo-Saxons took the appearance of the comet and the famine which followed the next year as omens of doom. It was commonly thought that at the end of the first millennium the agents of Satan would be unleashed upon the world, as had been foretold in the Revelation of St John. These dispossessions did not just affect the monks, but the laymen who worked on the monastic estates and their grievances against the resurgent nobility undermined national cohesion. A scribe wrote of Edward's reign:

> In his days
> On account of his youth
> The opponents of God
> Broke through God's laws;

> Aelfhere ealdorman,
> And others many;
> And marr'd monastic rules;
> Minsters they razed,
> And monks drove away,
> And put God's laws to flight ...

It did not help matters that despite his later sainthood, in life Edward was hot tempered and ungovernable. In 978 a council was held at Calne during which the building collapsed. Dunstan was miraculously saved by standing on a cross beam of the upper-storey but many others were killed and wounded. Then there came an even more shocking event:

> This year was King Edward slain, at even-tide, at Corfe-gate, on the fifteenth day before the calends of April. And he was buried at Wareham without royal honour. No worse deed than this was ever done by the English nation since they first sought the land of Britain. Men murdered him, but God hath magnified him. He was in life an earthly king he is now after death a heavenly saint.

This regicide was compounded by the fact that it was also (at least by proxy) fratricide. Edward had been hunting in the area and had decided to stay the night with his stepmother, Elfrida, and his young half-brother. Messengers must have been sent to expect his arrival and he suspected nothing as Elfrida awaited him at the gate entrance with ostlers to attend the horses. Elfrida proffered a goblet of mead and as Edward leaned forward to take this the ostlers suddenly grabbed his bridle and stabbed him repeatedly. The horse bolted but he bled to death and was hastily buried. The young Ethelred took no part in the actual murder, and may have been completely unaware of his mother's intentions. It was said that he became hysterical and could only be pacified when Elfrida thrashed him with candles so that bruises would not show on his now royal person. Ethelred would not allow candles in his presence ever again. The outpouring of emotion among the common people meant that Ethelred's accession was sullied and churchmen such as Dunstan were openly hostile. Whether true or not, it was believed that ealdorman Aelfhere had conspired with Elfrida to put Ethelred on the throne and had been prepared to stoop as low as foul murder to accomplish their aim. Stories began to circulate that Ethelred had sullied the font at baptism and that his mother was a witch and a harlot. To pacify the angry people Edward's body was disinterred and reburied at Shaftesbury Abbey. During the dissolution of the monasteries the grave was lost but was rediscovered in 1931. Edward's body was kept in a bank vault and was finally laid to rest as recently as 1984.

Even though his complicity in the act was not proven definitively, Ethelred's reputation was irretrievably damaged. This may have undermined his character from an early age and no subsequent monarch, even John or Henry VIII has attracted such an evil reputation. Dunstan and Oswald were alienated from the outset and promoted the cult of his predecessor. Shortly after his coronation there was yet another ill omen: 'This same year a cloud red as blood was seen frequently with the appearance of fire and it usually appeared around midnight: it took the form of rays of light of various colours, and at the first streak of dawn it vanished.' Probably this was a rare apparition of the Northern Lights, but to the superstitious Anglo-Saxons it was taken as a sign of divine vengeance on the king and his partisans. These included Aelfhere of Mercia who now governed on his behalf for four years, and his mother, Elfrida. In repentance for her sin, she endowed monasteries such as Wherwell where she remained in seclusion until her death. The unstable situation in England encouraged fresh Viking raids. In 981 Southampton was destroyed by a small Viking force and raids took place in Kent, Cornwall and Cheshire. The following year Dorset was the target, and finally London was attacked in 982 and a great fire engulfed the city. The years of peace and security were at an end and the old guard of nobles and churchmen who had done so much to safeguard the well-being of the kingdom died out. Aelfhere died in 983, Aethelwold the following year, and on Ascension Day 988 Dunstan died, having been warned by angels in a vision of his impending death three days previously. Two years before Ethelred had destroyed Rochester Cathedral in an act of violence, the reasons for which are not clear, but already he had a reputation for sudden violence followed by contrition. Now that he had come to adulthood his vacillation and slothfulness and self-indulgence knew no bounds. There was no one who could remonstrate with him or offer sound advice. The foundations of Edgar's peace were disintegrating and now the threat that had been removed since the time of Athelstan, the Vikings, returned. In 991 an English army was defeated by Olaf Tryggvason of Norway. The defeat was celebrated in an Anglo-Saxon poem 'The Battle of Maldon' which eulogised the English hero ealdorman Bryhtnoth who was killed in the fight along with most of his men. We can perhaps understand the reasons for the heroic poem about Brunanburh, but why write an epic about a lost battle?

The poem is the Anglo-Saxon equivalent of Tennyson's 'The Charge of the Light Brigade'. Bryhtnoth's doomed heroism stands as a valediction for a noble age of English military prowess, soon to be followed by years of cowardice, appeasement, extortion and treachery. Modern historians may doubt the veracity of the poem's account, because they have been inculcated with the notion of history as a branch of science – a German idea – but English history, which descends from Bede's *Historia* and the *Chronicle*, has a tradition of being a sub-division of literature, and Churchill's Nobel Prize was awarded for literature despite his subject matter being history. Bryhtnoth was a giant of a man, well over six feet tall. He was old, well into his sixties, when he drew his small army up to oppose the Vikings on the mudflats of Northey Island near Maldon in Essex. The Vikings could not get at the English except by means of a causeway which was covered over by the sea at high tide and were so close that they could shout across to them, demanding tribute. Bryhtnoth replied,

> We will give you spears for tribute
> You will not win treasure so easily;
> Point and blade
> Shall bring us together first,
> Grim battle-play
> Before we pay tribute.

The Vikings responded, asking that their men be allowed to cross over the causeway so that they could come to grips, for if they attempted to fight their way across they would be slaughtered in detail, which was probably Bryhtnoth's original plan, but now he allowed them to cross unhindered so that full battle could be joined. Ipswich had already been sacked and it was his duty to defend his lands. If the Vikings escaped they could lay waste the entire countryside. Rather than allow this he resolved to decide the matter one way or another even though he was probably outnumbered. As soon as battle commenced he became the Vikings' main target, easily identified by his stature, his fine armour and hoary beard. Soon he was sought out, overwhelmed and killed. This was usually the signal for retreat, but the English would not give in, intensifying their struggle:

> Thoughts shall be the harder,
> Hearts the keener, courage the greater,
> As our strength lessens.
> Here lies our leader all for hewn,
> The valiant man in the dust;
> May he lament forever who thinks now
> To turn from this battle-play.
> I am an old man; but will not hence,
> But I purpose to lie at my lord's side,
> By him so dearly loved.

It was the end of the English supremacy, of the peaceful times, of everything honourable and decent and just. Bryhtnoth joined the giants of olden times, the ranks of Anglo-Saxon heroes down the ages, the 'proud forgers of war', Beowulf, Hengist, Penda, Offa, Alfred and Athelstan. Corrupted, decadent, cowardly men took their place, under a king unworthy and cruel and treacherous, who would listen only to evil counsellors. His name, Ethelred, means 'noble counsel', but his people called him *unraed* as a pun, meaning 'no counsel'. On the advice of Sigeric, the new Archbishop of Canterbury, an unprecedented Danegeld of 10,000 pounds in silver was paid to the Vikings to leave England in peace. As the millennium approached, the Prophesy of St John, that the devil would be unleashed, was in all men's minds, and for many of them the king himself seemed a force for evil, Ethelred 'the Unready'.

II

THE SERMON OF THE WOLF

The payment of the *geld* or *gafol*, a tax levied on each hide of land in order to buy off the Vikings, was not a new innovation. Alfred himself had resorted to it when there was no alternative, and the Frankish kings had a long history of offering such tribute, but under Ethelred it became a policy of first not last resort and this was to have fatal consequences. The Vikings soon saw that a campaign of intimidation could bring them vast profits from organised expeditions in large fleets. Instead of the hazards and risks associated with hit-and-run raids, where their forces may be interdicted and their profits may prove somewhat unpredictable, it was now possible to rely on the mechanism of English government to collect their booty in the form of silver for them. As soon as this was known, confederacies of pirates formed such as the Jomsvikings, whose brigandage became organised and led by captains chosen from among their fraternities, and which relied on terrorist tactics to extort their ransoms and tributes. All this was known to the English and to Ethelred, and in 992 he gathered a fleet with the intention of mounting a surprise attack on the Vikings. Unfortunately, ealdorman Aelfric, one of Ethelred's own commanders, forewarned the Vikings and only one of their ships was destroyed, the rest making good their escape. The reason for this treachery is not stated, but we may presume that many English nobles who were charged with collecting the *geld* in their districts were involved in creaming off some of the silver for themselves, and so it was in their interests for the cycle of blackmail to continue, rather than risk their lives in combat with fearsome enemies.

This fiasco was observed all over Scandinavia and the Baltic, and in 994 Sweyn Forkbeard of Denmark combined with Olaf of Norway to attack London itself with a fleet of ninety-four ships. London, however, was one of the few towns in England which was capable of defying a Viking siege, thanks to Alfred's restoration of the Roman city walls and a large garrison, so the Vikings moved off to plunder elsewhere:

> Thence they advanced, and wrought the greatest evil that ever any army could do, in burning and plundering and manslaughter, not only on the sea-coast in Essex, but in Kent and Sussex and in Hampshire. Next they took horse, and rode as wide as they would, and committed unspeakable evil. Then resolved the king and his council to send to them, and offer them tribute and provision, on condition that they desisted from plunder.

The price on this second occasion was 16,000 pounds in silver, and this set the pattern for further lucrative Viking expeditions, as the *Chronicle* tells us. Three years later the Vikings returned, plundering Devon, Cornwall, the Severn Estuary and North Wales. The next year they were in Dorset before ensconcing themselves in the Isle of Wight, from which they could intercept merchant traders by sea as well as striking inland. Desultory attempts were made by the local militias to challenge them, but their failure to act in concert meant that they were easily defeated in detail, or their local commanders, for want of direction from the king, simply marched their forces away rather than face inevitable defeat. Ethelred's response was ineffectual, unmanly and derisory. In the year of the millennium, however, he was suddenly galvanised into action, but not against the main enemy. Instead he attacked Cumbria in a land invasion supported by a fleet. This has every appearance of an attempt to portray himself as a war leader in the mould of his illustrious ancestors. Perhaps amid the atmosphere of eschatological doom prevailing in that year it had become imperative for him to demonstrate some sort of leadership to prevent an uprising or a potential coup, but even this bizarre campaign went awry. Cumbria was cruelly ravaged but there was poor coordination between the land and naval forces, and the fleet was forced to content itself with a raid on Anglesey, hardly the epicentre of the threat to Ethelred's realm. The sense of despair which must have been felt by the common people permeates the *Chronicle* account, probably written after Ethelred's death but gathered from contemporary records.

Ethelred had been on the throne now for twenty-two years and was ultimately to reign for thirty-eight. It is incredible that England possessed the resilience to endure these privations and humiliations over such a long period, and in these days when every historical account is contested some scholars have doubted that Ethelred's reign could have been the total failure the *Chronicle* account portrays. How, they ask, could a king so utterly lacking in charisma and *fortuna*, good luck, have survived so long? That England became such a target for blackmail surely tells us that it must have been economically dynamic, wealthy, with a healthy balance of trade and a well-organised robust civil governance? There is some truth in this. The silver that was mined in Derbyshire and the Mendip Hills could not have been the only source for up to 10 million coins produced by England's seventy mints every three years. Much of it must have been imported from Germany in exchange for English-manufactured woollen stuffs exported overseas. As I write, a metal detector enthusiast has recently unearthed a hoard of over 5,000 silver coins dating from Ethelred's reign in Buckinghamshire. England was indeed wealthy and did have an advanced civil government, but under

Ethelred these achievements of his predecessors became a curse. The Vikings were content to operate their protection racket up to a point, but Ethelred's weakness began to make them wonder if the whole rotten edifice of the English state might collapse if they were to mount a serious invasion, taking the country for themselves. Ethelred must have been in a state of denial of the danger, leaving matters of state to his subordinates, allegedly taking to his bed for long periods. He was not just sleeping either. He had been a handsome young man by all accounts, and his first wife, Aelfgifu, bore him at least six children, before dying in labour with yet another. In this sphere at least, he was a most productive king. Such a man was bound to alienate men with a sound judgement of character and to retain those who saw their own advantage in telling him what he wanted to hear. Pallig, a Dane who was a relation by marriage to him, deserted him in disgust, but a young obscure *thegn* from the Shropshire borders, Edric 'Streona' ('the grasping one'), was rapidly elevated by ingratiating himself. Wulfstan II, Archbishop of York, wrote of the eight columns which supported lawful kingship when he was advising King Cnut a few years after Ethelred's death, and no doubt he knew very well that Ethelred had possessed none of them (truth, patience, liberality, good counsel, formidableness, helpfulness, moderation and righteousness).

Abbo of Fleury, the churchman who had founded the great library at Ramsey Abbey, tried to steady the nerves of the people during the millenarian expectation. He recalled preachers who had predicted that 'as soon as the number of a thousand years was completed, the Antichrist would come and the last judgement would soon follow'. Abbo did not subscribe to this view, but many others did, and although the world did not immediately end that year the Viking menace must have seemed like a demonic plague, destined in time to overwhelm the English state. Oswald, the half-Danish Archbishop of York, had died in 992 at Worcester while in the act of washing the feet of the poor, but he had been convinced that England's troubles were the result of divine punishment for national sin and apostasy. Wulfstan, his successor, looked to Gildas, the British monk who had seen the downfall of the British as a corollary of their sinfulness, and thought he saw this process at work in the disintegration of the English kingdom. Moreover, he perceived the degeneracy in sexual mores, the corruption, luxury and vice of the rich and the lack of potency among the nobility and royalty as excrescences feeding the growing power of Antichrist. The following year, 1001, all these fears seemed to be borne out:

> This year there was a great commotion in England in consequence of an invasion by the Danes, who spread terror and devastation wheresoever they went, plundering and burning and desolating the country with such rapidity, that they advanced in one march as far as the town of Alton; where the people came against them, and fought with them. There was slain Aethelweard, high steward of the king, and Leofric of Whitchurch, and Leofwin, high steward of the king, and Wulfhere, a bishop's thegn, and Godwin of Worthy ... and of all the men who engaged with them eighty-one. Of the Danes there was slain a much greater number, though they remained in possession of the field of battle.

Aethelweard was the historian who had once been a hermit at Bridgnorth, and the eminence of the casualties shows that the emergency had finally given impetus to a desperate resistance. The common folk could take no more and had taken their fate in their own hands rather than wait upon leadership from their dissolute, cowardly and discredited king, but nothing it seemed could rouse him into decisive action. The fighting continued all across the south of England, the heart of Ethelred's kingdom, but with the same dismal results. The Vikings ranged at will, leaving ancient towns burning in their wake, exerting a stranglehold on English trade by their possession of the Isle of Wight. Ethelred had only one answer: to raise yet another *geld*. This time the staggering sum of 24,000 pounds in silver was the price. By this time even Ethelred knew that this ordeal could not continue, and so he attempted to find a solution by resorting to diplomatic alliances. His first wife, Aelfgifu, had died leaving him with many young children including his heir, Athelstan. The Duke of Normandy, Richard, was approached with a proposal that his sister, Emma, should marry Ethelred. Normandy was the French equivalent of the Danelaw and had been settled by Scandinavians who had carved out a strong power in northern France. They were traditionally friendly to their Viking cousins and their harbours provided sanctuary for Viking ships, which had been damaged, and relief for their wounded, in exchange for English loot being traded through Norman ports. Ethelred's proposal was designed to eliminate this support for his enemies, which was in its way logical, but the sophistry of the plan was a poor substitute for waging actual warfare against them. As well as this, the alliance began a process which exposed England to interference from Normandy in its affairs, which was ultimately to lead to its downfall later in the century. Ethelred had another ingenious plan up his sleeve, however, which late in 1002 was to be enacted with calamitous consequences; the most infamous, despicable and dastardly deed in Anglo-Saxon, and possibly in all English history.

The long period of peace while Edgar reigned had encouraged people of Danish heritage in England to integrate on both an economic and cultural level. In the Danelaw this process had been underway for a long time, but now Danes were holding important offices of Church and State, such as Oswald, Archbishop of York, or Pallig, who had deserted the hapless Ethelred only to be reinstated. There were small Danish enclaves in the major towns all over southern England by 1000 and they were respectable Christian citizens making a valuable economic contribution as traders, merchants and manufacturers. As the English laboured under the demands made upon them for raising the *gelds* and their hardships increased exponentially, there was growing resentment against them which only required a lead from royal authority to turn it into active xenophobia. Ethelred's advisors, among them Edric Streona, used this febrile atmosphere to implant paranoid fears into

Ethelred's mind, to suggest that plots were being hatched against him and his court to murder him, and that the Danes were becoming a malignant cancer within his realm, 'cockles among the wheat' as he later put it himself. Therefore, a plot was hatched to eliminate them in a national pogrom. On St Brice's day, 13 November 1002, death squads would secretly gather in the southern English towns, and as the church bells rang out to summon the people for the feast day, this would be the signal for the English to fall upon those of Danish blood and slaughter them. Sir Frank Stenton thought that the plan could not have been operationalised in the Danelaw for obvious reasons and we only have actual written accounts of one attack, in Oxford, where the Danes shut themselves up in the church of St Frideswide and barricaded themselves in against the mob, but the English brought up faggots and set the wooden doors alight, then smashed their way in. Those Danes who fled into the streets to escape the holocaust were butchered with knives or clubbed to death. Later traditions say that sealed orders had been sent out to Tythings and the king's deputies in all the large towns to attack the Danes simultaneously while they were taking their traditional Saturday bath, though other experts say that 13 November fell on a Friday that year (appropriately). The Danes of Oxford could not have been the only victims. Pallig, the Danish nobleman mentioned above, was one of those murdered, but there was an even more eminent victim. Among the dead was the sister of Sweyn Forkbeard, the Danish king, and this callous killing turned him from being a mere raider bent on blackmail into an invader with a personal blood feud. From now on his fleets would no longer be just seasonal visitors – pirates who came for treasure – but an organised national army whose goal was to destroy Ethelred and take the English kingdom for good. This brutal act of ethnic cleansing had backfired in spectacular fashion.

Sweyn's revenge was swift and merciless. He had sworn on the 'bragging cup', a sacred oath to destroy England and kill Ethelred. Such a major national enterprise for the Danes required delicate negotiations with Duke Richard of Normandy who was persuaded to relinquish his previous agreement with Ethelred. His sister Emma might have been privy to these secret protocols. She had brought into England a retinue of haughty Norman knights who were despised in London, but one of them, Hugh, had been appointed as castellan of Exeter. Sweyn's fleet arrived near that town where the gates were opened to them and no resistance was offered. As a result the town was destroyed and the *Chronicle* specifically states that this came about through Emma's error in her appointment or, possibly more damning, her intrigue. From this strong base, Sweyn harried Devon and Dorset and then marched inland into Wiltshire. The men of Hampshire and Wiltshire hosted under ealdorman Aelfric and marched out to meet Sweyn's forces, but as soon as the armies drew up in sight of each other Aelfric feigned sickness and quit the field without a fight. As a consequence, Wiltshire was plundered before Sweyn returned to his ships. In 1004 they sailed to the coast of East Anglia to devastate that region. Norwich was sacked and burned and the local magnates decided that their only hope was to offer tribute to Sweyn so a truce was agreed. However, during the truce the Danes suddenly attacked Thetford within a month of destroying Norwich, but Ulfkytel, the ealdorman of East Anglia, had sent out scouts to observe their movements, and with the Danes far inland he now resolved to destroy the Danish fleet which was only lightly defended, while he, with a small English force obstructed Sweyn's army as it returned. It was one of the few occasions where an English commander showed any tactical or strategic insight, but unfortunately Ulfkytel lacked sufficient resources to carry it off. Sweyn's men sustained heavy losses in their attempt to dislodge Ulfkytel's blockading force outside Thetford, but eventually broke through. The English assault on the Danish fleet failed to materialise. If the main English army and the king had been there instead of a mere local militia the result could have been very different. As it was, the Danes received a nasty shock. They had come to see the English as weaklings and cowards but on this occasion, 'As they said to themselves, that they had never met with worse hand-play in England than Ulfkytel brought them'.

Sweyn now seemed unstoppable, but the constant ravaging and social dislocation had prevented the harvest being gathered in, and a terrible famine in 1005 affected the Danes as well as the hapless English peasantry. The Danes returned to their homeland but reappeared the following year. This time they included a fleet of privateers from the legendary Viking base at Jomsborg on the Baltic coast. They harried all the southern counties before retiring to their winter quarters on the Isle of Wight. Suddenly, at Christmas-tide they emerged and marched far inland to Wallingford, in a rapid forced march during which they lit beacons from the hilltops to indicate the route. Wallingford was easily overwhelmed, but Sweyn's force was now over fifty miles inland in mid-winter, and the situation resembled that at Thetford a few years before. The English prisoners gave out to Sweyn that a mighty English army was being mustered which would meet at a place called Cuckhamsley Knob on the Ridgeway, the burial place of Cwichelm the ancient king of Wessex. It was said that if the Danes met the English there they would never see their ships again. Sweyn was unconvinced and with supreme insolence immediately marched back to the coast in full view of the English capital, Winchester: 'There might the people of Winchester see the rank and iniquitous foe, as they passed by their gates to the sea, fetching their meat and plunder over an extent of fifty miles from the sea.'

The humiliation of the English was complete, and this Christmas expedition showed that the Vikings could strike anywhere at any time with complete impunity. While all this took place Ethelred skulked in far off Shropshire, well out of harm's way. Wessex, the most prosperous part of England, was a wasteland by now, and it at last dawned on Ethelred that something must be done.

Ethelred's policy seemed inflexible. In 1007 another huge *geld* was paid, this time of 30,000 pounds in silver. It may be that Ethelred's stay in Shropshire had something to do with the elevation of Edric Streona as ealdorman of Mercia. This shrewd and crafty individual had become a key advisor to Ethelred and despite his humble background he had now attained one of the great offices of state. Initially Ethelred's actions suggested that Edric's influence was a force for good. In 1006 Alphege, a churchman of impeccable character and sound political and moral judgement, was chosen as Archbishop of Canterbury. His advice to the king was uncompromising. There must be a national fast on herbs and water, and even nobles and the king himself must abandon their finery and jewellery and ask pardon for their sins in a national act of repentance. In 1008 Ethelred suddenly made preparations for war. A huge fleet was built and the smithies all over England busily worked to produce armour, helmets, swords and spearheads. What had happened to inspire this new martial spirit in the king? The answer was that the English kingdom was in meltdown. As royal authority had declined, poor people had been sold into slavery or been offered as sex-slaves to the Vikings and paganism and witchcraft had re-emerged in the moral vacuum left as the churches lost influence. Unless a supreme national effort, led by the king himself, was made, the contract between the king and his subjects must surely break down. The construction of the fleet and the provision of military equipment became imperative to national survival. The vast fleet gathered at Sandwich in readiness for the return of the Vikings in 1009. It was, however, to meet with the usual misfortune. Beorhtric, the brother of Edric Streona, was one of the fleet commanders and accused one of his fellow admirals, Wulfnoth of Sussex, of collusion with the Danes. In high dudgeon Wulfnoth took off with his own squadron of twenty ships and harried the south coast with them. Beorhtric begged the king to be allowed to pursue him with eighty of the best ships in the fleet, promising to bring him Wulfnoth's head, but his ships ran into a storm and were cast on shore where they were burned by Wulfnoth's men. It was a national disaster, and the remaining commanders abandoned their duties and went home. The remaining ships were brought to London where they sat uselessly in the Thames. The Danes were, of course, delighted with this news and immediately descended on Sandwich in unprecedented numbers. The catastrophe was so immense that it seemed nothing could go right for the English people, they had been abandoned by God and must be content to become slaves of a more vigorous and potent race. As this mood of doom gripped the nation, yet another disaster occurred.

The Jomsvikings under a leader called Thurkill 'the Tall' besieged Canterbury, with the object of taking Archbishop Alphege and ransoming him for 3,000 pounds in silver. Sweyn's army ranged all over southern and central England, wasting fifteen counties with horses taken from East Anglia, completely unopposed by any English forces whose local commanders refused to cooperate with one another. In 1011 Abbot Elfmar opened the gates of the city of Canterbury and allowed Archbishop Alphege and many other high-ranking churchmen and women to be taken hostage by the Vikings in exchange for his own life and property. This eminently practical Christianity was a sign of the complete moral collapse of the English, especially so as Elfmar owed his life to Alphege. The captives were taken to Greenwich to await their ransoms. Meanwhile, Ethelred was busy raising yet another *geld*, this time of 48,000 pounds in silver. Alphege refused to be ransomed and gave out instructions to English emissaries that any monies gathered for him should be distributed to the poor. He seemed genuinely content to stay among the Vikings and preach and make converts there, but when a shipload of French wine was seized en route to London his fate was sealed. In a state of barbaric drunkenness the Vikings marched Alphege to the hustings and demanded that he renounce his previous instructions and pay them their silver, which was refused. They tied him to a post and then pelted him with bones from the feast until he was almost dead, before a Dane who had been converted gave him the mercy stroke with an axe blow to the skull. The body was sent to London where he was buried at St Paul's. The sense of spiritual desolation and sorrow among the English now plumbed new depths, and even among the Vikings there was a sense of shame and guilt for this cruel and savage act. Ethelred had become hated among his own people, shutting himself up behind the impregnable walls of London, constantly in fear from the mob. It must have seemed only a matter of time before he fell. The only question was, who would destroy him, the Vikings or his own wretched people?

An extraordinary development now occurred. Thurkill 'the Tall', the commander who had taken Alphege prisoner, had not sanctioned his murder, and many among his own crew had converted to the Christian faith. The brutal killing was a signal that his authority was in question among his pagan compatriots, so he defected to Ethelred with forty ships' companies and volunteered to become his personal bodyguard and garrison London against Sweyn. Ethelred admitted them into the English army and promised them land in exchange for their service. This seemed like an ultimate act of treachery to the common people who were still in mourning for Archbishop Alphege whose murder had taken place as a direct consequence of Thurkill's abduction of the holy man. It was at this point that Archbishop Wulfstan composed a sermon known as '*Sermo Lupi ad Anglos*' 'the Sermon of the Wolf to the English'. Wulfstan had taken the pen name Lupus or 'the wolf', a pun on his own name, but this homily was no joke. It was a bitter excoriation of the English state and its condition, which he attributed to moral laxity, sexual immorality, the breakdown of law and order since Edgar's death, but above all the growing power of the Antichrist. It was disseminated to parish priests and monks throughout England to encourage repentance, but it also amounted to a political exhortation to the king and his ministers to change their disastrous policies:

> Dear Friends ... This world is in haste and is drawing ever closer to its end, and it always happens that the longer it lasts the worse it becomes. And so it must ever be, for the coming of Antichrist grows ever more evil because of the sins of the people, and then truly it will be grim and terrible in the world.

Although the Antichrist had failed to materialise at the millennium, many now thought that this would occur 1,000 years after the ascension, in 1033, and the millennial expectancy became associated in the popular imagination with the evident collapse of England and the lack of moral purpose and resolve of the king, Christ's representative in this world:

> The devil has deceived this people too much, and there has been little faith among men, though they speak fair words, and too many crimes have gone unchecked in the land ... Since King Edgar died the laws of the people have deteriorated altogether; holy places are everywhere open to attack, the houses of God are completely deprived of ancient rites, stripped of all that befits holiness; religious orders have now for a long time been greatly despised; many widows are forced to marry unrighteously; many are reduced to poverty; poor men are wretchedly deceived, most cruelly cheated and robbed of their innocence, sold out of this land to foreign slave-traders through foul injustice; children in the cradle are enslaved for petty thefts in this nation; the rights of freemen are suppressed and the rights of slaves curtailed, the duties of charity neglected; and to sum up, God's laws are hated and His commandments despised.

As for the Vikings, they are viewed as the instruments of Antichrist:

> We pay them continually, and they humiliate us daily. They ravage and they pillage and burn, plunder and steal and take all we own to their ships. And lo! What other thing can be clearer and evident to all in these events, if it be not God's anger?

This was a political bombshell which even Ethelred could not ignore. By now, though, he was unable to influence events, depending on Viking hard men to defend him even within the last bastion of London itself. Sweyn landed in the north with a huge fleet and 10,000 men and soon received the submission of the Danelaw, giving promises that the people of the north country would be spared if they owned him as their rightful king. Leaving his second son Cnut to guard the ships, he then set out to finally destroy southern England. His orders were explicit: south of the Watling Street every town was to be burned and all who refused to submit to him were to be destroyed. Even those who did homage to him were to give up all their possessions, including their children as hostages. Nothing could stand against this merciless horde, but the one final English redoubt, London, which refused to yield. The story at this point becomes understandably confused. An old tradition exists which says Sweyn attempted to force London Bridge from Southwark, but that this was prevented by Thurkill's Viking garrison who are supposed to have demolished London Bridge by attaching grappling irons to the ancient elm supports and rowing downstream. Some folk say that this is the origin of the famous children's rhyme 'London Bridge is Falling Down'. However it was achieved, somehow London held out, but by now Ethelred was doomed. The whole of southern England submitted to Sweyn and he was content to leave the London mob and the chief nobles to depose Ethelred rather than prosecute a useless siege during winter. Ethelred sent his wife and his young children by his second marriage away to Normandy by sea. At Christmas-tide he went to the Isle of Wight to spend what he must have thought would be his final Christmas in England, before sailing to Normandy himself in early 1014. The English king had been exiled from his own country and Sweyn prepared to march into London within a few months to be crowned as king.

The twists and turns in this incredible chapter of English history are so dramatic that an Elizabethan play *Edmund Ironside* was written about them anonymously (many think it was an early work by Shakespeare). For reasons of brevity I must condense the extraordinary events here. At Candlemas 1014 Sweyn suddenly died in strange circumstances at his encampment at Gainsborough. Many thought this was a divine punishment for his threat to raze the shrine of the blessed St Edmund, patron saint of the English. Cnut was immediately proclaimed king by the Viking army but he was a mere youth and the English nobles now sent letters to Ethelred advising that 'no sovereign was dearer to them than their natural lord, if he would govern them better than he did before'. This shows the deep-seated loyalty which bonded the English to their royalty, even in such desperate times. Ethelred made a bold decision. He sent over his young son by his second marriage, Edward, a handsome and godly youth, with messages of forgiveness to those nobles who had deserted him, saying he would be their 'faithful lord' and would ameliorate his behaviour, provided that all Danish kings were repudiated by them. This proved sufficient to reinstate him, and in Lent, just a few months after he had fled from London, he came home to a rapturous reception from the very people who a few months before had sought his blood. So invigorated was he at this display of loyalty, and so infuriated were the common people against the Danes, that he raised a large army and at long last took the offensive against the foe. Cnut was unprepared, and, leaving the wretched inhabitants of Lindsey to the tender mercies of Ethelred's army, he took ship and sailed away with his entire fleet. As a mark of his anger, he set ashore the hostages he had taken at Sandwich, with their hands and noses cut off. This left the Vikings at Greenwich to deal with, but they refused to budge until 21,000 pounds in silver was paid to them. This remarkable comeback marked the high point of Ethelred's reign but his popularity did not last long. In autumn a huge tidal wave, possibly caused by an undersea earthquake, engulfed the Severn Estuary, washing away thousands of people. Many thought this a divine punishment for having reinstated Ethelred. In 1015 Ethelred called a great council at Oxford which was designed to placate the chief men of the Danelaw following Ethelred's cruel devastation of Lindsey. The instigator of the council was the notorious Edric Streona who used the opportunity to abduct and murder the two chief men of the Danelaw, Sigferth and Morcar. These two were allies of Ethelred's son, Edmund, known as 'Ironside'. He had become the heir apparent following the death of his elder brother Athelstan, who had left him large estates and many valuable heirlooms, such as King Offa's famous Hunnic sword. However, Emma of Normandy had borne Ethelred two sons of her own, Edward and Alfred, and it was obvious that she would promote their succession with the backing of her brother, Duke Richard of Normandy. Edmund was a handsome, virile, brave and ambitious young man, the very antithesis of his father. Provoked by Streona's treachery he immediately gathered an army from the five boroughs and sent ultimatums to Ethelred. Streona was with the king at Corsham on Portsmouth harbour as Ethelred lay ill, and prepared to intercept Edmund's forces as the royal deputy, but seeing that the people were with the rebellion he took forty ships and went to Cnut, swearing loyalty to his cause. As his sickness worsened Ethelred retired once more to London to await the denouement. Cnut marched on the city and put it under close siege, digging dykes around it to cut it off from the outside world. As the Danes literally hammered at the city gates, Ethelred finally died on St George's day 1016. Cnut and Edmund both claimed the throne but it was obvious that the issue could only be resolved by armed conflict. The English nobles chose Edmund but it was difficult to see how he could prevail against the mighty Danish army around London save by prodigious efforts. Outside London, the English nobles who had sworn oaths to Sweyn were forced to acknowledge Cnut as his successor. It seemed that England was doomed to endure yet more strife, iniquity and bloodshed, but this humiliated, bankrupt and enfeebled people were about to rediscover their national spirit, for Edmund was no Ethelred. In him the courage and power of Alfred and Athelstan lived on, as the Danes were about to discover.

12

THE DANISH INTERLUDE

The treachery of Edric Streona, who had defected to Cnut, gave Edmund II, the new king of England, an enormous advantage in terms of attracting the loyalty of the common people. All their hopes rested upon him, the 'Ironside', a young man of proven military abilities with the courage to challenge their Danish tormentors. Unfortunately his power base, Wessex, lay in ruins and the nobles there had given oaths to Cnut. Edmund was forced to gather his army from the Danish-descended folk of the five boroughs who sought to avenge the murder of Sigferth and Morcar. Edmund had taken Sigferth's widow Eadgyth from the monastery at Malmesbury where she had been held captive and had married her, binding the people of the Danelaw to him. The small army the five boroughs could provide was, however, insufficient to challenge Cnut. Therefore Edmund decided to invade West Mercia and devastate the shires which belonged to the traitor Edric Streona. Cnut was not idle and his fleet of 160 ships, including Edric's contingent, disembarked and wasted Warwickshire in a winter campaign. Edmund's ally Utred, Earl of Northumbria, led his men home fearing that Cnut would devastate his lands and switched his allegiance to the Danish king. Despite this, Utred was murdered by Cnut and his earldom given to Eric of Hlathir, Cnut's Norwegian ally. In spring Edmund raised an army in Wessex, and the people flocked to his banner, desperate to get to grips with the hated Danes whether their lords had submitted to Edmund or not. Thus Edmund awaited Cnut's considerable and expert force with an army of peasants who were poorly equipped but whose morale was high. At Penselwood near Gillingham the two armies met and the result was a bloody draw. From an English point of view, however, it must have seemed like a moral victory, because after so many years of humiliation they had given the enemy battle and had not dishonoured themselves. In the summer another battle was fought at Sherston outside Malmesbury. It was hardly fought over two days and in desperation the traitor Edric hacked off the head of one of his own *thegns* who bore a very strong resemblance to Edmund, holding it up and crying out that the 'Ironside' was dead. The stunned English line recoiled thinking the king dead, but the situation was retrieved by the intervention of a local yeoman, John 'Rattlebone', so called because he wore armour constructed from animal bones. Rattlebone's men careered into the Danes and Edmund appeared prominently before his men. The infuriated English fell on the Danes and broke their line and Cnut, along with his English ally Edric and Thurkill 'the Tall' (who had now taken service with him), was forced to retreat, leaving the field of battle firmly in English hands. The victory sounded throughout the country like a trumpet blast. At long last Englishmen could hold their heads high, and the initiative lay with Edmund.

The Danish king, Cnut, was still young, and this terrific shock must have seriously damaged his confidence, but in Eric of Hlathir and Thurkill he possessed experienced commanders who could read the English situation precisely. This was what prevented a Danish rout, and they retreated to their stronghold around London which was still under siege. Even in the eleventh century, control of London was the key to England as a whole and Cnut fully expected an English assault from the south which would relieve the city. Edmund, however, knew that this was what Cnut would expect and so he made his plans accordingly. In a cunning move he manoeuvred his army across the Thames onto the north bank and swiftly marched towards London where it suddenly emerged near Clayhill Farm (the modern Devonshire Hill) at Tottenham, just north of the city. The Danish screen was thin and Edmund's forces soon brushed them aside and stormed into the city, where they were received with jubilation. The Danes fled in panic to their ships. Edmund rapidly pursued them to Brentford, but, for want of a ford, Cnut's forces escaped. Cnut's army was mounted and escaped Edmund's tired and pedestrian forces for that reason, but Edmund's obvious skill had galvanised the whole English nation into action. The English flocked to his banner and it was confidently expected that the Danes would be driven from England within the year.

In the period when Edmund was raising a new army, Cnut retired with his fleet into Essex and East Anglia, re-provisioned with stocks taken from raids into East Mercia and returned to the Medway to blockade London. Edmund then advanced into Kent, probably with the intention of preventing Danish reinforcement via Sandwich. Cnut attempted to make a stand, but at Otford his troops panicked at the sight of Edmund and rapidly retreated. The Danes fled to the Isle of Sheppey and at this point Edmund received a visit from the notorious Edric Streona, who, as Churchill would have described it, 're-ratted' at a meeting at Aylesford. Edmund must have hated him, but he was a relative by marriage (Edric had married Ethelred's daughter) and his forces held the balance of power. Edmund agreed to an alliance with him, 'than which no measure could be more ill-advised' as the *Chronicle* says, but at this stage Edmund had no choice other than to take such risks. The whole English nation now rallied to him, including Ulfkytel 'the valiant', hero of Thetford in 1004. With a vast English army Edmund confronted Cnut at Assandun, now Ashingdon in Essex, on 18 October 1016. This was the climactic battle of the second phase of the Anglo-Danish wars and decided the subsequent course of English history.

Cnut was outnumbered by the English who drew up in three huge columns, from Wessex, East Anglia and Mercia respectively. Edmund ordered the relics of St Wendreda to be brought from Ely to invoke divine blessing on the combined English force. The Danes were much more experienced and better equipped, however, and had the advantage of the high ground of Beacon Hill. The battle was desperate, but at the crucial moment Edric Streona, now fighting (supposedly) alongside his English countrymen, called out that the Danes were too strong, that all was lost, and riding hard to the rear with his own border troops on their little hobblers or ponies exposed the English flank. The fighting went on till nightfall but the Danes survived and in vast heaps the English dead lay in the moonlight, including Ulfkytel, Ednoth, Godwin of Lindsey, Wulsy, Aelfric, Aethelweard and a host of lesser noblemen. This was as great a disaster as Hastings was fifty years later, during autumn, the same time of the year, when it was virtually impossible for a defeated king to raise another army. Edmund retreated to the Forest of Dean with what stragglers he could extricate, hoping to survive there until the next spring, but this was on the borders of Edric's country and Cnut pressed the pursuit hard. It was later alleged that Cnut had bribed Edric to change sides at the last minute and this would seem entirely in character for this lowest of men. After some skirmishing, Edmund was alleged to have challenged Cnut to settle affairs by a personal combat, the Holm-ganga, whereby in Viking tradition the contenders would fight three rounds of sword-play on an island until one relented or was killed. Some traditions state that this duel was actually fought, on the Isle of Olney in the Severn, and that Cnut cried out for mercy from the 'Ironside'. What is a fact is that the two did meet nearby there, at Deerhurst in Gloucestershire, where they agreed to divide the kingdom as Alfred and Guthrum had once done.

In the ancient church at Deerhurst the two kings met and exchanged rich gifts and took the measure of one another. The broker of the treaty was Edric Streona who had served both men, and given Cnut's recent victory it was surprising that the terms were as good for Edmund as they turned out. Cnut was to retain Northumbria and Mercia and Edmund would keep Wessex. If either predeceased the other without living heirs their portion would pass to the survivor. London was to remain in Danish control but Edmund would be allowed to visit with a small bodyguard. The two parted as 'brothers' but this messy compromise was not destined to last long. On St Andrew's day at the end of November Edmund died. A later tradition attributes his demise to the villainous Edric Streona, but this story may come from a saga told later in order to vilify him. If the story is true then it was the saddest end which could be devised for this English hero. According to the legend two young lads were infiltrated into Edmund's household staff. When the king retired to the privy for 'a necessary purpose' a traitor waiting in the ordure pit beneath the lavatory was tipped off and stabbed the 'Ironside' in the posterior, either with a very sharp knife or, in more elaborate versions, an arrow fired using some malevolent contrivance from beneath. This story may be fictional, but somehow Edmund died and Cnut succeeded to the entire kingdom of England. Eadgyth and Edmund's two sons either fled the country or were transported by Cnut into Russia and the Ukraine, and from thence to Hungary. A tradition which rings true is that at Christmas 1016 Edric Streona was killed in his turn by Cnut for having disclosed his part in Edmund's assassination. Cnut had promised that one day he would set Streona 'higher than any man in England'. This promise was kept, or so the tale tells. Cnut flayed Edric alive, garrotted him, and decapitated him, throwing the body to the city dogs and then placing the head on a spike from the highest house on London Bridge. This satisfying folklore cannot disguise the fact that after centuries of bitter warfare England had at long last been overwhelmed by a foreign conqueror, Cnut, and the Danes had annexed England into a Scandinavian empire. Cnut's epic achievements cannot be contained within this brief chapter, but I propose to outline how they impacted upon the English state in particular. Suffice to say that the experience of subjugation by a foreign conqueror was by no means unknown to the English people in 1066, a fact which is still not sufficiently well understood.

Cnut is one of the few kings prior to the Norman Conquest who still lives in the popular imagination thanks to a tale which became widespread, which stressed his insight into the wiles of his fawning courtiers and his humility. Henry of Huntingdon in his *Historia Anglorum* recounts the familiar scene:

> When Cnut was at the height of his glory, he ordered his throne to be set on the sea-shore as the tide was rising, and said to the incoming sea: 'You are at my command, and the land where I sit is mine: there is none who dares resist my power. I therefore order you not to come up onto my land, nor to presume to wet the limbs or clothes of your lord'. The tide, however, rose in its usual manner, and without reverence soaked the king's feet and legs. He, jumping back, then declared, 'Thus may all the inhabitants of the earth see how vain and worthless is the power of kings. Indeed, I am not even worthy to bear the name of king before Him at whose behest heaven, earth, and sea obey the eternal laws.' Therefore King Cnut would never afterwards allow a golden crown to be put on his head: rather he would always place it on that of the image of Christ which hung on the cross.

What had caused this astonishing transformation? This was the same man after all who had mutilated hostages and committed devious murders, the son of one of the most notorious Viking kings. Certainly there was little for the Anglo-Saxons to celebrate during the first years of his reign. In 1018 a *geld* of 72,000 pounds in silver was levied and an additional 10,500 pounds was raised by the citizens of London to hasten the departure of Cnut's fleet. Some thousands of Danish elite warriors remained behind to guard Cnut, the so-called *hus-carls*. His chief commanders were given earldoms: Thurkill got East Anglia and Eric of Hlathir Northumbria. Sussex was detached from Wessex and given to an earl named Godwin who was to play such an important part in later events. In order to placate the Norman duke, Cnut put aside his first wife, Aelfgifu, and married Emma, Ethelred's widow, though her two sons by Ethelred remained in exile. The occupation was ultimately predicated on military might but Cnut's intelligent relations with the leading churchman, Archbishop Wulfstan, and his eagerness to promote the interests of the Church after such a long period of anarchy and strife laid the foundations for his subsequent reputation as a wise and godly ruler. These tales were promoted by the Church of course, but they must have some grounding in historical fact. Cnut even visited the tomb of his former adversary Edmund II at Glastonbury, where he laid a richly embroidered cloak depicting peacocks (symbolising resurrection) on the grave, which had been a gift to Cnut from Emperor Conrad. He raised a church on the hill at Ashingdon as a memorial to the thousands killed on both sides. Cnut did not overtly oppress the English people and was sensitive to their traditions and customs. At a great convention at Oxford he announced that henceforth

> I will be your grateful lord and a faithful observer of God's rights and just secular law. I have borne in mind the letters and messages which Archbishop Lifing has brought me from Rome from the Pope, that I should everywhere exalt God's praise and suppress wrong and establish full security by that power which it has pleased God to give me ... I thank almighty God for his help and his mercy, that I have so settled the great dangers which were approaching us.

Wulfstan's famous sermon had emphasised the decline in justice and order since the death of King Edgar and now Cnut proclaimed that he would reinstate his laws and ensure fair jurisdiction for all. Another bonus was that now that the Danes had subjugated England, ironically it was no longer under constant threat from raids or invasions from the Vikings. The price was high in monetary terms but this could be endured so long as there was peace and order. So in every sense Cnut's rule was preferable to the anarchy of Ethelred's long reign, and the surprising political acumen and expressions of seemingly genuine Christian faith (he even went on pilgrimage to Rome) while probably not endearing him to all English hearts, meant that his rule was not challenged, and Englishmen served in his military expeditions to Scandinavia.

Cnut's elder brother Harold had inherited the throne of Denmark but suddenly died without heirs in 1018. Cnut by now had a legitimate heir of his own by Emma of Normandy, Harthacnut. Cnut went to Denmark and secured the kingdom for his son, leaving the governance of England in the hands of Thurkill. An invasion of Sweden was repulsed, however, but Norway was incorporated into his northern empire. His growing power and reputation put him in the first rank of European monarchs. His daughter was married to the son of Emperor Conrad and this signified that the Vikings had at last been accepted as respectable Christian Europeans. Scotland was intimidated into accepting his overlordship. Cnut died in 1035 leaving two sons to dispute the succession. Harthacnut, Emma's son and Cnut's legitimate heir, was in Denmark, but Harold, his eldest son by Aelfgifu of Northampton, was in England and secured the backing of the chief nobles. Harold 'Harefoot' thus became the new king of England. The aggrieved Emma claimed that Aelfgifu, Harold's mother, had been a mere concubine and went so far as to dispute whether Harold was in fact Cnut's son. This campaign of denigration soon had tragic consequences. Alfred, Emma's younger son by Ethelred, took ship to Kent to visit her but was seized by agents of Godwin, Earl of Sussex, and handed over to Harold, who ordered that his eyes should be put out before throwing him into prison where he perished. This vile deed was to cast a long shadow over subsequent English politics.

Harold died in 1040 just as his half-brother was preparing to invade from Flanders where his mother was still in exile. Neither of Cnut's sons inherited his intelligence or humility and represented a reversion to the cruelty and barbarism of their Viking ancestors. In the two years he reigned over England, Harthacnut acted as a merciless oppressor. His first act was to have the body of his brother disinterred and thrown into a bog. His stewards extracted the huge *gelds* he demanded for the upkeep of his fleet by means of utmost brutality and this led to an uprising of the English in Worcestershire where two of his agents were lynched. In reprisal the city of Worcester was burned and the shire wasted. The citizens fled to an island in the Severn where fortunately they were overlooked by the king's men. Earl Eadwulf of Bernicia was murdered by Harthacnut in 1041 and the English must have feared for their future. Fortunately for them Harthacnut collapsed at a wedding through an excess of drink and fell into a seizure from which he died in 1042. The Danish interlude was at an end, for the only obvious claimant to the throne was Edward, Emma's surviving son by Ethelred. His long exile in Normandy and other French regions was almost at an end. The return of an Anglo-Saxon king of Alfred's line was an event of supreme national importance, almost a resurrection, and so some time passed before Edward 'the Confessor' returned for his grand coronation on Easter day 1043 at Winchester, his mother's old stronghold.

Few who attended the grand event, among them foreign dignitaries from all over Europe, could have guessed that the resurgent English state was doomed to extinction within a generation, and the remainder of this chapter comprises a brief account of the complex background to the eventual Norman Conquest. Edward's claim to the throne was uncontested and he was viewed as an Englishman returning to his rightful homeland, but in fact, on his mother's side, he was descended from Normans of Danish descent. His long exile had led him to adopt the manners and customs of Normandy and its adjacent French provinces, and he counted many Normans as personal friends and advisors, particularly churchmen such as Robert of Jumieges who was appointed as Bishop of London the year after the coronation. This Norman retinue was not entirely clerical, however. Norman warlords such as Richard Fitz-Scrob were settled on the Welsh March where they erected castles, a Norman innovation for holding down areas vulnerable to irregular warfare with a very small garrison. Edward had never forgiven the treachery of Earl Godwin who had kidnapped his brother Alfred and given him up to be murdered. Edward kept his Norman friends close and gave them so much power and influence in England as a means of self-preservation, a strong arm against assassination, a coup or localised uprisings. These tensions between the king and the powerful Godwin family were an extremely ominous cloud on the horizon. Immediately Edward had to deal with other pressing matters. As Peter Rex says in his *Edward the Confessor: King of England,*

> Shortly after the coronation, and as soon as he felt sufficiently established ... Edward dealt with the problem of Danish opposition to his rule by carefully calculated expulsions of those he regarded as centres of disaffection, and took care to reconcile leading magnates to his rule by continuing the policy of confirming various thegns in their sundry offices and lands and most especially took steps to ensure the continued support of the Church by renewing the privileges accorded to bishops and abbots.

So the Church was one cornerstone of Edward's rule, but he also required the financial wherewithal to govern the country, and the vast royal treasury was still held by his redoubtable mother, Emma. She had always favoured Harthacnut and her previous marriage to Ethelred had probably been loveless. In 1018 when her three children by him had fled for sanctuary to Normandy, she had left them to their fate. There was no love lost between Emma and Edward and the *Chronicle* states that

> it was advised the king, that he and Earl Leofric and Earl Godwin and Earl Siward with their retinue, should ride from Gloucester to Winchester unawares upon the lady; and then they deprived her of all the treasures that she had; which were immense; because she was formerly very hard upon the king her son, and did less for him than he wished before he was king, and also since: but they suffered her to remain there afterwards.

Now that he had enriched himself, Edward's obvious next step was to marry and to get an heir. The choice for his bride was surprisingly Edith, daughter of Godwin. Edward was probably persuaded by Church advisors who saw in the marriage a means by which Godwin's ambition could be contained and peace secured. She was a comely and accomplished young woman and through her mother was descended from the kings of Denmark. Godwin was a man on the make, as it were, and his English land-holdings were enormous, as were those of his sons, but the royal marriage of his daughter was his ultimate achievement, for in effect he had co-opted Edward into his own family, and any male issue meant that he would be the grand-sire of kings.

Unfortunately, Godwin's sons were a particularly unruly and turbulent clan. Sweyn, the eldest, had been given an earldom in 1043 which comprised much of Gloucestershire and Herefordshire. He intervened in the war between the kings of Gwynedd and Deheubarth in Wales on the side of the former, and on his return he abducted Eadgifu, Abbess of Leominster, with the intention of marrying her, but this was forbidden by the king. Sweyn was boastful and impetuous, claiming that his father was actually King Cnut, not Godwin. Eventually he was exiled, but then returned to beg the king's pardon in 1049. On his way to meet the king he murdered his own cousin, Beorn, for which crime he was banished yet again. He eventually died on a pilgrimage to the Holy Land. The second of Godwin's unfortunate sons was Harold, who was more level-headed and undoubtedly capitalised on his elder brother's misdemeanours. He held the earldom of East Anglia and was given Sweyn's lands while he was in exile abroad. Tostig, another of the numerous sons, was even more of a liability than Sweyn. He reportedly attacked his brother Harold after the invasion of Wales in 1063 while in the royal presence, tearing out his hair and kicking him while on the ground. When he was banished from court for this offence, he rode to one of Harold's residences where a banquet was being prepared for the king and killed the cooks and servants, hacking off their limbs and placing them on the mead and wine casks, leaving the message that Harold need not supply 'saused meat' for he had left it there in plenty for the king's visit. His later exile and his infamous return in 1066 were largely responsible for the English collapse that year. Two younger sons, Gyrth and Leofwine, were less troublesome, but the fact that they too were created earls shows that Edward was entirely enmeshed in this complicated family dynamic and probably not very cheerfully disposed to them.

In 1051 a minor incident ignited the latent hostilities which had been building up since Edward's return. The occasion for this was a diplomatic visit from Count Eustace of Boulogne to Edward. He was the king's brother-in-law. The previous autumn the Archbishop of Canterbury, Eadsige, had died and the monastic chapter and clergy elected Aethelric, one of their own, to be his successor. He was a kinsman of Godwin and in the context of Edward's complex relations with the earl, it is not difficult to see why the king objected to his appointment. Edward could not prevent Godwin's effective domination of England in secular affairs, but he regarded his own grip on the Church as being essential to his personal autonomy. Instead he appointed Robert Champart of Jumieges as the new archbishop. Robert used his influence with the king, which was considerable, to advance the positions of his own place-men and to diminish the power and influence of the Godwin family. No heir had been forthcoming from Edward's union with Edith, because the king wished to remain celibate (according to later texts whose aim was to sanctify him), or perhaps because his sexual tastes were towards men, or he was impotent, or he was asexual. These developments only required an incident to bring about a huge political crisis. It came about in this way: Eustace and his party of French knights were travelling from Canterbury to Dover where they intended to take ship for the return to France. They donned their armour and rode into the town demanding billets in a most arrogant display and an innkeeper refused to grant them lodging. The innkeeper was killed, which was a crime of murder under English law and in a spontaneous riot the townsmen of Dover set upon Eustace's men and slew nineteen of them. In retaliation a similar number of the Dover men were killed. Eustace rode hard to the king and accused the townsfolk of an unprovoked attack. This was all Edward needed to hear. He summoned Godwin and ordered him to devastate Dover and the surrounding area, which was his duty as earl, but Godwin refused to comply. Godwin and his sons could call on large numbers of troops personally loyal to them and he portrayed himself (probably correctly) as a patriotic Englishman defending the rights of the common man against foreign outrages. The 'French' garrisons on the Welsh March were denounced by Sweyn, Godwin's son, and a justifiable reaction against foreigners threatened to undermine Edward's royal authority. Edward played for time and as passions cooled he played his ace card, calling out the *fyrd*, the part-time militia whose oath of loyalty was to him personally. From this position of strength, Edward demanded that Godwin appear before him to face charges on pain of banishment. His bluff having been called, Godwin and his wife and eldest son were forced to seek refuge in Bruges. The Godwin tribe had seemingly received their comeuppance and the once over-mighty family were in disgrace, including Edith. Edward banished her from his bedchamber, if indeed she had ever ventured into that place, but there were many in England who sympathised with the exiled earl.

Godwin's powerful and ambitious ally, Count Baldwin of Flanders, married off his daughter to Tostig in hopes that the family would succeed in an invasion which he backed with money and ships. The family earldoms had been broken up and distributed among other nobles. Godwin set sail in summer 1052 and conjoined with a fleet brought over from Ireland under Harold's command. They proceeded to London up the Thames and the chief nobles immediately urged Edward to capitulate, which he grudgingly did. He thus became entirely captive to Godwin and his sons and his Norman and French appointees were forced to leave the country, including Archbishop Robert of Canterbury who was replaced by Stigand, Godwin's preferred candidate. This soured relations with the Pope to whom Robert appealed. Norman and French (the English called both Normans and French 'French' because of their speech) knights were forced to seek refuge in Scotland, for

Godwin's forces now controlled all the south-coast ports. Godwin was exonerated by the king of all charges against him and it must have seemed inevitable that Edward would become a mere puppet monarch of a man he despised. He was forced to take his wife back into the royal household which, we must presume, he found extremely distasteful. Edward was relieved, therefore, when Godwin died in spring 1053. In the vacuum left by his unexpected demise, it is alleged by later Norman chroniclers that Duke William of Normandy visited Edward in England and that the bewildered Edward promised him the throne after his death. One entry in the *Chronicle* (which may be a later interpolation) concurs that this meeting took place, but there is no real evidence for it, and strictly speaking, Edward had no right to make any such promise without consulting his chief men in council. The rising star in England was now Harold Godwinson, who, as we have seen, was the most intelligent of the Godwin brothers. He was also an extremely skilled soldier and this commended him for a task, which, while it was onerous, offered the chance for him to show his mettle, perhaps impressing the king sufficiently to be marked out as his heir.

Harold seized the opportunity with both hands. He had succeeded his father as Earl of Wessex, and his relations with the king were amiable. However, another candidate had emerged for the throne whose credentials were impeccable, namely Edward the son of Edmund who had been sent into exile. Ealdred, Bishop of Worcester, was sent on a mission to find and repatriate him. He had finally returned in 1057 only to die soon afterwards. This development concentrated the minds of both William and Harold on the succession. Harold invaded Wales, where Gruffydd ap Llewelyn of Gwynedd was attempting to unite the whole country under his rule. His large raiding into Herefordshire had demonstrated his resurgent military power and his confidence. Harold took charge of the campaign and in 1063 attacked Gwynedd during winter (an exceptionally daring feat) and so devastated the area that the Welsh murdered Gruffydd and sent his head to Harold. Harold appointed Bleddyn ap Cynfyn as king of Gwynedd and Rhiwallon, Bleddyn's brother, as king of Powys, taking upon himself the complex responsibility of a diplomatic settlement as well as his military command. This demonstration of his suitability for the throne caused Tostig, who had invaded Wales simultaneously, to lose face and it was this that had caused him to assault Harold and slaughter his servants. Tostig retired to his own earldom of Northumbria in disgust, where in 1065, after further outrages and abuses, he was driven out by the people and exiled. Harold was said to have set up stones across Wales bearing the inscription '*hic fuit victor haraldus*', which translates as 'Here Harold was victorious'. Clearly Harold was determined to exploit his victory to the maximum at this crucial time. The long struggle against the Welsh seemed to have finally been settled, and Earl Siward of Northumbria had invaded Scotland in similar fashion to eliminate the notorious King Macbeth in 1054. On the face of it, England seemed more powerful than at any time since Cnut, but Edward's failure to provide an heir left it hopelessly exposed to political and military strife after his death.

In 1065 the depredations of Tostig of Northumbria and his murder of a Bernician nobleman, Cospatrick, led to a major rebellion there. Morcar, the brother of Earl Edwin of Mercia, was chosen by the rebels as their new earl and Harold was forced to accept Tostig's banishment. This was a blow to Edward's authority. If we are to believe Norman accounts, Harold had been shipwrecked at some point during 1064 off the coast of France and was swiftly conveyed to William where he was tricked into swearing a sacred oath that he would promote William's succession. He was said to have been knighted by William for his feat of rescuing two Norman soldiers who had been trapped in quicksand near Mont Saint-Michel, apparently while serving in William's army against Breton rebels. If Harold was ever shipwrecked, and if he swore an oath obtained by trickery, both of which claims are frankly ill attested, then he would have immediately repudiated it upon his return to England for obvious reasons. To William, however, it was a binding oath, and to break it was an offence against his legitimate lordship. My own view is that this story was a later interpolation by Norman propagandists to legitimate their invasion and consolidate their conquest. Peter Rex in his *Edward the Confessor: King of England* says,

> But, if Edward had intended that William should be his heir, he did nothing to make it happen. Instead he either chose to seek out his nephew, Edward the Exile, or allowed the Witan to do so. If Edward the Exile had lived he would have been the natural choice. He was a member of the royal kin, the stirps regia and would have been acceptable to the Witan. William of Malmesbury, aware of this, suggested that King Edward gave the succession to the Duke after the death of the Exile, but that is contradicted by the Norman writers themselves. Had Edward intended Duke William to be his heir, then he ought to have been invited to England and put in possession of estates or even crowned or designated as the heir, but it never happened.

Soon this difficult controversy would be settled by force of arms. In January 1066, Edward took to his deathbed where he had a vision of two Benedictine monks he had known as a young man. They revealed that England would be assailed by the devil and that in a year and a day from his death his Anglo-Saxon kingdom would be conquered because of its sinfulness. Edward asked if there were any hope of repentance and resurgence for his fellow countrymen, to be told that this could only come about when a green tree, stricken in twain, should reunite and bear green leaves once more. Terrible storms did indeed rage that autumn and winter, and many trees were felled by them. Edward was regarded as a saint who could cure scrofula by his touch and perform many other miracles. On 5 January he finally expired, and 'even before the funeral meats were cold' Harold was acclaimed king by the Witan and it was recorded that Edward had finally indicated that he should succeed to the kingdom. If Harold was a usurper then he had the full backing of the chief men in England who saw in him their only hope of preventing a reversion to foreign rule. Thus began the brief and dramatic reign of the last of the Anglo-Saxon kings.

13

THE NORMAN CONQUEST

Harold had been elected as king and crowned by Archbishop Ealdred of York in preference to Edgar the Aetheling, the son of Edward the Exile and grandson of Edmund Ironside. Edgar was at least a descendant of Cerdic, the semi-legendary first king of Wessex, but he was only fourteen years old and could not seriously contend with the dangerous enemies gathering against England. Harold had the advantage of years of political and military experience behind him, especially his daring and conclusive campaign in Wales. He moved swiftly to reassure Earl Edwin of Mercia and Earl Morcar of Northumbria by marrying their sister Edith and putting away his lover, Edith 'Swan-Neck' who was a reputed beauty. Cnut's legacy of dividing the kingdom into powerful earldoms meant that the truly national requirements of self-defence at this time entailed personal sacrifices of this nature. Without the cooperation of Edwin and Morcar, Harold could not hope to mobilise a concerted military response. Yet for all his skills and distinctions, Harold was not strictly speaking 'throne-worthy' as Edgar was. We recall the portents and omens which had accompanied Ethelred's dubious succession and now a similar sign of divine displeasure appeared in the skies:

Then was all over England such a token seen as no man ever saw before. Some men said that it was the comet-star, which others denominate the long-hair'd star. It appeared first on the eve called Litania Major, that is on the eighth before the calends of May; and so shone all the week. Soon after this came Earl Tostig from beyond the sea into the Isle of Wight, with as large a fleet as he could get; and he was there supplied with money and provisions. Thence he proceeded, and committed outrages everywhere by the sea-coast where he could land, until he came to Sandwich. When it was told to King Harold, who was in London, that his brother Tostig was come to Sandwich, he gathered so large a force, naval and military, as no king before collected in this land; for it was credibly reported that (Duke) William of Normandy, King Edward's cousin, would come hither and gain this land ...

Harold, then, was faced with at least two powerful threats, and the anxious foreboding among the superstitious English people had to be met with a resolute response. Therefore, in spring, the *fyrd* was called out in an unprecedented muster and deployed to watch the south coast. Emissaries were sent to Denmark to recruit the most accomplished Danish *hus-carls*, men whose expertise was the ability to wield the Danish Great Axe. This powerful weapon was an axe with a foot-long cutting edge on a five-foot helve, which in the right hands could cut a man in half or decapitate a horse. There were such men in the English army, but the exemplars were still the Danes. The professional core of Harold's army were men like these but the mass of the army were the part-time militia who were equipped in more or less the same way as in Alfred's day. There may have been as many as 20,000 of these troops peering out to sea by the early summer of 1066 and a consensus has been propagated to the effect that they were doomed primitives facing a vastly technically superior enemy. Too much can be made of this, because on their day and with proper leadership they were the match of any army in Europe. Harold was a superb military commander who displayed rare daring and dash, and in the coming struggle the English acquitted themselves with tenacity, courage and patriotic devotion.

Tostig's fleet was driven off the East Anglian coast and so he sailed north to Scotland. The reckless and infuriated ex-earl now met with a stroke of good fortune. Harald Hardrada, King of Norway, had a claim to the English throne of sorts. It was claimed that Harthacnut had promised England to Magnus Olafsson, Hardrada's predecessor, and in theory this made Hardrada's claim a stronger one than Harold Godwinson's. Hardrada was a giant of a man, well over six feet tall, with a lifetime of piratical exploits and adventures behind him, including a spell as a member of the Varangian guard, the personal bodyguards of the Byzantine Emperor, recruited exclusively from elite Viking warriors. Seeing his opportunity to repeat Sweyn Forkbeard's exploits, he assembled a vast fleet of 300 ships at Trondheim, financed by wealth in gold and silver he had acquired from all over Europe. The Viking fleet made their way to the Orkneys where Tostig joined them with his own fleet. Tostig was still seething after his expulsion from Northumbria and his intense hatred for his brother, who had supported Earl Morcar against him, caused him to support Hardrada's claim to the English throne. So now, in addition to the threat from Normandy, the English were faced by an old-fashioned Viking invasion under a ruthless and daring leader who could deploy an army of perhaps 12,000 battle-hardened warriors. Meanwhile, the English fleet was deployed hundreds of miles away at the Isle of Wight and Harold was preoccupied with the Norman threat. All now depended upon the vagaries of the tides.

William's fleet was pinned down by contrary winds throughout July and August. He had taken great pains to persuade his chief nobles to support the invasion project and his patience must have been sorely tested as he waited for the winds to relent and the tide to turn. In order to protect the fleet from summer storms, as well as a possible pre-emptive strike by Harold (even Ethelred had raided Normandy with an English fleet in his day), the bulk of the fleet was concentrated at Dives-sur-Mer near Caen. As supplies grew scarcer and morale fell, it proved necessary to put to sea and the fleet hugged the Normandy coast as far as St Valery-sur-Somme, taking on reinforcements and food supplies for the men and 2,000 destriers, the warhorses that were William's shock weapon. These horses were trained to kick and bite opponents in battle, and controlling them for any length of time aboard ships in rough weather presented grave risks. William knew that his time was running out, for once the season of equinoctial storms commenced in a few weeks his entire fleet could be destroyed, even before it engaged the enemy. Fortunately for him, the long delay also presented problems for Harold. His ships had been patrolling the south coast in rough weather and needed an urgent refit. The *fyrd* was running low on food and was demoralised, and in a matter of weeks it would be harvest time when they were traditionally discharged to gather in their crops. Harold had no choice but to let them go on 8 September, but immediately the winds changed. The Vikings saw their opportunity and bore down on the north-east coast, appearing at the mouth of the Tyne. On 15 September they entered the estuary of the River Humber and disembarked at Riccall below the Ouse. With Harold still preoccupied in the south it was left to the earls, Edwin of Mercia and his brother Morcar of Northumbria, to oppose the vast and fearsome Viking force. Hardrada ordered an advance on York on 20 September in probable expectation that it would capitulate, but the days when the people of the north country greeted the Vikings as liberators were long gone. Edwin and Morcar, despite being heavily outnumbered, marched out to meet the Norwegians at Gate Fulford, a few miles beyond York. They blocked the approach road with their forces near an area of bogland, which they hoped would secure their flank. It was a brave but doomed enterprise. The ferocious Viking attack stormed their centre and drove their left wing into the marsh where they were trampled into the mire by Vikings who used their slain bodies as a bridge. York had no choice but to surrender and promised hostages and tribute as well as supplies for the Viking army. Hardrada, content with this for the time being, spared the city, returning to his warriors for a victory feast at Riccall. He must have been supremely confident, but he was about to receive a very nasty surprise. Harold Godwinson was about to pull off one of the most extraordinary military exploits in English history, which, had it not been for his defeat some weeks later, must surely have made him one of the greatest English heroes of any age.

Hardrada and a large contingent of his force, including Tostig, rode out to Stamford Bridge, a small village on the River Derwent, east of York, on 25 September in order to receive the hostages and supplies he had been promised. After the earlier, miserable summer weather it was a sultry day, so they had left their armour behind at the ships. The Vikings were sprawled beside the river sunbathing when some of them noticed a dust cloud rising in the distance. Initially they thought it must be the York dignitaries with their hostages, but on closer examination they saw the sunlight shimmering on thousands of mail-coats, spear-heads and helmets 'like sun on ice' as the later saga relates. Immediately Hardrada knew that he was in serious danger and dispatched messengers to the encampment at Riccall. The English army was coming on fast and Hardrada decided to stand and fight, rapidly forming up his men even though they had no body armour; 'without our hauberks do we go in array, to receive blows from whetted blades'.

Incredibly Harold Godwinson had marched 10,000 men all the way from southern England into the heart of Yorkshire in five days. The English roads, even the best ones, were mere dirt tracks, and the rapidity of the advance staggers the imagination, especially when we consider that each man had to carry weighty armour, a bulky shield and cumbersome spears, swords and axes as well as their provisions. The author doubts if any elite troops in any army in the world today could equal such a march, let alone fight a desperate battle at the end of it. How had Harold done it? This is not precisely known, but it seems that either he had taken the precaution of posting riders at relay stations along the main routes to the south, or, as Michael Wood postulates, that a system of beacons were lit which carried the news as in 1588 when the

Spanish Armada threatened. The leading elements, including the king, rode on ahead by day and night, and outriders summoned the men of Cambridgeshire, Nottinghamshire and other local *thegns* to join them en route until they arrived at Tadcaster on the evening before the battle to take a few hours' desperately needed rest. This tactic, a rapid and relentless march followed by a furious assault, had been perfected by Athelstan in his day and signified that there had been a renaissance of English martial vigour, and a new spirit of professionalism had emerged, probably inspired by the Anglo-Danish troops who formed the core of Harold's force. However, getting to the battlefield was one thing, to destroy the most famous warrior in Scandinavia would be quite another.

The *Saga of Harald Hardrada* says that before battle was joined negotiations took place but this must surely be a rhetorical device of the *skalds* for dramatic effect. Harold is said to have shouted across the river to Tostig, promising to restore his earldom if he would desert his new-found ally. In an unlikely response, Tostig asks what recompense Hardrada could expect, to which Harold replies jokingly, 'I will give him only six feet of English earth, or seven, for he is taller than other men!'

In reality, the English would have pressed on with utmost celerity to the little bridge over the Derwent across which they hoped to pour until they could form up opposite the Norwegian king. Hardrada had selected one of his biggest, toughest and strongest warriors to stand on the bridge alone with a great axe so as to buy time. The strategy worked, and for a long time he stood alone heroically defending the bridge, slaughtering all comers. Eventually a barrel or tub was found and an English spearman paddled downstream until he emerged beneath the giant, and then thrust upwards, skewering him in the nether regions. The English erupted onto the eastern bank of the river where before long they inflicted terrible casualties on the unprotected Vikings. The English tactics were sophisticated. As Trevor Rowley states in his *The Normans*, 'There is one source at least to suggest that Harold had used mounted troops and archers at Stamford Bridge both for advance and pursuit. According to the Heimskringla (the lives of the Norse kings) the English rode upon them from all sides and threw spears and shot at them.' Hardrada and Tostig were defended by their household troops in a tight knot below their banners. The giant Norwegian king was too distinctive to miss and was soon felled by an arrow in the throat. Tostig rallied the Vikings to him, resisting fanatically, but the English blood was up and before long vast heaps of Vikings lay in gory blood-rags and smashed shields. Harold offered the Vikings terms but they refused to give in. Soon Tostig was killed and all seemed over, but just then the Vikings from Riccall arrived to rescue their comrades. They had run over ten miles in the late summer heat in full armour and now they smashed into the English in true *berserker* style, many of them tearing off their padded under-tunics and armour so as to manoeuvre more freely. 'Orri's storm', as the saga refers to it, was how the Vikings remembered this ferocious assault, the last of its kind in the Viking age, presumably named after the Norwegian commander who led it. The English line recoiled briefly but the exhausted Vikings could not sustain the attack. They were finally overwhelmed by a coordinated attack of infantry, light cavalry and archers until virtually all were slaughtered. So few returned to Riccall that Olaf, Hardrada's son, who had been left to guard the ships, required only twenty-four ships of the original 300 to carry the remaining men to the Orkneys, where they limped in to tell their sorry tale a few weeks later. Hardrada's legendary treasures, including vast gold bullion were seized by Harold and left at York for safe keeping, but his body was carried back to his homeland. His countrymen were not so fortunate and their corpses were piled up to rot where they lay. A cairn of their bones was said to have still been visible there nearly a century later. Harold had covered himself in glory but he had paid a heavy price in English blood. While his exhausted troops rested and enjoyed the victory feast at York, a few days later a grimy, breathless messenger arrived there to tell him the catastrophic news. William had landed at Pevensey Bay and the Normans had a beachhead on the south coast.

William's fleet, led by his flagship *Mora*, a gift from his wife, Matilda, landed on 27/28 September. Initially the Normans disembarked and installed themselves in the ancient ruins of the Roman fort at Pevensey, but within two days a more secure harbour was sought and the fleet rowed round the coast to Hastings, which was easily defensible and had a road link to London. The Normans were nervous. When William stumbled and fell as he stepped ashore it was taken as an ill-omen until William took up handfuls of sand, joking that he had already grasped England with both hands. Fortunately for him there was plenty to keep the troops occupied, unloading the warhorses, fodder and supplies and erecting a stockade (it has even been suggested that a pre-fabricated wooden castle had been brought over from Normandy). William lost no time in scouting inland, where his first act was to terrorise the local population and burn their villages. This was not simply gratuitous terrorism. William knew that Harold must be provoked by this into hasty deployment in order to defend his stricken subjects. By the beginning of October, Harold had gathered his elite troops and had ridden hard for London. The casualties at Stamford Bridge had been heavy and so the levies of the Midland shires had been discharged. Messengers were sent ahead to London to summon a new army, but time was short. By 6 October the king was in London where he rested his weary *hus-carls* for four days while the *fyrd* of the southern shires and the local *thegns* came in. With the victory against the Vikings behind him, Harold may well have been over-confident. His victory at Stamford Bridge had been won by speed and surprise and perhaps at this crucial time he decided to gamble on using the same strategy against William. In this campaign, however, there were other factors in play. His elite troops were disaffected according to the *Chronicle* and other sources, not only from the hard fighting and rapid marching but because Harold had not distributed the booty from Stamford Bridge after the battle. Many of the Danish mercenaries may have deserted the king at this point and so the central core of the army that had triumphed at

Stamford Bridge was depleted and its morale poor. The situation among the shire levies was not much better. They had been on call all summer and had only just gathered the harvest in. However, the emergency was real and the Sussex *fyrd*, whose lands were being devastated, would have been anxious to get to grips with William. A rendezvous was arranged at the 'hoar-apple tree' atop Caldbec Hill on the London to Hastings road. Harold left London on 12 October and his forward elements arrived on the following evening. English probes ran into Norman pickets during the night and William was immediately alerted. Therefore Harold had no choice but to settle his troops down for the night where they foraged for timber and lit fires. To raise their spirits they began to sing hymns which the Normans took to be traditional English drunken carousing. Alerted, William ordered his army forward during the early morning while it was still dark. The Norman cavalry had slung their *hauberks* over their horses' backs, and in the twilight William put his on back to front which was taken as yet another ill-omen. Once again, William made a joke of this before mounting his Spanish destrier just as the sun rose. By now the whole Norman-led force was on the move, perhaps 10,000 men in all, and they drew up along Blackhorse Hill from which Harold's dispositions could be studied. Once the English position had been scoped, William arranged his forces into three sections: the French and Flemings were on the right wing, William and his Normans (and the bulk of the elite mounted knights) in the centre and the Bretons were placed on the left flank. Archers formed a screen along his front. William had denied Harold the opportunity to attack him and so the initiative lay with him, but the prospect before him was daunting, for Harold had been making his own preparations.

His attempt at a surprise attack foiled, Harold had no choice but to fight a defensive battle. His gamble of rapid deployment meant that his forces were still on the march and had not had time to form up into proper battle order. Like the Duke of Wellington at Waterloo, Harold had studied the position well beforehand, probably while supervising the coastal defences in the summer months, and it was a good one. The 1,000-yard-long ridge sloped steeply towards the Norman line, meaning that he had the advantage of higher ground. On either side it was protected by areas of quagmire. What would have aided Harold, and may have turned events to his advantage, was a steady downpour of rain which would have turned to mud under so many hooves, but no rain was forthcoming. Neither had he had time to impale stakes along his front line to obstruct the charges. Therefore Harold made the best of what resources he had to hand, and the English were arrayed in the traditional 'shield-wall' along the whole length of the ridge, each man interlocked with the next. The men of Essex and Kent formed the front ranks with ten more ranked behind them. If each man took up a yard of front then we can surmise that perhaps 12,000 men stood in readiness atop the ridge. Harold set up his banners – the dragon standard of Wessex and a 'fighting man' embroidered in golden thread – at the centre of the position. Around him the elite royal household troops were gathered, a formidable force of battle-hardened men who were sworn to protect the king's life and to guard his body even after death. Unfortunately, not all the English troops were of this quality. The *thegns* wore mail coats and helmets and were armed with spears, swords and axes, but the *fyrd* were yeomen who were unprotected. Their weapons were improvised – clubs, hatchets, sickles and bills – and their only head protection was straw-hats. There had been no time to properly brief their local commanders, the *thegns*, and there was no real central command. They operated on blind instinct or the last-minute muttered instructions which were passed down the line. Nevertheless they soon entered into the spirit of the event, beating their shields and shouting their war cry of 'Out! Out! Out!' By nine in the morning, William was ready and sent in his first attack, which was preceded by the Norman equivalent of a suicide attack. A Norman knight, Taillefer, advanced to the English line alone juggling his mace. The English line parted to let him through and he was rapidly dispatched. The first blood had been shed. By nightfall the entire ridge would be bathed in blood after one of the hardest-fought conflicts in English history, giving it the name by which it was to be remembered: Senlac, the 'blood lake'.

The Norman archers advanced and unleashed a desultory volley which the English took on their shields without any serious casualties. Behind the archers the Norman infantry closed on the English front to be met by the 'battle-shower', a deadly rain of rocks, clubs, javelins and hatchets which inflicted serious casualties. As soon as the Norman infantry came to grips with the English, they took grievous losses from the Anglo-Danish axe-men, and it seemed that they must have been repulsed. The Bretons on William's left flank were particularly hard hit and soon turned and ran into their own oncoming cavalry. The ill-disciplined English troops immediately pursued them down the slope, slaughtering them as they ran the scent of easy victory in their nostrils. It was a fatal error. William had observed the rout of the Bretons and charged into the English who retreated to a low hillock to defend themselves. Here they were rapidly overwhelmed until virtually all of them were killed. Harold's right flank had been almost completely destroyed thanks to this impetuous action, and he had no choice but to reinforce it by thinning out the line across the rest of his front. Order, of a sort, having been restored, both sides took a Saturday morning rest for an hour to refresh themselves. Of the two commanders, Harold's position was the most serious. His younger brothers, Gyrth and Leofwine, had been killed and he had lost well over 1,000 men in the foolish sally down the slope. However, William had to force a decision now or lose the day and his next attack was to be a much more effective one.

This time all three elements of the Norman attack were combined: foot soldiers, cavalry and archers. William was in the thick of the fighting and his mount was killed. The French and Flemings on his right flank took a severe mauling and recoiled from the axe-men in panic. A rumour spread that the duke was dead (he had been extricated with some difficulty from beneath his horse). Remounting, William removed his helmet so he could be plainly seen and rode along the centre of the line shouting 'Look here, I am alive, and with God's help we shall have the victory!' This had the desired effect and by now the Norman archers were finding their range, inflicting heavy casualties on the English rear ranks, many of whom had no shields. As the French and Flemish retreated once again, the indiscipline of the English amateurs showed itself. As soon as they ran after the French, the cavalry turned to cut them down. Trevor Rowley, in his *The Normans*, has suggested that these feigned retreats were a long-established Norman tactic and that they were used deliberately. Whether true or not, they had the effect of gradually wearing down the English line and opening up crucial gaps that the Normans exploited by riding in relays, stabbing down with their lances, and the archers supplemented these forays with close-quarter volleys. One of these archers found his mark, hitting Harold in the face with an arrow. The king fell, but his faithful household troops closed in a circle around him. In this furious climax of the battle, four Norman knights, seeing Harold's predicament (he may have been almost dead), rode into the troops around him and hacked their way through to the stricken king who was impaled in the chest, decapitated, disembowelled and, finally, cruelly emasculated. The terrible news spread along the whole English line and the rear ranks made their way to the woods in the dusk of late afternoon. The remaining *hus-carls* would not retreat. It was their bounden duty to fight to the last and the sacrifice of these brave men probably saved many English lives. There was one final twist. The Norman cavalry pursued the retreating English in the gloom of early evening and decided to charge a group of them. They fell into a ravine, later called 'Malfosse', or 'the evil ditch', and lay there helplessly. Seeing this, some of the retreating English returned to slit their throats. As William surveyed the scene of his triumph in the moonlight there was one final, heart-breaking episode. Edith 'Swan-Neck', the lover Harold had been forced to repudiate, arrived at William's tent, begging to be allowed to take his body for burial, promising him its weight in gold. She was allowed to search for it and eventually found what was left of him, which could only be recognised by 'certain intimate marks' known to her. It was taken for burial at Waltham Abbey where he was buried beneath a stone which read, '*Hic iacet Haroldus infelix*', in English 'Here lies the ill-fated Harold'. Below this a versifier added these poignant lines:

> In this tomb brave Harold rests
> Who once famed King of England was
> On whom renown, men, character and authority
> Conferr'd power and a kingdom
> A sceptre and a crown as well.
> Until he strove, a famous warrior
> To defend his own people,
> But died; slain by the men of France.

The thousands of lesser English dead suffered the same fate Harold had decreed for the Vikings after Stamford Bridge. William considered them traitors who had supported an excommunicated usurper. They were left to rot where they lay, among them many of the chief nobles of the land. Soon afterwards tales were told that Harold had not really died, but had survived and been taken to Winchester, where his grievous wounds were tended by a 'Saracen woman' skilled in secret medical arts. He then fled into exile, seeking allies, desperate to recover his kingdom, but failed to convince. He returned and wandered in disguise along the Welsh borders, the scenes of his glory days, until he finally received a divine summons to St John's church in Chester where he lived as a hermit until his death. These compensation myths of a defeated folk are told all over the world. Harold really was dead, and with him died the last hope of the Anglo-Saxon race, but our story is not quite over yet.

It is a common misconception that William's victory near Hastings was decisive and that it marked the end of Anglo-Saxon resistance. Certainly this is how the Normans wished to portray it.

William's mouthpiece, William of Poitiers, claimed he had 'Won the kingdom by a single battle', but this was part of the triumphalism designed to impress the subjects of the Norman duchy whose immense labour and sacrifices had made the expedition possible. It is true that Hastings was a catastrophic defeat, but there was no immediate capitulation by the English. Edgar the Aetheling provided an obvious focus for continued defiance of the invaders, and in the immediate aftermath of the battle the Normans needed time to recuperate from their own losses, which were very heavy, and await reinforcements. Piqued by this, William harried into Kent and assaulted Canterbury. At the onset of winter, disease spread through the Norman and allied soldiers, and William decided to force the issue by attacking London. Just as Sweyn Forkbeard had done, he captured Southwark and tried to force London Bridge, but his attack was repulsed by the London garrison under the titular leadership of Edgar the Aetheling. In reprisal, William set Southwark ablaze and marched in a circuit around the city burning villages and terrorising the population. As we have seen, England was no stranger to such horrors and London had a long tradition of resilience against besieging armies, but on this occasion the will to resist suddenly collapsed. Why was this? After all William's army was certainly inferior in numbers to Sweyn's or Cnut's. In part the reason for this has its origins in the Danish ascendancy some years before. The legacy of this former conquest was that England had been divided into several large portions or earldoms, which were in effect autonomous and looked to their own rulers. The concept of a unified English state, which had been Offa's dream and Alfred and Athelstan's achievement, had been dissipated, and petty sectional interests outweighed any sense of patriotism. The Battle of Hastings left many of the chief nobles of the land dead, and William had declared their estates forfeit. Most of them had had their estates in the south and the vacuum left by their demise led to a crisis of confidence. The memories of Ethelred's reign, when a boy king had proven ineffective against dangerous foreign enemies, made people wary of installing Edgar as king, and it was recalled by eminent churchmen that Cnut, a foreign interloper, had ruled efficiently and honoured justice. For all these reasons, England decided to come to terms with William. Edith, Harold's widow, surrendered Winchester along with the royal treasury and Archbishop Stigand of Canterbury personally endorsed William's claim. Ealdred, Archbishop of York, along with Edwin and Morcar, the chief earls, and Edgar the young Aetheling went to Berkhamstead where William was encamped and surrendered to him in late autumn. On Christmas Day, William was crowned in Westminster Abbey by Archbishop Ealdred who made him swear to 'so well govern this nation as any king before him best did, if they would be faithful to him'.

William visibly trembled during the ceremony. In the streets outside, large crowds had gathered to watch the proceedings watched by Norman armed guards. Inside the abbey, in a departure from normal procedure, the English nobles had been required to show their loyalty to the new king by loudly shouting 'Aye!' three times as he was hallowed. The nervous Norman soldiers outside heard this and thought there had been treachery against William so they immediately attacked the onlookers who they presumed were actually a mob purposely gathered to assist this. Buildings were set alight by the Norman troops and the whole ceremony was marred by this misunderstanding which revealed early on the tensions that were bound to emerge now that William was king.

This uneasy compromise was far from satisfactory. In the aftermath of the debacle at the coronation, William confirmed the ancient privileges of the City of London and restrained further abuses by the Norman army. He was explicit that there would be no victimisation of English nobles who had not served under Harold, but an early incident revealed how vindictive the new regime could be. William's wife, Matilda, had been infatuated with an English nobleman, Brihtric, in her youth, who had rejected her. As soon as William was crowned king she arranged for one of her agents (she was still in Normandy) to ride with all speed to Hanley Castle in Worcestershire, where the unfortunate man lived, and had him taken prisoner. After two years in a dungeon at Winchester the poor man was put to death, despite being entirely innocent of any crime. The earls and nobles of the Midlands and the north were required to do homage to William and this they were happy to do, but they soon learned the nature of their conqueror. Edwin and Morcar were effectively held as prisoners and together with Stigand they were taken to Normandy in 1067 where they were paraded through the streets as if they were subjugated captives, which in reality was the case. While he was away in his homeland, viceroys were appointed to rule England on his behalf: Odo, William's half-brother, controlled the south; and William Fitz-Osbern controlled the north. At the end of the year, William returned and was confronted by a centre of disaffection in the south-west, at Exeter. The constitution of the city did not permit a garrison within the circuit of walls and the citizens refused to comply with William's instructions that such a fortification should be constructed. Harold's mother and illegitimate sons were still in residence there and stirred up rebellion. William formed an army of Normans and loyal English troops and besieged the city, which capitulated after eighteen days, giving up hostages. This incident demonstrates one of the crucial tensions that had built up as a result of the Norman ascendancy, which was the construction all over the country of castles. Fitz-Osbern and Odo receive a small but revealing mention in a passage in the *Chronicle* (which continued to be compiled after the conquest): 'Bishop Odo and Earl William lived here afterwards, and wrought castles widely through this country, and harassed the miserable people; and ever since has evil increased very much.'

This 'evil' was entirely William's fault. He distrusted his powerful nobles and was in fact a paranoid personality due to a childhood spent in constant fear for his life as the bastard heir to the Norman duchy. Accordingly he parcelled out the estates seized from the Anglo-Saxon nobles killed at Hastings in widely dispersed packets, rather than grant large contiguous territories from which potential rivals may in time emerge. What this meant in practice was that when the Norman landlords arrived in their new holdings, they quickly constructed motte-and-bailey castles on high ground from which they could observe potential malcontents. Therefore, all over England these fortified garrisons were constructed, using forced labour impressed from the local populace. If there were any pre-existing structures where the Normans wanted to build a castle, they were ruthlessly demolished, even within ancient towns and cities whose charters exempted them from such military installations, as at Exeter. The resentment and fury this caused may be imagined. William's army was tiny and he could not be everywhere at once. All that was needed was some focus for a rebellion for the English to rise up and overthrow their foreign tormentors, whose arrogant behaviour and brutal persecution was resented everywhere. In the areas furthest from William's power base the people looked to their earls, Edwin and Morcar, to provide this leadership, and many considered that Edgar the Aetheling was in fact their rightful king. In 1068 it looked as if Edwin and Morcar would make such a move but William forestalled the rebellion by marching on York and constructing a castle there. Edgar fled for protection to King Malcolm of Scotland. The people of the north country had a long history of quasi-autonomous government and cultural particularism as we have seen many times in the preceding chapters. As hatred of the Normans grew they began to look back to olden times and became nostalgic for the days when they had been part of the Scandinavian scheme. The solution to their problems seemed obvious: all they needed to do to ameliorate their situation was to call in the Danes, whose customs and speech were akin to their own, and use their armies to throw off William's rule. All over England rebellions were simmering – in Devon, Shropshire, the Fenlands, Yorkshire and the north-east – and in 1069 the Anglo-Saxons and Anglo-Danes erupted into a furious insurrection.

14

THE LAST ANGLO-SAXON HEROES

There had been a Norman/French presence in England well before the Conquest. King Edward had implanted garrisons comprised of such troops in his reign on the Welsh Marches, where they were resented by both local English nobles and the Welsh. Even as far back as Ethelred's reign a Norman castellan had been given charge of Exeter, and now that William was king these isolated outposts were emboldened to ever more provocative shows of force. The *Chronicle* tells the story of the heightened tensions: 'And Edric Cild (Edric the Wild) and the Welsh became hostile; and fought against the garrison of the castle at Hereford, and inflicted many injuries upon them. And the king imposed a heavy tax on the wretched people, and nevertheless caused all that he overran to be ravaged.' This Edric 'the Wild' was a relation of that other Edric 'Streona', the notorious villain and traitor of Ethelred's reign, who had risen from obscurity to serve as chief minister to three successive kings and been awarded the title of Earl of Mercia. This later Edric was either a nephew or great-nephew of his infamous namesake, and by an extraordinary twist of fate he was destined to redeem the family honour and pass into the historical record, not only as a courageous resistance fighter, but as a legendary figure of the British mythical canon. His name 'the Wild' is very revealing. The actual term was Guilda, Latinised as Sylvaticus, which means literally 'the Forester'. After Hastings those who had served Harold, whether they had fought in the battle or not, were dispossessed of their lands and many had sought refuge overseas, in Ireland, Hungary and even as far as the Byzantine court where they enlisted in the Varangian guard to the emperor. Those who remained had become guerrilla fighters known as Sylvatici or 'salvages', in effect forest outlaws who carried out hit-and-run raids on the Norman/French garrisons. They were the ancestors of that mythical figure 'Robin Hood' (more of which later). Because William's garrisons were few and far between, a new law known as Murdrum was enacted, whose object was to discourage petty resistance of this type or selective assassinations. If a Norman were killed then the local Hundred courts were expected to give up the offender or suffer punishment of the entire region in which the murder had taken place. In stark contrast, William Fitz-Osbern permitted his men to commit rape, murder and pillage with no higher penalty than a one shilling fine on his troops. Under such a one-sided system of justice, Englishmen flocked to the woods to join their renegade leaders where they were expected to forego civilised amenities, such as a roof over their head, to become desperadoes. The country where Edric had held his manors, south-west Shropshire, was indeed wild and remains so to this day. The Clun Forest and Stretton Hills, the Stiperstones, Long Mynd and the Onny Valley were a warren of bogs, highlands and dense forests which were impenetrable to all but the most native folk. Any offensive action by mounted Norman knights here was doomed to failure for it was a perfect country for concealment and ambush. Bleddyn of Gwynedd and Rhiwallon of Powys, Edric's neighbours, had been faithful liege men of Harold and could be expected to offer refuge in emergencies to the English guerrilla fighters and in special circumstances to assist them by invading over the border. In short, this Shropshire outback country was a hornets' nest of discontent waiting to explode into rebellion at any time. Florence of Worcester, a later chronicler who must have had access to records of the insurrection says that

> there lived at this time a very powerful thegn, Edric, called 'the Forester' the son of Aelfric brother of Edric Streona. Because he scorned to submit to the king, his lands were frequently ravaged by the garrison of Hereford and by Richard Fitz-Scrob: but whenever they raided into his territories, they lost many knights and men-at-arms. Therefore, having summoned to his aid the princes of the Welsh, namely Bleddyn and Rhiwallon, this same Edric, about the feast of the assumption of St Mary, devastated Herefordshire as far as the River Lugg and carried off much plunder.

This was a few months before William's return from Normandy and was the first sign of the trouble that was to follow. For the moment, however, we must leave these developing skirmishes to return to the main strategic action, but we will hear more of 'Wild Edric' later on.

Meanwhile, a more serious challenge to Norman rule was developing in the north. Edgar the Aetheling had been driven onto the Scottish coast by a storm and had found refuge with Malcolm Canmore, King of Scotland. Malcolm offered to support Edgar in a bid for the English throne, and the Bishop of Durham was involved in these intrigues. The Norman garrison of Durham and their commander Robert of Commines were massacred while they slept and soon afterwards the Normans of York were surprised by the citizens and besieged in the castle. William marched north, drove out the force that Edgar had brought with him from Scotland and constructed a new castle at York. As soon as William returned to the south the insurrection flared up again and Edgar returned from over the Scottish border. William was forced to turn around to face this renewed threat just as Harold's sons were raiding the south-west coast with a fleet they had gathered in Ireland. Harold's sons had not inherited their father's military acumen and were repulsed without the need for William's presence, returning to Ireland. However, a new and much more dangerous development followed. King Sweyn Estrithson of Denmark, with a fleet of 240 ships containing not only Danes but Poles, Norwegians and Lithuanians, arrived in the Humber. They secured the northernmost area of Lincolnshire and then marched on York with their jubilant Anglo-Danish allies who had secretly summoned them. This was the most serious crisis of William's reign so far, but the redoubtable Norman immediately responded by marching north yet again. This time, however, there was method in the rebel plan, and as soon as William marched north simultaneous rebellions emerged in the south-west, in Devon and Cornwall and Somerset, and also in Staffordshire and Shropshire. The leader of the Shropshire revolt was Edric 'the Wild' who besieged Shrewsbury Castle, and in Cheshire the Welsh princes invaded to link up with disaffected rebels from Chester. To put down rebels was second nature to William but the prospect of facing down a large Viking army was quite a different matter. In fact, William's military resources were not equal to the task, and so he resorted to that time-honoured strategy of paying them to desist from their project. This proved fruitful and the Danes returned to their ships where they encamped for the winter. William took York again and spent Christmas there. It had been an infuriating year which had almost cost William his throne and so now he put into effect a plan which would prevent any recurrence of these irritating attacks; it was to be one of the most dastardly deeds in all English history.

During a bitterly cold winter, William sent out his troops to systematically ravage habitations and destroy all human and animal life between York and the River Tyne; this was the so-called 'harrying of the north'. This was no longer mere warfare but a policy of extermination and genocide. There had always been a cruel streak in William. As a young man he had besieged a town where the inhabitants had goaded him by hanging tanned leather hides over the city battlements and beating them, to remind him that he was the bastard son of a tanner's daughter, Arleve. When the town fell he ordered all the inhabitants to be blinded and to have their hands and feet chopped off. This terrible revenge on the poor folk of Yorkshire and Durham was on an altogether different scale. All seed corn was burned, all ploughs destroyed and all livestock slaughtered. As people fled to the offshore islands and dense woodlands they were hunted down remorselessly and none were spared. By the time the devastation was over the entire area was an uninhabitable wasteland. People resorted to cannibalism in their dire distress and tried to sell themselves into bond-slavery, but there was no one left with the resources to employ them or feed them. It is said that on his deathbed William expressed deep remorse for this savagery, and while we must probably discount this, such a shameful act gave every cause for contrition. For generations this entire region, once one of the most populous and prosperous in England, fell into decay and ruin. Orderic Vitalis, the Shropshire chronicler was appalled, writing, 'On many occasions I have been free to extol William according to his merits, but I dare not commend him for an act which levelled both the bad and the good in one common ruin by a consuming famine ... such barbarous homicide should not pass unpunished.' 100,000 people perished: the equivalent of more than 1 million today. It goes without saying that the troubles in the north were settled by this brutal campaign and so William was free to return south, to subdue his other enemies.

Resolved to utterly destroy the remaining English resistance, and in a mood of fanatical vengeance, William now demonstrated his extraordinary qualities of determination and leadership. Instead of marching back the way he had come, William decided to take his army up over the Pennine passes during a desperately cold winter. Almost all the horses perished and many men were lost to frostbite and disease, and he came within an inch of inducing his men into mutiny, but his indomitable will prevailed and in spring he emerged onto the Midland Plain. Chester was swiftly taken and a castle built there. Next he assaulted the Stafford rebels who were awaiting reinforcement from Edric but a conjunction of their forces was prevented. Stafford was taken and a castle constructed there, and the Norman garrison of Shrewsbury was relieved and its castle rebuilt. In the south-west the rebellion collapsed as soon as it was known that William was approaching with his army. There can be no doubt that William displayed admirable courage, determination and skill, as well as the ability to recognise the limits of what could be achieved by purely military means. Yet he had also shown the ruthlessness, barbarity and callous indifference to human suffering which characterised the Norman Conquest and which left a legacy of hatred towards the regime among the English population which endured for hundreds of years, as we will see. The Norman occupation was now an ineluctable fact, a condition the Anglo-Saxons had to learn to endure as best as they could, but there were still some men who would not submit, whose spirit could not be broken: the last of the Anglo-Saxon heroes.

A contingent of the Danish fleet under the command of Jarl Asbiorn had sailed south to the East Anglian coast in search of further plunder during the summer of 1070. They emerged in the Fenlands near Ely with the object of plundering the monastic settlement of Peterborough, one of the richest foundations in England. They were joined by Hereward 'the Exile' who had been the leader of a group of outlaws a few hundred strong whose refuge was in the impassable Fenlands. The Danes were content with their vast loot and left for Denmark, but Hereward's company still remained as renegades in their hidden stronghold. As a result of the terrible harrying of the north, Earl Morcar and some hundreds of other failed northern rebels joined Hereward and put up a stubborn guerrilla war against the local Norman authorities, which proved so troublesome that eventually William had to come in person to put it down. These are the bare facts, but this bold defiance of the Normans was to pass into legend, and Hereward became an English folk hero, but who was this man? As with the later Robin Hood, the accretions of folk tales have rather obscured the core of historical truth in Hereward's case. Most of what we know derives from an account by Richard, a monk of Ely in the twelfth century, which he explicitly says was drawn on evidence from contemporary witnesses. Richard's version and others state that he was the son of Leofric, Lord of Bourne in the fens. According to Richard, Hereward had been driven into exile as a young man because of his 'hell-raising' behaviour, participation in blood feuds, fighting and duelling. With a faithful companion, Martin Lightfoot, and his famous mare called Swallow, equipped with his famous sword, the Brain-biter, the young hero hired himself out for military service abroad. Most of the tales told about this period as a soldier of fortune are typical mead hall stories designed for entertainment, but Peter Rex in his *Hereward the Last Englishman* adduces strong evidence that the story of his exile and mercenary service in Flanders is probably true. Here he served in the army of the Count of Flanders in his protracted war with the Count of Guines. While enlisted in his service, Hereward fell in love with a lady called Torfrida who possessed magical powers. He also attracted a group of like-minded young soldiers into his service who accepted him as their leader. A mercenary named as Herivvardi is described as being present in Cambrai in 1065 and may well have been the same man. Peter Rex, despite the subtitle of his book, thinks that the story of Hereward's noble origins should be discounted, and that he was in fact the son of a minor Anglo-Danish *hold*, the equivalent of an English *thegn*. This seems reasonable because his name is Danish, and as we have seen there existed a long tradition of Danish men hiring themselves out as mercenaries, so the strange thing is that one of the greatest heroes of English folklore, and the man who embodies in the popular imagination unyielding resistance to the Norman yoke, was probably descended from the Vikings. However it was, at some point Hereward returned to his homeland to find it under the heel of the Norman tyranny and it is at this point that things get interesting.

We saw at the commencement of this book how the invasion of an irresistible foreign conqueror led on to a blurring of historical and folk-mythical accounts of events. Whereas the Anglo-Saxon consolidation had taken two centuries, allowing the subjugated people time to develop a myth of a heroic resistance fighter, for the English this process took place in one man's lifetime. Their crisis of confidence, to put it mildly, was so extreme and the transformation so swift that they projected their most deeply held racial myths onto the very last heroes of the resistance. In many ways, and as I have sought to stress throughout this story, *the myth was a more coherent and genuine* reflection of their experience than a straightforward history. That is why I do not apologise for repeating some of the themes which have been a cypher for the English national consciousness of these times. Though they are not strictly historical they led on to the emergence of their own idea of a hidden racial messianic redeemer, just as the Celts had resorted to in their time.

In legend at any rate, Hereward returned by night to his old manor at Bourne. At some inn or similar meeting place, he disguised himself and made enquiries after his family and estates. The news was bad. Only the previous day a party of Normans had come thither to sequester the family holdings. Hereward's younger brother had defended the threshold, shielding his mother from a fate worse than death, and had killed two of the intruders before he was killed in turn. The Normans had decapitated the lad and set his head up as a trophy atop the gatehouse. Soon the Normans could be heard carousing nearby and this was enough to resolve Hereward on a traditional course of action. While whores and minstrels cavorted before the wine-sodden foreigners, one of the girls shouted a warning, 'Do you not forget that the lad you have slain has a brother, the famous Hereward who is in Flanders now and I tell you all, if he were here none of you would see sunrise on the morrow.' This sage advice was predictably ignored and the minstrels took up their theme of the glorious Norman triumph the previous day. It proved to be their last such entertainment, for immediately Hereward threw back his hood, unsheathed Brain-biter and first clove in the musicians' skulls before turning on the inebriated Norman soldiers who were annihilated before they even had time to go for their weapons. Their heads were taken and set up on the familial gatehouse (a very ancient British theme), and now there was no going back. Hereward was an outlaw and a very dangerous one, and in no time he had a small army and a secret unassailable base from which to launch his forays.

Support soon flocked in, not only from his own tenants on his own estates but from all over the country, including some of the most eminent nobles and churchmen. Just as in the legend of Robin Hood (which I believe was in some respects based on the stories of Hereward's exploits), the cruellest, most villainous and efficient of the Norman knights were sent to apprehend or kill Hereward, but were always outdone or tricked by his cunning ruses. Just as in the Greenwood of Sherwood Forest, the rebels are provisioned by God in the vast larder of the Fens, with its abundance of eels and other fishes, fowls, as well as what could be taken from itinerant 'French' in raids. The marshes also offered a defence and a sanctuary provided by nature herself. A Norman soldier wrote of the hostile swamps in the same way a GI might remember Vietnam in the twentieth century:

> The bogs would hardly bear a man or an animal, and you would be struck by arrows from afar, stumbling from firm ground onto man-traps full of spikes. Heavy rain, too, flooded rivers and streams instantly and what had been reeds suddenly became pools dragging men to their deaths in the bottomless abyss. Just as you were proceeding well great fissures would suddenly appear.

It was impossible to fight a conventional war, especially against a skilled, ruthless and experienced leader such as Hereward. This was no desperate last stand. Hereward was able to control events and defy the Normans with ease, and this is why the more powerful men joined him. William, as they knew, had other problems on his hands, namely a rebellion against him in Maine overseas. There was just a chance that if they could hold out, other major rebellions may follow.

It could not be allowed to continue of course. After many bungled attempts by his subordinates had failed, William took charge of the campaign himself in his own inimitable style. A causeway was painstakingly constructed at a place called Alreheth or Aldreth, made out of timber and stone piles driven in to the mud, with tree-trunks slung on ropes between, onto which inflated hides and fleeces were affixed. Ingenious though it was, it was also vulnerable, for those crossing it were funnelled into a hail of arrows and missiles, and in their haste to make the shore they overloaded the structure. Many hundreds sank into the swamp where in their heavy armour they were sucked down to oblivion. William was crestfallen. The victor of Hastings had been outwitted and outfought by this swamp-man of no account, a mere nobody. What was to be done? The answer came from one of William's notorious henchmen, Ivo de Tallebois. He knew of a cunning woman, a witch, whose powers could be obtained at a suitable price, who could undermine Hereward by *magick*.

Her secret arts soon bore fruit. Edwin and Morcar, most of the powerful nobles who had been sheltering with Hereward and churchmen such as Bishop Aethelwine whose support gave the insurgency a cloak of legitimacy, deserted the cause. Hereward with his hard core of loyal supporters escaped but William enforced a total blockade by land and sea and set his troops to patrol the fens in boats. Meanwhile, a new causeway was in the process of being prepared and the witch was busily casting spells to poison water sources the rebels might use. Four gigantic observation towers were constructed so as to direct the fire of war-engines, such as ballistae, which would bombard the crossing points. As a last insurance policy, the witch was sent atop one of these towers to invoke curses on Hereward and his gang. But Hereward had advanced notice of the plans and suddenly emerged to attack the siege-engines and burnt the towers, the hag included. The Norman troops panicked and fled into the fens where they were drowned in their hundreds.

Once again Hereward had outwitted the king, even with his diabolical aid, and so William resorted to other means. Where the devil had failed perhaps God may prevail, and so Abbot Thurbrand was suborned to denounce the rebellion from the pulpit and to promise forgiveness for those who would inform on the rebels. This was the prelude to a final effort by William. This time he personally led his forces into the swamps and the Normans broke into the isle where they inflicted a bloody slaughter. Somehow Hereward and his core war band escaped. Those taken alive by William were cast into dungeons, blinded and mutilated, or, in lesser cases of treason, imprisoned. Hereward would not give in even now. He escaped into the Bruneswald, a great forest in the East Midlands, and here, surely, he became the prototype for the later legend of Robin Hood. His coterie of exemplary companions, his excellence in the arts of disguise and trickery, his female companion with magical powers and his exploits with weapons and animals whose powers only respond to him personally are typical folk motifs. Hereward's ultimate fate is not clear, but a story goes that eventually the exasperated William offered him and his men royal pardon if they would agree to serve him. There is no reason why the story should not be true, but if so it could only end badly. The Norman knights, knowing how easily provoked Hereward was, arranged for one Ogger to goad him into a fight. Predictably Hereward responded by wounding Ogger and was immediately overpowered and thrown into prison. The jailer tipped off Hereward's friends on the outside about when he was to be transported and his comrades rescued him. William once again arranged for Hereward to surrender and receive a conditional pardon, and some think that the condition included military service in William's campaigns against the French rebels in Maine. As soon as he joined the Norman ranks he was a marked man and was probably slain by a party of Norman/French knights en route to Maine, his nemesis being a knight called Halselin. The most serious English threat to the Normans since Harold's death had been vanquished, though not without a valiant struggle, but at about the same time another English guerrilla fighter was about to pass out of mere history and into legend.

Hereward's was not the only doomed compromise with William. Over in the Welsh Marches, Edric finally came in and submitted too, and his fate seems similar. He was probably in the king's retinue when William invaded Scotland in 1072. This was a time-honoured method of putting one dangerous enemy to use against another. Somehow Edric survived and returned to his estates in Shropshire, but they were no longer his. A Norman knight, Sir Ralph Mortimer, had seized all Edric's manors in his absence. What was more disturbing was that by colluding with William, Edric had violated the 'Sovereignty of the Land', the ineffable bond between the folk territories and their mortal ruler. The most obvious expression of this theme, what Adolf Bastian would have called the Volkergedanken is indicated by his fairy bride, 'Lady Godda'. She is the mistress of the earth, the queen of the forests, guardian of the holy wells, in fact no less than the goddess Cuda Stephen J. Yeates has identified with post-Roman and early medieval paganism. While wandering in the Clun Forest with a squire, Edric perceives light coming from an inn and the two decide to approach the place at nightfall. Walter Map, a later storyteller, records the traditional tale:

> It was a kind of drinking den which the English have in every parish which they call 'Guild Houses'. Coming closer they saw light within and looked inside to see nine young maidens ... provocatively clad in elegant shifts, they were taller and of nobler bearing than human women. One among them struck him especially ... more desirable than the mistress of any king ... seeing her he was wounded to the heart, could scarcely bear the love-fire of Cupid's darts.

Such moments make for rash and passionate actions, and, of course, Edric seizes the girl and rides off with her after a desperate struggle with her sisters. She pines away, refusing to speak with him or to eat, though she permits sexual intercourse but without passion. Eventually she relents and says she will behave as a wife should and bear his child on the strict condition that he *never mentions* her sisters. Taboos are made to be broken and of course Edric inevitably offends. His fairy bride dematerialises and broken-hearted he searches endlessly for her in his old heartlands on the Welsh border. What had once been a man fades likewise and becomes a dweller on the threshold of Annwn, the Celtic otherworld. The lead miners of the Stiperstones used to say that he could be heard moaning and wailing for his lost love in the deepest tunnels, begging forgiveness for ever having bargained with William 'the Bastard', the 'Cong Kerry' as the border people remembered him. This may seem a digression, but in fact represents in mythical terms the passing of the Anglo-Saxon age. Edric never truly dies, for he is doomed to an eternal penance, the price he must pay on behalf of the race for having lost the land. Beneath the weird outcrops of the Stiperstones he waits to emerge for a while, but only in special circumstances when England goes to war. Then he rides out with his hearth companions and his trustiest comrades, and beside him rides his green-clad bride, as on demented steeds, leading a pack of red-eared hell-hounds the 'Wild Hunt' rides across the Shropshire Hills. They were seen in Napoleon's time and before the Crimea, before the Boer War and the First World War. Any Anglo-Saxon of any age would recognise the spectral company, for the 'Wild Hunt' had originally been Woden and his divine companions of the ancient pagan pantheon, the most sanctified elemental core of the consciousness of the people. When a civilisation is finally overwhelmed there is nowhere left for its gods and heroes to go except underground. It is perhaps fitting that the Anglo-Saxon story ends in the liminal country near Offa's Dyke in what had been the most enduring physical expression of all that they had achieved over so many centuries. The Anglo-Saxon age had passed.

15

THE ANGLO-SAXON LEGACY

Very little remains of the Anglo-Saxon world, at least in the physical environment. A few precious churches from the era, Offa's Dyke and similar earthworks and a scattering of Anglo-Saxon way-crosses are all that are left to us. The Anglo-Saxons mainly built in timber, which explains the paucity of visible structures. This can make them seem like a people who vanished from history like the Tylwyth Teg or 'fair-folk' of Celtic myth, the aboriginal inhabitants of these islands in pre-history, recorded only in hazy legends. The true Anglo-Saxon legacy to us is not to be found in physical structures or even (though it is extremely important) in archaeology. It is rather to be found all around us, in flesh and bone and blood, in speech, customs and rituals, the place names of countless towns and villages and fields. It is a very human inheritance and is all the more loveable for that. By contrast, the Norman imprint, while it is exceedingly well-marked by enduring structures in stone, made hardly any impact on the gene pool, except of course that of a privileged alien elite. No more than 50,000 Normans and Frenchmen crossed the sea to colonise England and for many of these their primary residence still remained in the duchy. Half of the land mass of England was divided out between just a dozen men, most of them blood relations to the king. Actually William proclaimed himself to be the ultimate landlord of the entire country, but in practice it was necessary to compromise, yet the entire Norman feudal apparatus was in the hands of just a few hundred men. The Church was ethnically cleansed of virtually all Englishmen (only Wulfstan II at Worcester survived after 1075), not only because bishops may prove a rallying point for disaffection as in Durham, but because the papal authorities extracted heavy fines from William when they heard of the monstrous abuses of the English people, and William needed his own men in charge to prevent any meddling from the Pope. The new regime made absolutely no effort to integrate. It was 300 years before the ruling elite grudgingly began to use English speech. They refused to adapt to even such amenities as the village ale-houses and drank in their own taverns or *bouteilleries*, butteries where wine was served. Exclusive areas were set aside in English towns where 'French-towns' were implanted next to the old English settlements, where the two populations even attended different churches, as at Nottingham. Walls often divided such areas within what were already quite small towns. In fact it was pointless to attempt any kind of national reconciliation in these early stages. The Conquest was what it said it was: brutal military occupation by a hostile foreign power, and the most obvious symbol of this was the castle. These, of course, still stand all over England and Wales, Scotland and Ireland, enduring testimony to the iron grip of the Normans. The afforestation of a third of England's land area, much of it the personal property of the king, was accompanied by harsh Forest Laws, for William's love of the hunt was legendary: 'The King, William, set up great protection for the deer and legislated to the intent that who so ever should slay hart or hind should be blinded ... He loved the high deer as if he were their father.'

It was forbidden for forest folk to keep a hound higher than their knee, and even these smaller creatures were 'lawed' by mutilating the front paw if their cottages lay too near the game. Although, and it is to their credit, they abolished slavery, we should perhaps consider that this came about due to the general reduction in the status of the common peasant. In practice every low-born Englishman became little more than a serf, so slavery was scarcely necessary. It is not my intention to trespass too much on the Norman period, but I hope the above conveys something of the miseries which the occupation brought for the oppressed Anglo-Danish population. What they needed were tales of the deeds of a hero, and in the heart of ancient Mercia he emerged from the deep woods.

Robin Hood, of course, belongs to a slightly later stage of the Anglo-Norman relationship, but the mythical elements of his stories are probably earlier. A strange cult of Mary existed among the Anglo-Saxon and Anglo-Danish peasantry. This was extremely complex, but it seems that much of this cult was the transference of even more archaic religious traditions, which venerated Brigit, originally a goddess of poetry, onto Mary, who in turn had many different aspects. One of these, 'Mary Gypsy', or 'the Egyptian', was a prostitute who had arrived in the Holy Land by the ingenious expedient of sleeping with the entire crew of a ship bound to take pilgrims there. From this story of a very human saint another Mary emerged, called 'Marian', or Marion, who becomes the special companion of Robin Hood. One of the few means of escape from the wretchedness of the Norman regime was the opportunity to go on pilgrimages. Under the umbrella of protection pilgrims' status conferred on them, these palmers were free to tell tales around the campfire of an English hero who was still at large in the woods. He was, of course, one of the old Anglo-Saxon gods, Rof Breoht Woden, who morphed into a character known as Robin Goodfellow. As Robin Hood he became the supreme English national folk hero. Robert Graves in his *The White Goddess* says that Hood or Hud meant 'log', referring to the sacred oak log kept at the back of the fire in every humble cottage, and his intuition that the cult was a survival of ancient forest rituals, which seem to have their origin in pre-historic times, seems entirely reasonable. At Abbots Bromley in Staffordshire, the 'Horn Dance' is performed ritually each September to this day. In the cult, conventions and oppressive restrictions could be cheerfully cast aside. Dubious friars could bless marriages which were unofficial and unrecognised by the Church. The English had to live now to some extent against the established order and many of them did retire into the dense woods to become brigands. Like Edric 'the Wild' and his legend, the mission of the outlaw hero cannot be finally accomplished 'until all wrong is made right', and this is a classic example of a myth reversing the usual process of justice. It is not the outlaw who is the villain but the legitimate authorities, in this view, and this simple theme lingered on in the English popular imagination. It was easy to exclude the Normans from these tales because they were told exclusively in English, and by refusing to learn the 'barbarous' speech of the English the Norman ruling elite failed to acknowledge cultural achievements (albeit in remote places and in virtual secrecy) which the English were bringing about, writings that were to preserve a precious seed of Anglo-Saxon culture which in time would grow into the giant oak of English literature.

Just as Aethelweard had retired to the banks of the Severn to write his history of the English, in the late twelfth century another hermit preacher sought the solitude of a cave on the riverbank to produce a poetic history of his own. His name was Layamon, and at Arley Redstone nearby the modern town of Stourport-on-Severn in Worcestershire, he set up a rock-hewn chapel at a crossing on the Severn which was the main ferry for drovers leading their flocks from Wales to London. His name is either English or Viking, the 'Y' in Layamon being the ancient runic character 'thorn'. He was licensed to 'read book', meaning that he was a clerk licensed by the rural dean of Martley in Worcestershire. One in twenty adult men were clerks in post-Conquest England, not ordained priests as such but men whose literacy gave them a certain cachet and whose preaching fell on the ears of people whose labour precluded regular church attendance, such as charcoal burners, trow-boat pilots and Welsh drovers. The monetary offerings for prayers said for their safety at the river crossing provided Layamon with a small living, and in quieter times a cave hermitage where, by the light of tallow candles, he took on an enormous literary project. At around the same time a strange obsession with ancient Celtic stories of 'King Arthur' had gripped the ruling Norman aristocracy and royalty. About 1200 a Jersey man called Wace had produced an adaptation of Geoffrey of Monmouth's *Historia Regum Britanniae*, which was an amalgamation of ancient Welsh and Breton tales with various other sources alleging a divine outworking of British national destiny. These historical tales became central to the court entertainment and deportment of the French speaking elite, and were soon translated into German, Spanish, Italian, but not into English. The English were too low in the social scale to benefit from these tales of courtly love, and anyway the hero of the stories, Arthur, had been the bitterest enemy and most implacable foe of their ancestors. Layamon had access to Welshmen who waited on the ferry dock. They told him *original* stories of Arthur, ones that had not been included in Wace's *Roman de Brut* and Layamon decided to make it his life's task to write a 16,000-line poem, a Brut of his own, tracing the legendary history of Britain from the earliest times. What was different was the language in which he wrote – English – and this little-regarded but epic work laid the foundation for later English writers such as Chaucer, Langland and Shakespeare. Written in the unfashionable and barbaric English language, they remained obscure for a long time, and this was probably intentional. I have postulated elsewhere that Layamon's work may have been a covert attack on the tyranny of King John, whose murder of his nephew called Arthur of Brittany made him guilty not just of potential regicide but also a sort of deicide (many Celts saw the young prince as a reincarnation of King Arthur). It seems to me that Layamon's obscure project did two things simultaneously. First it took the tales out of the hands of the ruling elite and rendered them in an accessible form for the common people, the *English* people. Secondly it identified the English as a folk whose long relationship with the land of Britain made them worthy of record, the inheritors of the 'matter of Britain', a people with a symbiotic relationship with the land which they and their ancestors had kept for hundreds upon hundreds of years. Layamon clearly intended that the English people should not only preserve their cultural heritage, but also see it in the context of the longer history of earlier cultures and races which had once held sway, and this stubborn refusal to abandon their language, and even extend its cultural influence, eventually won out. Even today the 100 most-used words in modern English are almost exclusively Anglo-Saxon in origin, and famously when Winston Churchill made his rousing appeals in defiance of Nazi invasion in 1940 the words he used were of a similar Anglo-Saxon derivation. As a result of British and United States imperial expansion, English is one of the most widely used and influential languages in the world today. The shouted exclamations of ships' crews as they rowed ashore on the coast of eastern Britain in the fifth century share many common words with the voice of the airline pilot which comes over the intercom on transnational flights in the twenty-first.

In this way, the Norman hegemony was eventually tamed, and after the loss of Normandy during the reign of the infamous King John, the Normans, robbed now of their ancestral homeland, began at long last to integrate, to learn the speech of the despised English and to become in their turn one with the land. The tensions about inequity and the concentration of power in a few hands did not disappear, however, and in the turmoil of the English Revolution of the seventeenth century the Parliamentarian side and its independent allies saw their struggle as a historical battle with the forces of Norman oppression. Gerrard Winstanley, the leader of the ultra-radical 'Diggers' (a proto agrarian-communist movement), thought that the Conquest of 1066 could be equated with the fall of man:

The Reformation that England now is to endeavour, is not to remove the Norman Yoke only, and to bring us back to be governed by those Laws which were before William the Conqueror came in, as if that were the rule and mark we aim at: No, that is not it; but the Reformation is according to the word of God, and that is the pure Law of righteousnesse before the Fall, which made all things, unto which all things are to be restored; and he that endeavours not that, is a Covenant breaker.

The revolution was seen as a political opportunity to restore England to a time before privilege and elitism, and cynical oppression by a foreign interloper had ruined it, and the gentry were seen as the inheritors of the Normans who had crossed with William in 1066 when their ancestors had 'killed an English man, and took his possessions'. William the Bastard 'and his armed Banditti' had established the ruling elite on a basis of 'fraud, deceit and oppression' and the 'Clargey' were little better, and it was a common belief that it would 'never be a good world so long as there was a Lord in England, for the whole rabble of Duke, Marquesse, Lord, Knight, Gentlemen by patents ... I find no room for in Scripture'. Needless to say this pre-Norman Utopia was that most dangerous phenomenon, a 'history as wished for'. It was quite true that descendants of William's henchmen still wielded inordinate power in England in the seventeenth century, and probably they still do, but Anglo-Saxon England was not a prelapsarian paradise as we have seen. Those on the political left who persist in seeing it in this way are deluding themselves in just the same way as those on the right who hark back to a racially pure insular Eden, uninfluenced by Europe. That is why we need now, more than ever, to estimate these times correctly, to try to know the nearest to the truth about them as we can.

They were times of terrible and unremitting violence. First, there was the 200-year war with the British, followed by a roughly similar period of wars between the English heptarchic realms. Then, there came another two centuries of vicious struggles against the Vikings. In fact any analysis of the Anglo-Saxon age cannot be complete without also being a study of the British and the Scandinavians among whom they lived, albeit in a constant state of warfare. In all that time only in Edgar's reign was there a brief respite from conflict. This scarred the English psyche and made war a natural condition which they expected, rather than the failure and calamity which it actually is. The constant warfare did not end in 1066, of course, but for almost 1,000 years England has been immune from foreign conquest. I believe that this has left a sort of myth of invincibility in the English popular imagination. My father often used to say that even in the days following the Dunkirk debacle in 1940 he and his school-fellows never doubted victory for one moment. The Anglo-Saxons were fearsome warriors indeed but for every Alfred or Athelstan there was an Ethelred. They were capable of incredible stoicism and heroism but also deeds of barbaric cruelty, such as the St Brice's Day Massacre, and acts of cowardice and oafish bungling. In short, they were just like the people of today. I have written this book with James Ingrams' translation of the *Anglo-Saxon Chronicle* beside me as a constant companion. I find that the people who I read about in its pages seem strangely familiar, like those one may hear about on the news. When I walk the streets of the Black Country towns near my home I hear the lilting dialect of my neighbours and recall that theirs is the speech most strikingly similar to that of the Anglo-Saxons. Their bawdy, irreverent humour, their love of dogs, their sweet tooth and frank talk are typical traits of their ancestors from 1,400 years ago. Their more recent ancestors shocked the world by their inventiveness and industry, and in the coalfields and nail-shops of South Staffordshire they inaugurated a new age which completely reconfigured the world economy.

So, it is time for our journey to come to its end. I do not claim to be a professional historian and much of what I have set down in the foregoing pages is a personal view based on many decades of research. Many of the books from which I have quoted can be found in the attached bibliography and will repay the reader who wishes to develop their interest in the period by more serious study. I am a Mercian and my obvious bias towards the contribution of that country to English and British national life is something I make no apologies for. After all, the Northumbrians, the West Saxons and the Normans have all depicted English history according to their own regional squint before me. We are all products of the land that bore us, and all of us exult to see the well-trodden pathways. As Layamon wrote, 'Cador proceeded over wealds and over wilderness, over dales and over downs, and over deep waters. Cador knew the way that towards his country lay.' There is a deep-seated fatalism in the English which is a definite legacy from the Anglo-Saxon ancestors. They believed in a concept called *Wyrd* or 'that which will be'. A poem called *The Fortunes of Men* considers the differing fates of men:

> Hunger will devour one, storm dismast another,
> One will be spear-slain, one hacked down in battle,
> One will drop wingless, from the high tree,
> One will swing from the tall gallows,
> The sword's edge will shear the life of one
> At the mead-bench, some angry sot
> Soaked with wine. His words were too hasty,
> One will delight a gathering, gladden
> Men sitting at the mead-bench over their ale
> One will settle by his harp
> At the feet of his lord and be handed treasures,
> One will tame that arrogant wild bird,
> The hawk on the fist, until the falcon
> Becomes gentle enough for jesses'.

Our fates are diverse and mysterious, and our times are dangerous. Another poem *The Lament of Deor* is a similar contemplation on the destinies of men, all the joyful, glorious, terrible and heartbreaking events that make up the tapestry of life. For every such life event it returns to the same refrain: 'That passed over, this may too.'

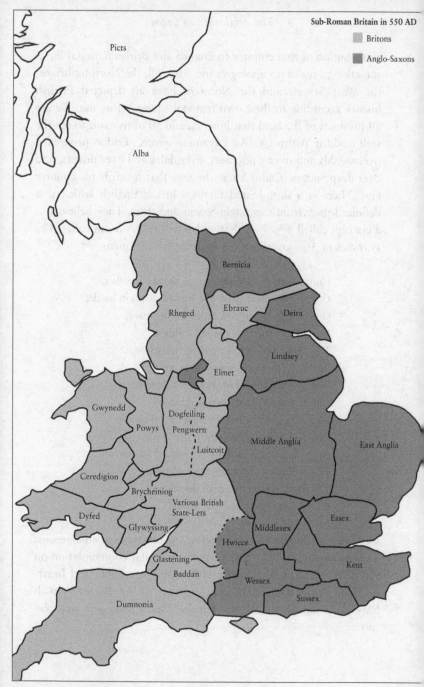

Sub-Roman Britain in 550 AD

Britons
Anglo-Saxons

Picts

Alba

Bernicia

Ebrauc

Rheged

Deira

Lindsey

Elmet

Gwynedd

Dogfeiling
Pengwern

Luitcoit

Middle Anglia

East Anglia

Powys

Ceredigion

Brycheiniog

Dyfed

Various British
State-Lets

Glywyssing

Middlesex

Essex

Hwicce

Glastening

Kent

Baddan

Wessex

Dumnonia

Sussex

All maps drawn from rough sketches provided by the author.

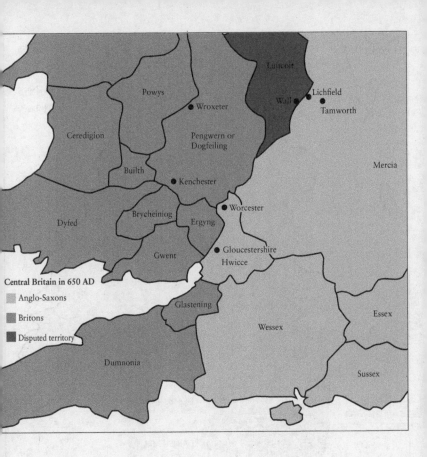

Central Britain in 650 AD

- Anglo-Saxons
- Britons
- Disputed territory

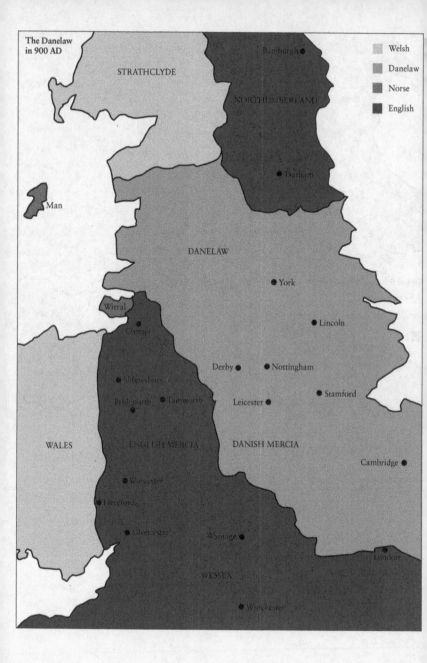

The Danelaw in 900 AD

Welsh
Danelaw
Norse
English

STRATHCLYDE

Bamburgh

NORTHUMBERLAND

Durham

Man

DANELAW

York

Lincoln

Wirral

Chester

Derby Nottingham

Shrewsbury

Stamford

Bridgnorth Tamworth

Leicester

WALES

ENGLISH MERCIA

DANISH MERCIA

Cambridge

Worcester

Hereford

Gloucester Wantage

London

WESSEX

Winchester

BIBLIOGRAPHY

The Real Middle-Earth: Magic and Mystery in the Dark Ages, Bates, Brian, London, Pan, 2002

English Heritage Book of Anglo-Saxon England, Welch, Martin G. London, Batsford, 1992

The Black Country, Chitham, Edward, Stroud, Amberley, 2009

The English Settlements: Oxford History of England, Myers, J. N. L, Oxford, Clarendon Press, 1986

Anglo-Saxon England: Oxford History of England, Stenton, Frank M. Oxford, Oxford Paperbacks, 2001

The Age of Arthur: A History of the British Isles from 350 to 650, Morris, John, London, W&N Publishing, 2004

Religion and Literature in Western England, 600-800: Cambridge Studies in Anglo-Saxon England, Sims-Williams, Patrick, Cambridge, Cambridge University Press, 2005

The Tribe of Witches: The Religion of the Dobunni and Hwicce, Yeates, Stephen J. Oxford, Oxbow Books, 2008

A Shropshire Lad, Houseman, A. E, London, 1896

Bloodfeud: Murder and Revenge in Anglo-Saxon England, Fletcher, Richard A. Oxford, Oxford University Press, 2004

Mercia and the Making of England, Walker, Ian W. Stroud, Sutton Publishing, 2000

The Anglo-Saxon Kings, Venning, Timothy, Stroud, Amberley, 2011

In Search of the Dark Ages, Wood, Michael, London, B.B.C Publications, 1981

The Anglo-Saxon Age: The Birth of England

Edward the Confessor: King of England, Rex, Peter, Stroud, Amberley, 2013

The Normans, Rowley, Trevor, Stroud, History Press, 2009

The White Goddess, Graves, Robert, London, Faber & Faber, 1961

Radical Religion in the English Revolution, McGregor J. F & Reay B. (Eds.) Oxford, Oxford University Press, 1988

The Anglo-Saxon Chronicle, Ingram, James, London, Everyman, 1823

The Way and the Light: An Illustrated Guide to the Saints and Holy Places of Britain, Sharp, Mick, London, Aurum Press, 2000

Folk Heroes of Britain, Kightly, Charles, London, Thames & Hudson, 1982

The Likeness of King Elfwald, Collingwood, W. G, Kendal, Titus Wilson, 1917

The Year 1000, Lacey, Robert & Danziger, Danny, London, Little, Brown and Company, 1999

Hereward, Rex, Peter, Stroud, Amberley, 2013

INDEX